Federal Criminal Law Doctrines

Federal Criminal

Law Doctrines / The Forgotten

Influence of National Prohibition

Kenneth M. Murchison

Duke University Press   Durham and London   1994

© 1994 Duke University Press

All rights reserved

Printed in the United States of America on acid-free paper ∞

Designed by Cherie Holma Westmoreland

Typeset in Melior by Yankee Typesetters, Inc.

Library of Congress Cataloging-in-Publication Data appear on the last printed page of this book.

Contents

Acknowledgments

Many people have contributed to bringing this project to fruition. The most direct contribution was that of Morton Horwitz. His initial encouragement was instrumental in persuading me to begin graduate studies at the Harvard Law School, and he served as advisor for the dissertation from which this book is adapted. As advisor, Morton sharpened my analysis with his comments and questions, but he always allowed me to pursue my own ideas even when they diverged from his own.

Other teachers and advisors have also made important contributions. The problem that I was assigned to complete for Welsh White's criminal procedure class when I was a second-year law student at the University of Virginia gave me the first glimpse of prohibition's impact on federal criminal law. David Flaherty organized the legal history program at the University of Virginia that sparked my interest in the subject, and his legal history course gave me the first opportunity to analyze the impact of prohibition on American law. When the project almost died at an early stage, William Harbaugh agreed to serve as a replacement advisor at the last moment so that the entrapment section could become my M.A. thesis at the University of Virginia.

A number of individuals assisted me in revising the dissertation for publication. The late George Armstrong offered useful hints regarding style, Gaines Foster read portions that were particularly difficult to rewrite, Michael Blumm reviewed the manuscript and offered helpful words of encouragement at a particularly discouraging point in the process, and John Devlin graciously critiqued last-minute changes as soon as they came out of the word processor. My research assistant, Janet Britton, rechecked all the sources and proofread the entire manuscript with great care. At the Duke University Press, Rachel Toor has been the model of a supportive editor.

Over the years, librarians at various institutions—Harvard Law School, the University of Virginia, Louisiana State University, and the University of Richmond—provided much needed help. I owe particular thanks to Charlotte Melius and Madeline Hebert, research librarians of the Paul M. Hebert Law Center of Louisiana State University. They consistently helped me locate difficult sources that were often out of print.

The Paul M. Hebert Law Center has assisted me in other ways as well. Financial support enabled me to finish my research after completing my year in residence at Harvard, and an invitation to make a presentation at a faculty colloquium helped to bring my work to a conclusion. The services of five able typists—Susan Roshto, Toni Fontenot, Debby Broussard, Laurie Knight, and Linda Duplessis—transformed my rough drafts into a finished project.

Portions of earlier drafts of the manuscript have previously been published in the following articles: *The Entrapment Defense in the Federal Courts: Emergence of a Legal Doctrine*, 47 Miss. L.J. 211 (1976); *Prohibition and the Fourth Amendment: A New Look at Some Old Cases*, 73 J. Crim. L. & Criminology 471 (1982); *Property Forfeitures in the Era of National Prohibition: A Study of Judicial Response to Legislative Reform*, 32 Buff. L. Rev. 417 (1984); *The Dual Sovereignty Exception to Double Jeopardy*, 14 N.Y.U. Rev. L. & Soc. Change 383 (1986). Those portions are reprinted here with the permission of the respective reviews and, in the case of the *Mississippi Law Journal* article, with the permission of Fred J. Rothman and Company.

Finally, a special word of thanks must go to my family, which allowed itself to be uprooted and moved across the country so I could undertake the research on which this work is based. Above all, I am indebted to Eloise who has helped me throughout the project. Not only did she provide the financial support that enabled me to begin my legal studies, she has also supported me in countless other ways during the last twenty-five years.

Kenneth M. Murchison
February 1994

1 / The Prohibition Backdrop

The era of national prohibition is a fascinating and significant chapter in United States history. In 1920 the nation began the "noble experiment"[1] of federal control of intoxicating liquors. The ratification of the Eighteenth Amendment prohibited the manufacture, sale, and transportation of intoxicating liquors as well as their importation into, or exportation from, United States territory.[2] Just thirteen years later, the experiment ended in failure. The Twenty-first Amendment abolished national prohibition,[3] and the Eighteenth Amendment became the first (and only) constitutional amendment to be repealed.

As a failed attempt to regulate national morals, the prohibition experiment has drawn the attention of contemporary policy analysts as well as historians. Both commentators and scholars have, however, generally overlooked the importance of the experiment for the development of legal thought, and that omission is unfortunate. Studying the prohibition era not only clarifies the historical development of federal law and the impact prohibition had on the intellectual culture of the nation. It also suggests the need for a revision of the conventional wisdom regarding the Supreme Court of the 1920s and offers an illuminating case study of how legal doctrine responds to changing social conditions.

Much contemporary interest in national prohibition derives from the desire to draw parallels to modern problems. In particular, analysts have tried to draw parallels with respect to current regulations of alcohol and other drugs.

Recent years have seen the emergence of new and stricter controls on liquor consumption. For example, most states have strengthened their laws against driving while intoxicated. Responding to federal pressure, states have also raised the legal age for purchasing alcoholic beverages to twenty-one.[4] Certainly no one has advocated a return to prohibition. Nonetheless, one study has suggested the future may produce "new, extensive regulation of the liquor industry . . . integrated into a paradigm of environmental safeguards and corporate responsibility. . . ."[5]

For other drugs, the current political mood is more ambivalent. The past has emphasized suppression through criminal prosecution, and the dominant voices still call for stricter controls and better enforcement. However, an increasing number of commentators have begun to advocate abandoning the traditional reliance on the criminal process.[6] Here the alleged parallel is not to adoption of the Eighteenth Amendment establishing prohibition but to the repeal of prohibition by the Twenty-first Amendment.

The frequent analogies to the prohibition experiment in the contemporary debates invite, if they do not compel, study of the experiment. Fortunately a large body of literature exists because the era of national prohibition has attracted considerable attention from professional historians over the last three decades.

The primary historical inquiry has been to define the significance of the era of national prohibition in United States history. On that issue, much of the debate has focused on two issues: whether prohibition was part of the nation's general reform tradition, and whether prohibition was an instrumental response to a significant social problem.

In the 1950s, Richard Hofstadter initiated the modern debate about the nature of the movement that led to the adoption of the Eighteenth Amendment; that is, whether national prohibition was a progressive social reform, as its adoption at the end of the Progressive Era suggests, or whether it was a pseudoreform, as its repeal at the beginning of the New Deal indicates. Hofstadter's general history of the American reform tradition described prohibition as "a ludicrous caricature of the reforming impulse," a "reaction against the progressive temper," and a "pinched, parochial reform."[7] Andrew Sinclair's 1963 history of prohibition accepted that view,[8] and it probably still remains the general view of most nonhistorians.

As early as 1963, James Timberlake disputed the Hofstadter thesis by documenting the links between prohibition and the progressives.[9] Moreover, recent scholarship has developed a growing consensus that rejects the Hofstadter characterization. This revisionist review increasingly accepts prohibition as part of the conflicting impulses of the progressive movement in the United States.[10]

Sociologist Joseph Gusfield raised the question of whether prohibition was an instrumental or a symbolic reform. His 1963 study of the temperance movement argued that prohibition was largely a symbolic issue. He contended that prohibition—and indeed the entire temperance movement in the United States—was not primarily an effort to reduce the consumption of intoxicating liquors. Instead, the reform was largely a symbolic conflict between a traditional nation centered in rural, middle-class, Protestant values and an emerging one identified with cosmopolitan, urban, and immigrant values.[11]

Subsequent studies have substantially modified the Gusfield thesis, although few modern scholars completely reject the symbolic importance of prohibition.[12] The more recent scholarship has demonstrated that the periods of temperance and prohibition reform involved real social problems associated with alcohol. In addition, the newer studies have also shown that prohibition was far more effective than previously thought. Per capita consumption of alcohol decreased sharply during the prohibition era and did not return to its pre-prohibition level for many years.[13]

The focus of historical scholarship has shifted in recent years as scholars have increasingly explored how national prohibition affected American life and culture. Considerable debate has continued over the issue of whether prohibition stimulated the growth of organized crime.[14] Scholars also have argued that prohibition has had a variety of other effects: encouraging single-issue pressure groups,[15] diminishing support for all governmental programs designed to reduce the consumption of alcoholic beverages,[16] glorifying the consumption of alcoholic beverages as a form of social protest,[17] discouraging other proposals for governmental regulation of personal affairs,[18] defeating moderate attempts to promote temperance,[19] and weakening the labor union movement.[20]

Historians have frequently noted prohibition's pervasive impact on legal institutions like prisons and courts.[21] They have, however, generally ignored its impacts on American legal thought.[22] The present study provides a partial correction to that omission by analyzing the prohibition-era changes related to federal criminal law.

This introductory chapter sets the stage for detailed assessments of five particularly important areas of federal criminal law. It begins with a brief history of prohibition and then offers an overview of the personnel and decisions of the United States Supreme Court during the era of national prohibition. From this background, the chapter describes a pattern that is characteristic of the Supreme Court's decisions in the prohibition era. That pattern provides a model for the analysis of individual areas of legal doctrine and the concluding assessment of prohibition's importance.

A Summary History of Prohibition

In colonial America and in the early republic, nearly everyone consumed alcoholic beverages. Even crowds at religious gatherings imbibed large quantities of liquor. Temperance proposals usually encouraged only abstention from spirits, not from malt liquors. Such partial abstention was, for example, the recommendation of Dr. Benjamin Rush, one of the earliest temperance advocates. The well-known revolutionary leader from Pennsylvania based his advice on some of the earliest scientific research into the ill effects of intemperate use of spirits.[23]

Market forces led to dramatic increases in the consumption of alcohol during the first half of the nineteenth century. The expense of transporting corn from the Midwest to eastern markets encouraged farmers to distill the grain into whiskey. The new supply of whiskey led, in turn, to a rapid increase in consumption.[24]

As reformers became concerned about the problems associated with increased drinking, the first organized temperance movement arose in the United States. Prominent among the early reformers were evangelical church leaders from New England. In 1826 temperance reformers founded the American Society for the Promotion of Temperance, the organization that began the first mass temperance movement. The society achieved considerable success, and reform efforts of the 1830s expanded the temperance program in two important ways. First, the temperance organizations began to urge, and then to demand, total abstinence from malt beverages as well as distilled liquors. Second, the first effort to impose legal restrictions appeared in the form of the "no-license" campaigns that encouraged local governments to refuse to license any retailers to sell liquor.[25]

During the 1840s, leadership of the temperance movement shifted to reformers who concentrated on moral persuasion rather than legislation to accomplish their goals. The most successful of the groups relying on persuasion techniques were the Washingtonian societies. Their members were reformed drunkards who conducted revival-style meetings to advance the temperance cause.[26]

The pendulum shifted to coercion in the 1850s, and reformers made the first concerted effort to enact prohibitory laws. Neal Dow, the mayor of Portland, was the leading advocate of state prohibition.

Maine followed his leadership by enacting the first statewide prohibition law in 1851, and a number of other states followed Maine's lead.[27]

This first wave of prohibition receded rapidly. Judicial decisions invalidated the statutes in several states, and the temperance movement never mounted a serious effort to overrule them. By 1869 statewide prohibition remained the law in only six states.[28] Scholars have traditionally attributed the collapse of the prohibition effort to the rising sectional conflict over slavery, but recent studies have emphasized the failure of the statutes to achieve the temperance goal for which they were designed.[29]

Prohibition reappeared as a significant political force in the second half of the nineteenth century. Some reformers took the third-party approach and formed the Prohibition Party, the first political party to make national prohibition its goal. The party played a pivotal role in the defeat of James G. Blaine in the presidential election in 1884, and it continued to increase its percentage of the vote until 1892. Nevertheless, the party never attracted wide support; after 1892 it declined rapidly as an independent political force.[30]

In the 1870s, the campaign to abolish intoxicating liquors got a new lift from a series of anti-saloon crusades. Sparked by an evangelical clergyman, women throughout the Midwest marched and held prayer vigils in front of local saloons. The prayer crusades closed a number of saloons and led to the formation of the Women's Christian Temperance Union (WCTU) in 1874. The WCTU supported nonpartisan referenda to establish statewide prohibition, and its strategy sparked a second wave of state prohibition. This second wave also receded, however. By the early 1890s, the number of states that retained prohibition statutes with statewide effect again dropped to six.[31]

The story of national prohibition really begins in 1893 when a small group met at Oberlin College. They founded the Anti-Saloon League, a nonpartisan organization equally dedicated to the abolition of alcohol and political pragmatism. Commentators have long recognized the league's political innovation: It was the prototype of the single-interest pressure group. A more recent history has also documented the extent to which the league employed the new organizational techniques of modern business organizations.[32]

The league always focused on achieving political success. As a contemporary observer noted, even the league's name reflected this pragmatic orientation.

> The very name Anti-Saloon League was chosen to focus interest on the institution which was the fountain of the poisonous product which the "Pledgers" shunned and the WCTU would outlaw. Moderate drinkers and total abstainers, who balked at the ideal of absolute prohibition, were willing to admit that the American saloon had become a noisome thing.[33]

A popular history has called attention to another indication of this pragmatic bent, the league's willingness to overlook personal indiscretions of legislators who voted for its positions.

> [O]ne congressman served a term in prison for accepting a bribe of five thousand dollars in a case involving the withdrawal of four thousand cases of whiskey in Pittsburgh. When he was released he ran for reelection and was supported by the Anti-Saloon League; he had always voted dry.[34]

The league gradually built an effective political base. Following a model established in Ohio, the league would initially concentrate its resources on securing local option ordinances. As public temperance sentiment grew stronger, the league would begin to lobby for prohibition on the state level. These efforts prompted the third wave of state prohibition laws. Always careful to avoid outdistancing public opinion, the league did not always insist that these laws be "bone dry." In many states, it accepted statutes that recognized limited situations in which intoxicating liquors could be lawfully possessed and consumed.[35]

The league achieved an impressive series of victories prior to the adoption of national prohibition. At the state level, the league secured the enactment of prohibitory laws in a majority of the states. At the federal level, it persuaded Congress to use its power to regulate interstate commerce to make the state laws more effective.

The Supreme Court's interpretation of the Commerce Clause of the Constitution[36] initially precluded states from taxing goods shipped in interstate commerce so long as they remained in the "original package" in which they had been shipped.[37] A few months after the Supreme Court decision establishing the original package rule, Congress passed the Wilson Act, which subjected intoxicating liquor to state law upon its "arrival" in the state.[38] Although the Supreme Court upheld the constitutionality of the Wilson Act,[39] subsequent decisions narrowly construed the act to exclude intoxicating liquor that was shipped into a state if the sale occurred outside the state's boundaries.[40]

Congress closed the transportation loophole in 1913 when it passed the Webb-Kenyon Act.[41] The new federal statute reinforced state prohibition laws by forbidding the transportation of intoxicating liquor into a state in violation of state law. Four years later, Congress added a "bone dry" amendment to the Webb-Kenyon Act; the amendment forbade interstate shipment of intoxicating liquor into any state that prohibited its manufacture and sale, regardless of whether the state also banned importation of intoxicating liquor from outside the state.[42]

In 1913 the league decided the time had come to push for national prohibition, and it led the successful battle. Within five years, the league had secured the submission of a constitutional amendment achieving its goal.

Initially the league seized on patriotic fervor associated with World War 1 to obtain the enactment of wartime prohibition. Relying on the need to conserve food to aid the war effort, supporters of prohibition persuaded Congress to impose liquor regulations that became increasingly strict as the years passed. A 1917 statute forbade the importation of distilled spirits; banned the use of foods, fruits, food materials, or feeds to produce distilled spirits for beverage purposes; and authorized the president to extend the ban to malt or vinous beverages. The following year, Congress first authorized the president to establish prohibition zones around "coal mines, munitions factories, shipbuilding plants, and . . . other plants for war materials" and then forbade the sale of distilled spirits and malt or vinous liquors beginning June 30, 1919.[43]

The league quickly followed up its wartime victory and achieved its ultimate goal. In 1918 it persuaded Congress to propose the Eighteenth Amendment. Less than fourteen months later, the states ratified the proposed amendment, and national prohibition became part of the constitutional order of the United States.[44]

The Eighteenth Amendment included two substantive provisions and one procedural innovation. Section 1 became effective on January 16, 1920, one year following its ratification. It forbade the manufacture, sale, or transportation of intoxicating liquors in the United States as well as their importation and exportation. Section 2 granted Congress and the states "concurrent jurisdiction" to enforce the provisions of the amendment. Section 3 required ratification of the proposed amendment within seven years of its submission to the states.[45]

Congress passed an enforcement statute after the Eighteenth Amendment had been ratified but before its effective date. Technically named the National Prohibition Act, the statute was popularly known as the Volstead Act after its chief sponsor, Representative Andrew Volstead of Minnesota.[46] Title I of the act expanded the scope of wartime prohibition and continued the wartime restrictions until the effective date of the Eighteenth Amendment. Title II exercised Congress's enforcement power under Section 2 of the Prohibition Amendment.

The Volstead Act added a number of offenses to the list of federal crimes. It prohibited the manufacture, sale, barter, transportation, importation, exportation, furnishing, or possession of any intoxicating liquor in violation of the act.[47] In addition, it defined the maintenance of any property where intoxicating liquors were manufactured, kept, sold, or bartered in violation of the act as a "common nuisance."[48]

The act contained other important provisions in addition to its criminal proscriptions. It broadly defined the term "intoxicating liquor" to include any beverage that contained more than one-half of 1 percent alcohol by volume,[49] and it included several noteworthy enforcement provisions. One section provided for the forfeiture of vehicles used to transport intoxicating liquor in violation of the act. Another gave federal courts power to issue "padlock injunctions" that could order establishments where intoxicating liquor was sold to be closed for a year. A third authorized federal courts to enjoin certain sellers of intoxicating liquors from continuing their activities in the future.[50]

Notwithstanding these provisions, the Volstead Act was not as extreme as it was sometimes portrayed by opponents of prohibition. For example, manufacture (but not sale) of ciders and fruit juices was exempt from the one-half of 1 percent definition of intoxicating liquor.[51] Neither possessing liquor in one's private residence nor purchasing liquor was a crime, although subsequent possession of the liquor by a purchaser could be a misdemeanor punishable by a $500 fine.[52] Furthermore, the act allowed searches of residences only when the prohibition authorities presented evidence showing that liquor was being sold at the residence or that the residence was being used in part "for some business purpose,"[53] and its forfeiture provisions protected the rights of innocent property owners.[54]

Penalties under the Volstead Act were relatively mild. All first offenses were misdemeanors; even for second offenders, the act authorized lengthy prison sentences only for manufacturing and sale offenses. The act prescribed the harshest maximum penalty, a $1,000 fine and imprisonment for one year, for the offense of maintaining a common nuisance. For first offenders, manufacturing and sale violations were punishable by a $1,000 fine and six months imprisonment; subsequent offenses were punishable by a $2,000 fine and imprisonment for five years. Maximum punishments for other violations of the Volstead Act were a $500 fine for the first offense, a $1,000 fine and imprisonment for ninety days for the second offense, and a fine of not less than $500 and imprisonment for two years for third and subsequent offenses.[55]

No precise measurements of public opinion during the prohibition era exist, and historians disagree on whether a majority of United States citizens supported prohibition when the Eighteenth Amendment was adopted. Nonetheless, most agree that prohibition enjoyed substantial public support at the time the Eighteenth Amendment was adopted and throughout the first half of the 1920s. A variety of evidence supports that hypothesis. Not only was prohibition approved by the requisite two-thirds majority in both houses, it was also ratified by forty-six states. Moreover, the required two-thirds of the states completed the ratification vote in less than fourteen months, and the majorities favoring prohibition were substantial in most states.[56] Once the ratification process was complete, Congress quickly adopted the relatively strict Volstead Act by a huge majority,[57] and it enacted a group of even stricter amendments to the act in 1921.[58] Finally, the number of representatives and senators who had been endorsed by the Anti-Saloon League continued to grow throughout the first half of the 1920s.[59]

A number of factors contributed to the ultimate repeal of the Eighteenth Amendment. Even as the nation was embracing prohibition, changing social conditions were undermining the pietistic moral values on which the Anti-Saloon League had based its successful campaign. More concretely, the increasingly obvious inadequacies of prohibition enforcement steadily increased public dissatisfaction. Organizational structures also played an important role. The political effectiveness of the Anti-Saloon League declined appreciably after the death in 1927 of Wayne Wheeler, its longtime general counsel, and groups opposing prohibition were much better organized by the late 1920s. Ultimately, however, the onset of the Great Depression in 1929 shifted the political balance of power in the United States and made repeal possible.

Public sentiment began to shift during the second half of the 1920s as it became obvious that widespread violations of the law were occurring. Not surprisingly the press—especially the newspapers in large cities—became increasingly critical of prohibition enforcement. In addition, an organized business opposition appeared in the form of a revitalized Association Against the Prohibition Amendment. In response to the growing criticism, Congress held hearings on prohibition in 1926. Shortly after President Hoover took office in 1929, he appointed a National Commission on Law Observance and Enforcement, which was headed by George Wickersham, a former attorney general.[60]

Despite the rising tide of complaints in the press and in Congress, the Anti-Saloon League and its allies retained political control throughout the 1920s. At the end of the decade, supporters of prohibition viewed the Eighteenth Amendment as impregnable. Mabel Willebrandt, formerly Assistant Attorney General in charge of prohibition enforcement, declared in 1929: "Repeal of the Eighteenth Amendment and the Volstead Act law, or material modification that would permit government distribution of liquor or sale of light wines and beer, is practically impossible."[61] A year later, Senator Morris Sheppard, the author of the Senate Resolution that became the Eighteenth Amendment, proclaimed: "There is as much chance of repealing the Eighteenth Amendment as there is for a humming-bird to fly to the planet Mars with the Washington Monument tied to its tail."[62]

Congress consistently turned a deaf ear to most proposals for modifying the Volstead Act as well as to calls for repeal of the Eighteenth Amendment. The two amendments to the Volstead Act that Congress passed did nothing to mitigate its strictness. The first merely reorganized the Prohibition Bureau and brought its employees within the coverage of the civil service laws.[63] The second, the Jones Act of 1929, actually increased the maximum penalties for most prohibition violations, although it did instruct judges to distinguish between commercialized operations and casual or minor violations.[64] By making sale of intoxicating liquor a felony, the Jones Act also established the basis for the claim that the purchaser of the liquor was violating the federal misprison statute by "helping" the seller.[65]

After 1930 opposition to prohibition increased significantly. The Depression enabled opponents to add the economic arguments that repeal would mean more jobs and increased taxes to their earlier claims that repeal would safeguard personal liberties.[66] Even the handpicked members of President Hoover's national commission gave national prohibition no more than nominal support when the commission issued its final report in 1931. All but one of the commissioners signed the report's declaration that the commission was "opposed to repeal of the Eighteenth Amendment." However, each of the members added a separate statement, and most advocated significant modification of the existing system of prohibition.[67]

In 1932 the Democrats embraced repeal of the Eighteenth Amendment. According to Arthur Schlessinger, Jr., the reading of the platform plank advocating repeal received the biggest ovation at the Democratic Convention. After hesitating throughout the nomination process, Franklin Roosevelt unequivocally embraced the repeal platform in his speech accepting the Democratic nomination.[68]

Following Roosevelt's victory in 1932, the final battle for repeal began.[69] When the lame-duck Congress submitted the Twenty-first Amendment to the states on February 6, 1933, it required that the amendment be ratified by special conventions rather than by state legislatures.[70] Using this procedure, the states ratified the Twenty-first Amendment even more rapidly than they had ratified the Eighteenth. When Utah completed the ratification process on December 5, the prohibition era was over. While the repealing amendment was being approved by the states, the new Congress took office. It quickly amended the Volstead Act to permit the sale of light beer and wines.[71]

The Supreme Court in the Prohibition Era

Personnel

In contrast to the dynamic political developments summarized above, the prohibition era produced no dramatic changes in the membership of the Supreme Court. Of course, new appointments occurred, and fifteen justices served during the thirteen years the Eighteenth Amendment remained in effect. Table 1 on the following page lists the justices who served on the Court during the period and gives the appointing president in parentheses.

A majority of the Court served together for eleven of the thirteen years of national prohibition. Three justices—Van Devanter, McReynolds, and Brandeis—were members of the Court throughout the period, and two others Butler and Sutherland—served from 1922

Table 1. Supreme Court Justices during the Prohibition Era

	Chief Justice	2	3	4
1920	Edward White (Taft)	Willis Van Devanter (Taft)	Oliver W. Holmes (Roosevelt)	James C. McReynolds (Wilson)
—	William H. Taft (Harding)			
—				
—				
1925				
—				
—				
—				
—				
1930	Charles Evans Hughes (Hoover)			
—				
—			Benjamin N. Cardozo (Hoover)	
—				

5	6	7	8	9
Louis D. Brandeis (Wilson)	William R. Day (Roosevelt)	John H. Clarke (Wilson)	Joseph McKenna (McKinley)	Mahlon Pitney (Taft)
	Pierce Butler (Harding)	George Sutherland (Harding)		
				Edward T. Sanford (Harding)
		Harlan F. Stone (Coolidge)		
				Owen Roberts (Hoover)

until the end of the era. In addition, Justice Holmes was a member of the Court from the beginning of prohibition until Justice Cardozo replaced him in 1932, and Chief Justice William Howard Taft served from 1921 to 1930.[72]

The first change in the Court's personnel came in 1921 when William Howard Taft replaced Edward Douglas White as chief justice.[73] Although the two chief justices came from different political parties, the new appointment did not represent a major ideological shift. Indeed, Taft had appointed White as chief justice in 1910. In any event, the change occurred so early in the prohibition era that it preceded all of the Supreme Court's prohibition decisions except for the initial opinions upholding the validity of the Eighteenth Amendment and the Volstead Act.

Four associate justices joined the Court between 1922 and 1925. In 1922 Senator George Sutherland replaced Justice Clarke, and Pierce Butler replaced Justice Day. Less than a year later, Edward Sanford was appointed to Justice Pitney's seat. Harlan Fiske Stone replaced Justice McKenna in 1925.[74]

The new appointees did not significantly alter the ideological composition of the Court as a whole. All four justices were appointed by conservative Republican presidents, and Taft was intimately involved in the selection of the first three of them. The appointment of Justice Sutherland strengthened the more conservative wing of the Court, but Justice Stone quickly allied himself with Holmes and Brandeis. In the 1930s, he was one of the most consistent supporters of New Deal programs.

The 1930s brought three additions to the Court. In 1930 President Hoover appointed Charles Evans Hughes to replace William Howard Taft as chief justice and Owens Roberts to replace Edward Sanford, who had joined the Court as an associate justice in 1923. Two years later, Hoover named Benjamin Cardozo to take the seat of Oliver Wendell Holmes, Jr.[75] Although the three justices later joined together to sustain the legislative initiatives of the New Deal,[76] they had no such decisive impact in prohibition cases. Indeed, they did not constitute an organized block in prohibition cases.

In short, the doctrinal changes of the prohibition era—unlike those involving the New Deal legislation of the 1930s—cannot reasonably be attributed to changes in the philosophical makeup of the Court. Although some changes in personnel occurred, the changes were not decisive in altering the course of decisions. For the most part, the new justices simply joined other members of the Court who changed their position.[77]

The attitudes that the justices displayed toward prohibition do not follow any easily discernible ideological pattern. Both Chief Justice Taft and Chief Justice Hughes opposed the adoption of the Eighteenth Amendment, but—as explained below—they took different positions once prohibition became the law of the land. Associate justices who expressed views on prohibition also divided along unusual lines. On one hand, two progressives (Brandeis and Clarke) and one conservative (Van Devanter) supported the reform.[78] On the other hand, a moderate (Roberts)[79] and a conservative (Butler) opposed constitutional prohibition, although Justice Butler had previously prosecuted at least one saloonkeeper as a state's attorney.[80]

Taft's response to prohibition was both unusual and interesting. Prior to the adoption of the Eighteenth Amendment, he expressed hostility to national prohibition, insisting that the issue was properly a local one. In letters published in a Connecticut newspaper in 1918, he opposed ratification of the prohibition amendment.[81]

Once prohibition became part of the Constitution, Taft's attitude shifted appreciably. A moderate drinker prior to the adoption of the Eighteenth Amendment, Taft personally abstained from the consumption of alcoholic beverages once prohibition was established as federal law. In an article published in the *Ladies Home Journal* in 1919, he declared himself "strongly in favor of the most practical laws to secure the rigid enforcement" of the Eighteenth Amendment. Similarly, his private correspondence criticized those "wets" who continued to drink intoxicating liquors after ratification of the Eighteenth Amendment and enactment of the Volstead Act.[82]

Taft's campaign for effective enforcement of the Eighteenth Amendment was consistent with his general legal philosophy. He consistently advocated strict enforcement of all criminal laws and emphasized the citizen's duty to follow the law, especially the Constitution, even when the citizen disagreed with it.[83] As chief justice, Taft authored a number of important Supreme Court opinions involving prohibition enforcement in which he always supported enforcement authorities.

Even during the 1920s, not all of the justices took as absolute a view of their personal responsibilities to support prohibition as Taft did. Justice Holmes appears to have been as indifferent to prohibition as he was to other legislative reforms. When presented with champagne at his eightieth birthday party 1921, Justice Holmes offered the following defense of his decision to consume the champagne:

> The Eighteenth Amendment forbids the manufacture, transportation, and importation. It does not forbid possession or use. If I send it back, I shall be guilty of transportation. On the whole, I think I shall apply the maxim *de minimis,* and drink it.[84]

Holmes's indifference to reform did not lead him to challenge the legislation that adopted it. Early in the prohibition era, he liberally construed the Volstead Act to override a preexisting treaty with Great Britain. His opinion offered the following defense for his approach to the prohibition legislation: "The 18th Amendment meant a great revolution in the policy of this country and presumably and obviously meant to upset a good many things on as well as off the statute book."[85]

By the second half of the 1920s, Taft recognized that the Court was increasingly divided over prohibition issues. In private correspondence, he declared that "something about the [Volstead Act] . . . seems to engender bitterness" among the members of the Court. He complained that "Frankfurter and that crowd" exercised influence over Brandeis and that Stone "wobbles a good deal on the subject."[86]

Despite his support for prohibition, Brandeis was probably the justice most sensitive to the excesses of prohibition enforcement. The condemnation of wiretapping in his dissent in *Olmstead v. United States*[87] remains a classic of constitutional law. Moreover, he also lobbied Felix Frankfurter to aid in blocking a $500,000 appropriation for undercover work to enforce prohibition.[88]

One personnel change from the 1930s does merit special notice: Hughes's replacement of Taft as chief justice. Like Taft, Hughes was a Republican who opposed the adoption of the Eighteenth Amendment. Their reactions to the new constitutional provision differed significantly, however. Although Hughes authored an amicus brief urging the validity of the amendment, he continued to believe prohibition was a mistake and to satisfy his personal fondness for good liquor when the occasion presented itself.[89]

One might expect Hughes to have been more sympathetic to violators of prohibition, and the Court's opinions after 1930 were more favorable to prohibition defendants. Nonetheless, it seems unreasonable to give Hughes credit for the change. Except when he wrote a narrow opinion recognizing the defense of entrapment, Hughes's personal contribution to the prohibition-related opinions of the 1930s was small. Moreover, Hughes's lack of control over his colleagues on other issues[90] cautions against accepting the change of the chief justice as a complete explanation for the dramatic doctrinal developments of the prohibition era.

Decisions

No one has yet written the definitive history of the Supreme Court during the prohibition era, especially a completely persuasive account of the Taft Court of the 1920s.[91] Conventional wisdom treats the Court of the prohibition era as a preparation for the showdown with the New Deal in the 1930s. Thus, the Taft Court (like its remnants in the early 1930s) is remembered primarily as a Supreme Court that opposed economic and social legislation enacted both by the states and by the federal government at the same time that it accepted restrictions on freedom of speech and other civil liberties.[92]

The conventional wisdom contains more than a kernel of truth. As early as 1930 Felix Frankfurter noted: "Since 1920 the Court has invalidated more legislation than in fifty years preceding."[93] According to Alpheus Mason's count nearly four decades later, the Court invalidated nearly one-fourth as many federal statutes during the 1920s as had been invalidated in the 140 years prior to 1925.[94]

The statutes the Taft Court held unconstitutional included significant legislative reforms of both the states and the federal government. Taft himself wrote the opinions that invalidated the Arizona statute forbidding labor injunctions and the federal child labor tax.[95] Other important decisions invalidated a minimum wage law for the District of Columbia, a state statute that banned the use of "shoddy" material in bedding, and a state licensing requirement for those who sold tickets for transportation to and from foreign countries; required compensation under the Eminent Domain Clause when state regulations were too restrictive; and mandated the use of replacement value in setting railroad rates.[96]

One can also reasonably charge the Taft Court with insensitivity to the civil liberties of unpopular minorities. Over the classic First Amendment dissent of Justice Holmes, the Court tolerated criminal prosecutions based on the "dangerous tendencies" of the speeches of antiwar activists.[97] The Court also allowed the federal government to deny citizenship to conscientious objectors and permitted states to discriminate against Japanese aliens and to sterilize inmates of mental institutions.[98]

The conventional wisdom gives only a partial picture of the decisions of the Court in the prohibition era. In the 1960s, Stanley Kutler noted that Chief Justice Taft recognized the need for an expansive definition of federal power to regulate interstate commerce and that his Court upheld federal regulatory power in many contexts.[99] Similarly the Court first upheld the validity of state zoning laws during the 1920s.[100] Perhaps most importantly, the Court also rendered some expansive opinions regarding civil liberties. Although a majority of the Court narrowly defined the substance of the First Amendment, the Taft Court was the first to apply the guarantees of the amendment to the states.[101] Even prior to the New Deal revolution, the Court occasionally relied on the First Amendment to reverse state criminal convictions, and it refused to approve injunctions that prohibited a newspaper from publishing certain articles.[102] In addition, the Court also extended the Due Process Clause to protect noneconomic rights as well as to defend property interests.[103]

When an adequate history of the Supreme Court of the prohibition era is written, the prohibition decisions will occupy a prominent place. Between 1920 and 1933, the Court decided scores of decisions relating to the Eighteenth Amendment and the Volstead Act. In doing so the Court displayed far more sensitivity to changing social attitudes than conventional wisdom would predict.

Despite the relative continuity in its personnel, Supreme Court doctrine regarding prohibition issues was far from stable. Not only did the Court decide a large number of cases involving prohibition enforcement, but the trend of the Court's decisions parallels the political conflict over prohibition. Nearly all of the Court's early decisions favored enforcement authorities; opinions from the middle years showed incipient doubts coupled with continuing support; and the decisions after 1930 restricted enforcement options and expanded individual rights. Furthermore, many of the major exceptions to the general pattern involved some type of property right. Even in the early and middle years of the prohibition era, the Court was willing to protect vested property interests.[104]

The overwhelming majority of the decisions prior to 1925 favored the government, including one handed down before the Eighteenth Amendment became effective on January 16, 1920. The Volstead Act's definition of intoxicating liquors to include all beverages with more than one-half of 1 percent alcohol by volume also applied to wartime prohibition, and the Court sustained that definition even before the amendment went into effect.[105]

Early in the decade, the Court emphatically rejected a series of innovative procedural and substantive attacks on the validity of both the Eighteenth Amendment and the Volstead Act. One 1920 decision refused to allow a state to conduct a referendum on repealing its legislative ratification of the Eighteenth Amendment.[106] A second confirmed that the Eighteenth Amendment "had become part of the Constitution and must be respected and given effect the same as other provisions" and that the Volstead Act could define intoxicating liquors to include beverages containing as much as one-half of 1 percent of alcohol by volume.[107] The following year the Court affirmed the power of Congress to limit the period for ratification,[108] and a 1925 decision ruled that Congress could constitutionally enact the Volstead Act before the date on which the Eighteenth Amendment became effective.[109]

The Court also recognized broad federal enforcement powers. For example, it construed the Volstead Act to cover international shipping of intoxicating liquors[110] and upheld Congress's power to tax the intoxicating liquors that the act made it illegal to produce.[111] It also allowed federal prosecutors to use bills of information rather than grand jury indictments to charge misdemeanors under the Volstead Act.[112]

The Court was equally generous when defining state enforcement power in the early years of national prohibition. A Georgia law established a presumption that persons who occupied the real property on which a distilling apparatus was found knew of its existence. A 1922 decision sustained the presumption.[113]

On the other hand, the Supreme Court was not sympathetic to the rights of criminal defendants. It consistently adopted narrow constructions of the scope of individual rights under the Fourth and Fifth Amendments and the federal habeas corpus statute. For example, the Court recognized the open fields exception to the Fourth Amendment's search and seizure provisions[114] and allowed states and the federal government to initiate successive prosecutions for the same overt act.[115] It also refused to allow the habeas corpus statute to be used as the vehicle for lodging a constitutional challenge to a misdemeanor conviction under the Volstead Act.[116]

The number of decisions related to prohibition enforcement increased significantly during the second half of the 1920s. In general their tenor was similar to those of the early years. For the most part, they supported enforcement officials.

The Court continued to recognize broad regulatory authority for both state and federal governments. At the state level, it affirmed a conviction under a law that banned mere possession of intoxicating liquor.[117] At the federal level, the Court affirmed congressional power to limit the authority of physicians to prescribe intoxicating liquors[118] and upheld the Volstead Act's "padlock" provisions authorizing the closing of premises on which certain liquor violations occurred.[119] Finally, the Court still narrowly constructed the rights of criminal defendants under the Fourth and Fifth Amendments.[120]

During the middle years of prohibition, Supreme Court opinions also continued the generous construction of the Volstead Act. The Court interpreted the act to reach a conspirator who never entered the United States as a member of the conspiracy,[121] to allow the Commissioner of Internal Revenue to deny permits to persons the commissioner determined were unfit to deal in nonbeverage alcohol,[122] and to give federal officials considerable authority to forfeit property used to transport intoxicating liquors.[123] The Court also construed the income tax law to require individuals to report gains from illicit traffic in intoxicating liquor.[124]

Notwithstanding this overall trend, a close look at the decisions from the second half of the 1920s reveals some incipient doubts about prohibition enforcement. The Court rendered several decisions favorable to defendants where the opinions were not based on vested property rights.[125] Dissents became somewhat more common, and the Court even divided five to four in two highly publicized cases involving wiretapping and congressional control over physicians.[126]

After 1930 the trend of decisions shifted noticeably. The most dramatic illustration of the change occurred not in the Supreme Court, but at the district court level. Conceding that he was likely to be reversed, a federal judge ruled the Eighteenth Amendment itself invalid. He accepted the argument of prohibition opponents that the subject of the amendment fell outside the amending power conferred by Article V of the Constitution.[127]

In the Supreme Court, the shift was less dramatic but still quite substantial. The government still prevailed on occasion, as in the appeal from the district court that declared the Eighteenth Amendment invalid.[128] The Court, however, rendered decisions adverse to the positions advocated by prohibition enforcement authorities in a variety of areas. Most of these cases involved the Volstead Act; in them, the contrast with the sympathetic construction in the opinions from the 1920s is vivid. The new opinions declared that purchasing liquor was not a crime under the act,[129] allowed judges to reduce sentences imposed under the act,[130] construed a treaty with Great Britain to deny customs officials authority to board British vessels,[131] and severely restricted the government's ability to forfeit the interests of innocent owners of property used to transport intoxicating liquors.[132] The decisions from the 1930s also expanded the rights of criminal defendants by rediscovering the rule requiring liberal construction of Fourth Amendment rights,[133] denying the government the power to recover civil penalties for acts that had formed the basis for a prior Volstead Act conviction,[134] and allowing a defendant's wife to testify on his behalf.[135]

Following repeal the Court—like the country as a whole—tried to put the prohibition experience, and the problems associated with prohibition enforcement, behind it.[136] Less than a year after the ratification of the Twenty-first Amendment, the Court held that the adoption of the repealing amendment operated to abate pending prosecutions.[137] Later it expanded that ruling to cover cases in which convictions were being appealed.[138]

A Preliminary Assessment

The general symmetry between the political and doctrinal developments of the prohibition era provides the hypothesis for this study. It suggests, and the chapters that follow demonstrate, how studying the legal developments of the prohibition era can illuminate the historical significance of prohibition, increase our understanding of the Supreme Court's history, and illustrate how law responds to changes in public attitudes.

The historical claim is the most obvious. The decisions described in the preceding pages document that the Supreme Court faced a host of new problems in prohibition cases, and many of those problems remain important in federal criminal law today. Moreover, the overall decisional pattern of the prohibition cases follows changing public opinion during the prohibition era. Taken together, these factors indicate that legal doctrine contains some of the most significant and enduring impacts of national prohibition.

The prohibition cases also provide an interesting window for viewing the Supreme Court during the 1920s and early 1930s. The pattern reflected in the Court's prohibition cases offer a framework that may lead to a more complete understanding of the Court's decisions.

Finally, the prohibition cases illuminate, in a more general way, the relationship of legal doctrine to the political and social situations to which it responds. The volume and pattern of the prohibition cases identify the prohibition experience as the decisive factor in shaping federal criminal law doctrine during the 1920s. At the same time, the pattern is too complex to support a reductionist claim that the judicial decisions of the prohibition era reflect prohibition politics. The occasional contrary decisions, especially decisions affecting property rights, indicate that other influences were also important. Furthermore, the prohibition cases also confirm the importance of legal ideology in shaping doctrine. Most of the major decisions of the early years remained authoritative at the end of the prohibition era because of the court's preference for distinguishing rather than overruling prior decisions.

The remainder of this study is a detailed analysis of the foregoing claims regarding the doctrinal developments of the era of national prohibition. The substantive chapters review the changes that occurred in five areas related to federal criminal law: the defense of entrapment, the Fourth Amendment's protection against unreasonable searches and seizures, the Fifth Amendment's prohibition against double jeopardy, property forfeitures, and the jury trial guarantees for criminal proceedings. The concluding chapter then uses the information from those chapters to show that the legal developments of the prohibition era are important in order to analyze the historical impact of national prohibition, to understand the Supreme Court of the prohibition era, and to appreciate how law changes and develops.

2 / Entrapment: The Emergence of a Legal Doctrine

The defense of entrapment excuses a defendant from criminal liability because the actions of government officials produced the crime of which the defendant stands accused. Entrapment is an accepted part of contemporary law, but, at least as far as federal law is concerned, the doctrine is a creation of the twentieth century.

Even before the Eighteenth Amendment became effective in 1920, two federal circuits had articulated a rudimentary doctrine of entrapment. The realities of prohibition enforcement encouraged defendants to raise the defense more frequently. As a result, the federal courts had to define the parameters of entrapment doctrine with more precision. For the most part, the courts of appeal were the architects of the doctrine. Not until the very end of the prohibition era did the Supreme Court recognize and endorse the new defense.

Entrapment Doctrine before Prohibition

In 1908 California immigration agents suspected that Woo Wai, a Chinese American businessman in San Francisco, had information about a smuggling ring operating on the Pacific Coast. The officials resolved to catch Woo Wai in a smuggling violation so they could compel him to tell what he knew about other suspected smugglers. Unable to secure evidence that would support Woo Wai's prosecution on any charge, the agents decided to trap him into violating the immigration laws, and an agent sought to enlist his participation in a plan to smuggle alien women into the country through Mexico.[1]

Woo Wai refused to have anything to do with the immigration officials' plot. Undismayed, the agents continued to press the scheme on their unsuspecting victim for nearly eighteen months. They assured him that the plan was foolproof. Twice they transported him to San Diego at government expense so immigration supervisors could assure him that they would offer complete protection. Woo Wai finally capitulated, and he carried out the smuggling operation that the government agents had conceived and arranged.

As Woo Wai crossed the border with the aliens, immigration agents arrested him. After the arrest, the agents who had originally enlisted Woo Wai in the plot offered him immunity from prosecution if he would testify against others whom they suspected of membership in a smuggling ring. When Woo Wai denied any knowledge of the ring's activities, the immigration authorities prosecuted him on a charge of conspiracy to smuggle aliens into the United States.

Seven years later, the criminal defense of entrapment made its first appearance in the reported decisions of the United States federal courts as a direct result of this tale of intrigue.[2] At trial the district judge charged the jury that Woo Wai had stated no defense recognized by the law even if the jury believed all of his testimony about the governmental involvement in the scheme. After receiving these instructions, the jury convicted Woo Wai and all of his coconspirators who were not immigration officials. On appeal the United States Court of Appeal for the Ninth Circuit expressed its disapproval of the trial court's charge and of the immigration department's subterfuge. It voided Woo Wai's conviction and remanded the case for a new trial because "[W]e are of the opinion that it is against public policy to sustain a conviction obtained in the manner which is disclosed by the evidence in this case." "Sound public policy," said the appellate court, "can be upheld only by denying the criminality of those who are thus induced to commit acts which infringe the letter of the criminal statutes."[3]

A casual survey of the federal criminal law in 1915 illustrates the innovation that the Ninth Circuit introduced in the *Woo Wai* case.[4] The Supreme Court precedents in a series of mail fraud cases were contrary.[5] Moreover, the court of appeals did not cite any reported decisions of the lower federal courts even by way of analogy. Similarly the criminal law texts,[6] legal encyclopedias,[7] and legal dictionaries[8] failed to cite any federal cases supporting the defense.

The decision overturning Woo Wai's conviction does not seem to have occasioned any significant scholarly comment. In fact, the *Index to Legal Periodicals* does not even list it among the cases decided in 1915 that were discussed in the legal periodicals of that year.

Judicial acceptance of the entrapment defense proceeded slowly during the five years following the *Woo Wai* decision in 1915. The Ninth Circuit ordered new trials on entrapment grounds in two more cases. Only the Seventh Circuit followed suit.

One of the Ninth Circuit cases involved an immigration scheme similar to that of Woo Wai's case. Sam Yick approached a customs inspector and asked him to prepare some false immigration papers. Instead of prosecuting Yick for the violation, the inspector enticed him into a plan for bringing Orientals into the country and later had Yick prosecuted for the more serious crime of conspiracy to bring aliens into the country illegally. According to the court of appeals, the trial record contained no evidence indicating that the conspiracy crime originated with Sam Yick. Nevertheless, the trial judge had refused to submit the entrapment defense to the jury, saying in his instructions that "the fact . . . that government officers incited or aided defendants to commit the crime charged against them . . . is no bar to a prosecution by the government." Because this instruction was inconsistent with its recent decision in Woo Wai, the appellate court reversed Yick's conviction and ordered a new trial: "[W]here the officers of the law have incited the party to commit the crime charged and lured him on to its consummation the law will not authorize a verdict of guilty."[9]

One other Ninth Circuit entrapment case reversed a conviction prior to 1920. It involved the wartime offense of selling liquor to soldiers in uniform. The defendant testified that government undercover agents had harassed her for over three hours before she agreed to sell them any beer. The district court refused to submit the entrapment defense to the jury and gave the following charge:

> There is a class of offenses, *like the unlawful selling of intoxicating liquor,* . . . [where] it is difficult to secure the evidence by any other means, except by the use of decoys; and you are instructed that if it appears in this case that the officers had information which led them to believe and they were justified in believing that the premises occupied by the defendant was a place where . . . the defendant was engaged in selling intoxicating liquor to members of the military service, while in uniform, it was very proper for them to initiate an investigation, and if the two officers . . . went there and solicited beer and offered to buy it, and urged her to sell it to them, the fact that they urged her to sell the beer to them is no excuse.

The court of appeals held that this instruction was contrary to the "settled rule in this circuit," reversed the defendant's conviction, and remanded the case for a new trial in the district court.[10]

The third appellate case to follow the *Woo Wai* decision and to overturn a conviction because the trial court erroneously instructed the jury on the entrapment defense arose in the Seventh Circuit. Unable to induce the defendant into a knowing violation of the federal law that prohibited selling liquor to Indians, government agents devised a scheme to trick him into violating the statute unwittingly.[11] The agents disguised an individual to resemble the Mexican laborers who were working on a road gang in the area and sent the disguised individual to the defendant's establishment. The defendant sold the disguised Indian some liquor, and government agents immediately arrested him. Later he was convicted in the district court when the trial judge refused to submit the entrapment issue to the jury. The Seventh Circuit reversed the conviction, remanded the case for a new trial, and leveled this blast at the conduct of the government agents:

> Is our government of the superman type that releases the ruler from the obligations of honesty and fairness that are imposed on the citizens? Is one's liberty or reputation as a law-abider to have less protection than his property? We are strongly of the view that sound public policy estops the government from asserting that an act which involves no criminal intent was voluntarily done when it originated in and was caused by the government agents' deception.[12]

These three cases, however, remained isolated exceptions in the federal criminal law of 1920. A majority of the reported federal decisions continued to uphold convictions for mail fraud,[13] selling liquor to soldiers in uniform,[14] and maintaining a house of ill-fame within five miles of a military reservation[15] against entrapment challenges. Some of the opinions in these cases went so far as to deny the existence of the entrapment defense.[16]

Increased Acceptance in the Lower Federal Courts

The Early Years of Prohibition

The defense of entrapment attracted little interest from academics during the first five years of the prohibition era. The *Index to Legal Periodicals* did not include it as a subtopic until 1924, and only two short articles on the subject appeared before 1925.[17]

By contrast, judicial attention to the defense increased appreciably during the early years of prohibition. Between 1920 and 1924, thirty-two appellate opinions addressed the entrapment defense. All but three[18] involved criminal charges related to prohibition or the narcotics laws,[19] and they were nearly evenly divided between alcohol[20] and drug offenses.[21] Only the Eighth Circuit actually reversed convictions on entrapment grounds, and it did so in two cases. Both involved narcotics violations and reflected outrageous police conduct similar to the cases that had recognized the defense prior to prohibition.

The first of the reversals involved a conviction of Clarence Butts, an admitted morphine addict, for selling narcotic drugs. Butts had become addicted to morphine while taking the drug to relieve the pain from eighteen operations for tuberculosis of the bones. He had, however, never sold morphine prior to April 1920 when an acquaintance approached him for help in procuring a small quantity of the drug.

According to Butts's testimony, the friend played on his sympathy by claiming that he was in severe pain that he could not stand if he did not get some morphine. After several plaintive pleas, Butts procured a small amount of the narcotic and sold it to his friend at no profit. Butts then learned that the supposed friend was working as an undercover agent to avoid prosecution on an earlier narcotics arrest. On the basis of the single sale to the informer, federal officials prosecuted Butts on the offense of selling narcotic drugs. The trial court refused an entrapment instruction, and the jury convicted him.

The Eighth Circuit reversed. Emphasizing that the "first duties of the officers of law are to prevent, not to punish, crime," the court reminded the officers that "it is not their duty to incite to and create crime for the sole purpose of prosecuting and punishing it." In Butts's case, the court continued, the evidence strongly tended to prove that the officials had caused the crime in order to punish it. The court ordered a new trial, declaring that it

is unconscionable, contrary to public policy and to the established law of the land to punish a man for the commission of an offense of the like of which he had never been guilty, either in thought or in deed, and evidently never would have been guilty of if the officers of the law had not inspired, incited, persuaded, and lured him to attempt to commit it.[22]

In the other decision that reversed a conviction on entrapment grounds during the 1920–1924 period, the bizarre feature was the district judge's charge to the jury, rather than the police conduct. The defendant testified that a female government informer enticed him into selling her narcotics. According to the summary of the evidence contained in the opinion of the court of appeals:

> There was evidence tending to show that the defendant had never theretofore dealt in narcotics, that the officers participated in devising the criminal act, aided the informer in inducing it, and sent her after the defendant with money and the beguiling pleas of a woman's tongue when he had dropped out of the proposed plan and was about to escape.[23]

The trial judge severely limited defense attempts to elicit further evidence of government inducement by cross-examining government witnesses. Moreover, he made conviction almost a religious duty in his instructions to the jury. In his charge, the district judge recalled "the beautiful story that Jesus of Nazareth gave to the world when He was here" and "the tragedy of His crucifixion." He reminded the jury that "on the night before the crucifixion, Jesus went down to Jerusalem even though He knew He would be betrayed." "It may be argued," the judge said, "that by going to Jerusalem, Jesus tempted Judas Iscariot; that He could have remained away and saved Judas Iscariot from committing the despicable crime . . . of betraying his master. . . ." It might be said that Jesus was urging Judas to commit the crime, "but it was in the heart of this man. It was really giving him the opportunity to commit crime if he was disposed to commit the crime."

From this scriptural allusion, the judge drew the following homily for the jury:

> These officers, in going there with the informer and having her call this man at the room at 516 Cordova Hotel, were only giving this man an opportunity to commit crime if he were disposed to commit a crime, and there was no other method whereby they could detect men who were violating the act.

"So," he informed the jury, "the court must charge you that there was no entrapment in this case."[24]

Terming the entrapment illustration "incongruous," the Eighth Circuit concluded that a jury could not act "without passion and prejudice in such an atmosphere." In the appellate court's analysis, it was important to find out all that had transpired between the informer and the government agents. Whether the agents stopped with setting a decoy for a suspected lawbreaker or whether they enticed an innocent citizen into a violation "raised an issue of fact . . . and it was error to refuse . . . to instruct the jury on that subject." The court reversed the conviction and remanded the case for a new trial.[25]

The Eighth Circuit decisions were the only decisions that actually reversed lower court verdicts. However, other circuits also embraced the defense. The Ninth Circuit confirmed the rule it had laid down in its decision in the *Woo Wai* case.[26] In addition, opinions from the Second, Third, Fourth, and Seventh Circuits also verbally acknowledged the defense.[27]

The Second Half of the Decade

The years after 1925 saw increasing interest in the entrapment defense among legal commentators. Each of the last five years of the 1920s produced at least one law review article on the subject. These articles were usually short comments on recent cases by law student authors. They contain little critical comment. Instead, they are content with a recitation of the court ruling under discussion, a collection of the leading cases, and a statement as to whether the decision accords with the majority of decided cases.[28] They reflect a widespread acceptance of the defense,[29] although an occasional author expresses some reservations about the general practice of submitting the defense to the jury rather than to the court.[30] Most of the authors regarded the essence of the defense as a factual question appropriate for jury consideration: They identify the issue raised by the defense as whether the police conduct induced a particular defendant to violate a statute that the defendant would not otherwise have violated.

As early as 1922, the defense was well enough established for the Lawyer's Cooperative Publishing Company to publish an annotation that collected a large number of state and federal cases dealing with entrapment.[31] The criminal law treatises and general legal references also show a growing recognition of the entrapment defense in the federal courts during the 1920s. The 1927 edition of Clark and Marshall's criminal law text discusses the defense approvingly and cites federal cases supporting the doctrine.[32] Similarly the 1929 Supplement to *Ruling Case Law* also reflects the increased acceptance of the defense by citing federal cases that recognize the doctrine.[33]

The second half of the decade also produced growing acceptance of the defense by the federal judiciary. The number of reported opinions in the federal courts of appeal was constant, but the prohibition flavor of the doctrine became more pronounced. Twenty-one[34] of the thirty-three entrapment opinions involved offenses related to prohibition.[35] In addition, the number of reversals increased to seven, all but one of which involved prohibition offenses.[36] Moreover, the growing acceptance of the defense is also evident in the fact that in many of the cases that were affirmed on appeal, the trial court had submitted the entrapment issue to the jury.[37]

The emphasis in the reported opinions shows a decidedly more legalistic bent. Burden of proof and evidentiary problems associated with assertion of the defense begin to appear.[38] In general the decisions turn less on unique fact situations than on the relatively unemotional question of whether the defense offered any credible evidence tending to show that the criminal intent originated with the government. If there was any such evidence, the trial court risked reversal by refusing to submit the issue to the jury.

The legalistic emphasis is particularly evident in the opinions of the Eighth Circuit, which reversed three prohibition convictions on entrapment grounds in 1927 and 1928. In the first, one of several defendants testified that he had made the illicit liquor sales only after repeated pleas and pressure from governmental agents. The Eighth Circuit ruled that this testimony presented "a question of fact for the jury upon the issue of entrapment."[39] Similarly the defendant in the second case testified that he became involved in the scheme to violate the Volstead Act only after prohibition agents had repeatedly pleaded with him over a period of several days. Again, the appellate court reversed the conviction and remanded the case for a new trial, holding that "where the evidence on the question of entrapment is in conflict it presents an issue of fact for the jury on proper instructions."[40] In the third case, federal authorities prosecuted a prohibition agent for accepting a bribe from a person against whom the agent was scheduled to testify in a separate criminal action. Testifying at his own trial, the agent said that he took the money merely to obtain evidence that would support a bribery prosecution against the man who offered the bribe. The court ruled that the agent's testimony raised an entrapment issue that should have been left for the jury.[41]

There were similar reversals in the First,[42] Fifth,[43] Sixth,[44] and Ninth[45] Circuits, and other appellate decisions that affirmed convictions also treated the entrapment defense as raising an issue for the jury.[46] In fifteen years, the defense had grown from an ad hoc weapon to handle bizarre cases to a legal doctrine that was regularly asserted in federal courts on appeals from liquor and drug convictions.

The 1930s

The trend toward increased acceptance of the defense of entrapment by legal commentators continued during the 1930s. The 1933 edition of *Black's Law Dictionary* added entrapment to the list of words it defined,[47] and the supplement to *Corpus Juris* expanded its treatment of the topic.[48] In addition, the number of articles discussing the defense increased from two in 1930[49] to five in 1931.[50]

Not surprisingly the pattern of decisions in the courts of appeals also continued to reflect acceptance of entrapment as a defense. Both the number of opinions[51] and reversals[52] dropped. However, the percentage of the cases that involved offenses related to prohibition continued to increase.[53] Entrapment was now an accepted part of the fabric of federal criminal law.

By the early 1930s, all of the federal circuits had recognized the defense of entrapment.[54] The exact parameters of the defense were not always clear.[55] However, the reported opinions generally emphasized the "origin" of the defendant's intent to violate the criminal law. Whenever there was conflicting evidence on this question, the appellate courts required instructions that, in effect, asked the jury to decide whether the defendant was a law-abiding citizen who had been tempted to crime by overzealous government agents or a confirmed criminal that the government had finally tricked into a violation for which a conviction could be obtained. Typical and widely quoted was the following articulation of the defense by the Eighth Circuit:

> It is not denied that, in cases where the criminal intent originates in the mind of the defendant, the fact that the officers of the government used decoys or untruthful statements to furnish opportunity for or to aid the accused in the commission of a crime, in order successfully to prosecute him therefor, constitutes no defense to such a prosecution, . . .

But when the accused has never committed such an offense as that charged against him prior to the time when he is charged with the offense prosecuted, and never conceived any intention of committing the offense prosecuted, or any such offense, and had not the means to do so, the fact that the officers of the government incited and by persuasion and representation lured him to commit the offense charged, in order to entrap, arrest, and prosecute him therefor, is and ought to be fatal to the prosecution and to entitle the accused to a verdict of not guilty.[56]

Supreme Court Recognition

During the decade and a half that the federal courts of appeals struggled to create, to define, and to restrict the entrapment doctrine, the Supreme Court gave little guidance to the lower courts. On twelve occasions, the Court declined to review entrapment decisions of the intermediate appellate courts by denying petitions for writs of certiorari.[57] The only case to mention the doctrine was *Casey v. United States*,[58] a 1928 decision in which the Court granted certiorari to determine whether a statutory presumption in the Harrison Anti-Narcotic Drug Act was constitutional. In *Casey* the issue was raised inadvertently when the record revealed an entrapment claim that the defendant had never pursued.

Federal narcotic agents suspected that Casey, an attorney, was supplying jail inmates with illegal drugs. They persuaded a prisoner and the wife of a second prisoner to help them trap the attorney into a violation. The plan was for the prisoner to request a conference with Casey. At the conference, the prisoner would attempt to purchase some morphine. The agents installed a dictaphone in the attorneys' cage where the attorney and the prisoner were to confer, and they arranged to listen in surreptitiously on the meeting. According to the agents' testimony, Casey agreed to sell the morphine, accepted payment from the prisoner, and agreed to deliver the narcotic to the woman who was also secretly cooperating with the agents. The next day, Casey delivered a towel to the woman. Chemical tests revealed that the towel contained morphine.

Justice Brandeis wrote a dissenting opinion, in which Justice Roberts concurred. He refused to discuss the statutory presumption that the case was intended to present "for, in my opinion, the prosecution must fail because officers of the Government instigated the commission of the alleged crime." He argued that "the obstacle to the prosecution is . . . that the act for which the Government seeks to punish is the product of a criminal conspiracy by government agents to induce its commission." While "the Government may set decoys to entrap criminals," he wrote, "it may not provoke or create a crime and then punish the criminal, its creature." The dissenting justices attached no legal significance to Casey's failure to object on the ground of entrapment, "either below or in this Court." This prosecution, he reasoned,

> should be stopped, not because some right of Casey's has been denied, but in order to protect the Government. To protect it from illegal conduct of its officers. To preserve the purity of its courts. In my opinion, the judgment should be vacated with direction to quash the indictment.[59]

Justice Holmes authored the majority opinion holding the statutory presumption constitutional. He did not consider the entrapment problem. "A court," he said, "can rarely act with advantage of its own motion, and very rarely upon grounds that the record was not intended to present." Describing the agents' conduct as no "worse than ordering a drink of a suspected bootlegger," he concluded: "[W]hatever doubts we may feel as to the truth of the testimony we are not at liberty to consider them on the only question before the Court."[60]

Five years after the *Casey* decision, the Supreme Court finally addressed the merits of the entrapment defense.[61] The case that eventually reached the Supreme Court began on November 30, 1930, when the grand jury for the Western District of North Carolina indicted C. V. Sorrells on two counts of violating the Volstead Act. The first count of the indictment charged that, on July 13, 1930, Sorrells unlawfully possessed one-half gallon of whiskey with intent to sell it. Count two charged that, on the same date, Sorrells sold one-half gallon of whiskey to R. V. Martin.[62]

A week later, Sorrells was tried in the United States district court. The government's principal witness, R. V. Martin, testified that he had purchased a half gallon of whiskey from Sorrells on July 13, 1930, for five dollars. When cross-examined, Martin said that he had gone to Sorrells's home on July 13 in the company of Fanning Lowe, E. D. Jones, and C. J. Snyder and that Fanning Lowe introduced him to Sorrells. He admitted that the first time he asked Sorrells for some whiskey Sorrells refused, saying that he did not fool with liquor.

Explaining the transaction in more detail, Martin acknowledged that Sorrells did not produce the whiskey until Martin had asked him three times and that Sorrells did not complete the sale until thirty minutes after Martin arrived. Martin also conceded that, after discovering that he and Sorrells had served in the same division in the world war, he had reminisced with Sorrells about war experiences for some time. Martin agreed that he was the only person to mention anything about securing liquor and that he went to the Sorrells home with the express purpose of indicting and prosecuting Sorrells for violating the Volstead Act.[63]

When Martin completed his testimony, the government rested. After the district judge denied Sorrells's motion for a directed verdict of acquittal, Sorrells presented his defense. The eight defense witnesses did not deny that Sorrells sold the whiskey. They tried, however, to establish that Martin had trapped Sorrells into the violation.

E. D. Jones, the first witness for the defense, testified that he, along with Martin and two other men, visited the Sorrells home on July 13 and that he had introduced Martin to Sorrells. He admitted that Sorrells had obtained a half gallon of whiskey for Martin. He said, however, that Sorrells had made the sale only after four or five entreaties from Martin that attempted to play on his war comradeship with Sorrells. He also claimed that Sorrells had left his house for twenty to thirty minutes to obtain the whiskey he sold to Martin. On cross-examination, Jones stated that he had never heard of Sorrells being in the liquor business and that he believed that one former war buddy would get liquor for another.

The next defense witness, C. V. Stevens, testified that Sorrells's character and general reputation were good. He said that, as time-keeper of the company for which Sorrells worked, he knew that Sorrells had held his job continuously without missing a payday since March 1924.

The defense also called C. J. Snyder and Fanning Lowe, the other two persons present at the sale, as witnesses. They corroborated Jones's testimony concerning the circumstances under which Sorrells had sold the whiskey to Martin. Other defense witnesses attested to Sorrells's good character and their lack of knowledge about him ever selling any liquor. When these witnesses completed their testimony, the defense rested.[64]

In rebuttal, the government introduced evidence that, subsequent to July 13, Sorrells had sold whiskey to prohibition agents. The government also called several witnesses who said that Sorrells had the general reputation of being a rum runner. When the government rested again, Sorrells renewed his motion for a directed verdict of not guilty. The court overruled the motion. He refused to give any of the entrapment instructions Sorrells requested. Instead, he gave the following charge to the jury:

> Gentlemen of the Jury, the defendant takes the position that this evidence shows that this man was induced or entrapped to sell liquor. The court holds as a matter of law that was not the case, and the court instructs that if you believe the testimony of Mr. Martin, the witness who said he bought a half gallon from the defendant, you will convict him then. You will take the case and go out with it or you can form your opinion here.

The jury found Sorrells guilty, and the court sentenced him to a prison term of eighteen months.[65]

Sorrells appealed his conviction to the United States Court of Appeal for the Fourth Circuit. His brief in the appellate court relied primarily on his entrapment claim. He argued that the evidence showed entrapment as a matter of law or, alternatively, that the evidence presented a factual question on the entrapment issue that the trial judge should have submitted to the jury under an appropriate instruction.[66] The government's brief did not challenge the legitimacy of the entrapment defense when government agents induced criminal violations. Instead, it contended that there was no entrapment issue for the court or jury because the evidence showed without conflict that the government agent did no more than offer to buy the whiskey.[67]

A divided court affirmed Sorrells's conviction. Judge Parker's majority opinion, which Judge Northcott joined, held that the district court "properly instructed the jury that there was no evidence of entrapment." Breaking the uniform pattern of doctrinal development during the prohibition era, Judge Parker proceeded to define entrapment much more restrictively than any other federal appellate court had done. Relying on old Supreme Court mail fraud cases and an annotation written in 1882, the opinion recognized the defense of entrapment "only where, as a result of inducement, the accused is placed in the attitude of having committed a crime he did not intend to commit, or where, by reason of the consent implied in the inducement, no crime has been committed." The defense applied, the majority said, only in prosecutions for crimes such as larceny where the victim's consent negates an essential element of the crime and in mistaken identity cases where the inducement negates any intent to violate the law.[68]

Judge Parker acknowledged that "courts in some of the federal circuits have seemingly given their approval to the broad doctrine that inducement on the part of government officials is a sufficient defense for one charged with the sale of intoxicating liquor in violation of law." He declared, however, that "such holding is contrary to the weight of authority on the subject" and cited a long list of state and older federal cases. He also attempted to distinguish *Newman v. United States*,[69] a recent Fourth Circuit case that had recognized the defense of entrapment. According to Judge Parker:

> the Newman Case is authority for the proposition that the defendant there was not entitled to certain instructions on entrapment . . . but insofar as the language of the opinion goes beyond this, it is not controlling. . . . If the Newman case be understood as laying down the rule that one who knowingly and intentionally violates the law, and entertains the criminal design to violate it, is to be excused . . . because his crime was induced by the act of an officer of the law we cannot follow it.[70]

"Many decisions," Judge Parker argued, "deal with the subject of entrapment as though the enforcement of the law were a game in which the law is to be penalized because officials do not play according to the rules." These opinions, he continued, "apply a false doctrine of entrapment based in some decisions on estoppel and in others on shadowy grounds of public policy." "Neither ground," he concluded, "will withstand analysis." He rejected the estoppel argument because of the rule in civil cases that the government cannot be estopped by the conduct of its officers. "As for public policy argument there is no higher public policy than that all men should obey the law."[71]

Judge Soper dissented. He argued that the court's opinion was contrary to its former decision in *Newman*, which had recognized a rule that "has been accepted in every federal circuit." He distinguished the precedents relied on by the majority with the observation that the Supreme Court "has had no occasion to say in any case before it that the accused had been improperly trapped." "It is of course true," Judge Soper wrote, "that no conduct on the part of the officers of the government can authorize or excuse a violation of the law." Nevertheless, "it has been thought by the federal judiciary with striking unanimity that the government should not be allowed to prosecute a man who has been transformed from a law-abiding citizen into a criminal by the activities of its agents." When the proof established such inducement of the defendant, he argued, "fair dealing demands that the prosecution shall fail." Admitting that "it is likely enough that the rule of entrapment now generally accepted in other federal circuits is an extension of the law," Judge Soper said that "the development illogical though it may be has taken place, and we should gain nothing if we should now retrace our steps."[72]

Analyzing the evidence against Sorrells, the dissenting judge said:

the jury might have found that the defendant had been an industrious law-abiding man, who had never violated the National Prohibition Law . . . prior to the sale charged in the indictment, and that he was overpersuaded on that occasion by the persistent requests of his former comrades in arms to leave his home and procure the liquor they desired.

On the other hand, he conceded, "the jury might have concluded that the agent had reason to suspect that the defendant was a lawbreaker, and that the event proved this to be true when once the defendant was convinced that he might safely do business with his visitors." In Judge Soper's view, this situation

was not a case for peremptory instructions by the District Judge either way, if improper entrapment is a valid defense, for conflicting inferences might reasonably have been drawn from the evidence, and a question of fact for the determination of the jury was presented.[73]

After the Fourth Circuit affirmed his conviction, Sorrells petitioned the Supreme Court of the United States for a writ of certiorari. In his petition, he argued that the Court should review the case because of the conflict among the circuits created by the Fourth Circuit decision.[74] The government's memorandum in response admitted that "if the doctrine is correctly stated in the other Circuit Courts of Appeals, the defense of entrapment in this case raised issues which should have been submitted to the jury under appropriate instructions." As a result, it "did not oppose" the Supreme Court's granting the petition.[75] The Supreme Court granted the writ of certiorari on October 10, 1932, and limited its review to the question of whether the evidence was sufficient to go to the jury upon the issue of entrapment.[76]

Sorrells's brief on the merits urged that the government's evidence alone was sufficient to establish the entrapment defense.[77] The government's brief did not strenuously argue for affirmance of the holding of the court of appeals, although it did note that the Supreme Court had never upheld an entrapment claim previously. Instead, it placed primary reliance on the argument that the entrapment defense had to be pleaded as an affirmative defense and was not available on a general plea of not guilty.[78]

Only Justice McReynolds dissented from the Supreme Court's reversal of the decision of the Fourth Circuit.[79] Eight justices agreed that entrapment was a defense recognized by federal law, but they split five to three in explaining the nature of the doctrine.

Chief Justice Hughes wrote the majority opinion. After summarizing the proof presented at Sorrells's trial, the chief justice said the evidence would support findings:

> that the act for which defendant was prosecuted was instigated by the prohibition agent, that it was the creature of his purpose, that defendant had no previous disposition to commit it but was an industrious law-abiding citizen, and that the agent lured the defendant, otherwise innocent, to its commission by repeated and persistent solicitation in which he succeeded by taking advantage of the sentiment aroused by reminiscences of their experiences as companions in arms in the World War.

According to the majority opinion, "such a gross abuse of authority given for the purpose of detecting and punishing crime, and not for the making of criminals, deserves the severest condemnation, but the question whether it precludes prosecution or affords a ground of defense, and, if so, upon what theory, has given rise to conflicting opinions."[80]

Noting that "this Court has not spoken on the precise question," the chief justice pointed out that "the weight of authority in the lower federal courts is decidedly in favor of the view that in such cases as the one before us the defense of entrapment is available."[81] The chief justice then discussed the objections to the doctrine raised in the opinion below—that the conduct of government agents may not estop the government and that the legislature is the final arbiter of public policy. "These arguments," he concluded, "rest entirely upon the

letter of the statutes," and "literal interpretation of statutes at the
expense of the reason of the law and producing absurd consequences
or flagrant injustice has frequently been condemned."[82] According to
the chief justice, "this established principle of statutory construction
is applicable to the [Volstead] Act," and he continued:

> We are unable to conclude that it was the intention of the Congress in
> enacting this statute that its processes of detection and enforcement
> should be abused by the instigation by government officials of an act on
> the part of persons otherwise innocent in order to lure them to its
> commission and to punish them. We are not forced by the letter to do
> violence to the spirit and purpose of the statute.[83]

Despite its recognition of the entrapment defense, the majority refused "to approve the view that the court, although treating the statute
as applicable despite the entrapment, and the defendant as guilty, has
authority to grant immunity, or to adopt a procedure to that end." In
the chief justice's view, it was "the function of the court to construe
the statute, not to defeat it as construed." Thus, if the statute was
applicable, any correction for improper conduct by government officials would have to come from the executive because "judicial nulli-
fication of statutes, admittedly valid and applicable, has, happily, no
place in our system." The Court's task was simply "to ascertain
whether in the light of a plain public policy and of the proper administration of justice, conduct induced as stated should be deemed to be
within the statutory prohibition." This approach, the opinion declared, "carries its own limitation." Therefore, the case presented "no
occasion to consider hypothetical cases of crimes so heinous or revolt-
ing that the applicable law would admit of no exceptions" because
"no such situation is presented here."[84]

The chief justice next turned to the problem of what evidence a
court should permit the jury to consider when a defendant asserted an
entrapment defense. He identified the controlling question as
"whether the defendant is a person otherwise innocent whom the
Government is seeking to punish for an alleged offense which is the
product of the creative activity of its own officials." In such a case,
the Court ruled:

> The Government . . . is in no position to object to evidence of the
> activities of its representatives in relation to the accused, and if the
> defendant seeks acquittal by reason of entrapment he cannot complain

of an appropriate and searching inquiry into his own conduct and predisposition as bearing upon that issue.[85]

Finally, the Court answered the government's contention that a defendant had to plead entrapment as an affirmative defense and that the defendant could not raise it on a plea of not guilty. The majority concluded that the defense required no special plea because "the defense, if the facts bear it out, takes the case out of the purview of the statute." The judgment was reversed, and the case was remanded to the district court for further proceedings consistent with the views of the majority.[86]

Justice Roberts filed a separate opinion that Justices Brandeis and Stone joined.[87] The three justices agreed that the judgment should be reversed, "but for reasons and upon grounds other than those stated in the opinion of the court." Writing for the three concurring justices, Justice Roberts defined entrapment as: "the conception and planning of an offense by an officer, and his procurement of its commission by one who would not have perpetrated it except for the trickery, persuasion, or fraud of the officer."[88] His view of the defense called for "no distinction between crimes mala in se and statutory offenses of lesser gravity; require[d] no statutory construction[;] and attribute[d] no merit to a guilty defendant." Instead, it recognized "the true foundation of the doctrine in the public policy which protects the purity of government and its processes." He criticized the majority's "new method of rationalizing the defense" as "a strained and unwarranted construction of the statute," which "amounts, in fact, to judicial amendment."[89] Moreover, he chastised the majority for ignoring the question of "whether a similar construction will be required in the case of other or more serious crimes." The majority's opinion, he said, announced no rule "as to when a statute shall be read as excluding a case of entrapment." Nor did it suggest any principle of statutory construction "which should enable us to say that it is excluded by some statutes and not by others."[90]

According to the concurring justices, the correct basis of the entrapment doctrine was "a court's authority to protect itself from such prostitution of the criminal law." Under their view, the question was one for the court rather than the jury because "the protection of its own functions and the preservation of the purity of its own temple belongs only to the court."[91] The minority's analysis viewed the majority's solution of submitting the case to the jury and permitting a "searching inquiry" into the defendant's past character as allowing the prosecution to pivot conviction in entrapment cases "not on the commission of the crime charged, but on the prior reputation or some former act or acts of the defendant not mentioned in the indictment." Therefore, although the three justices concurred in the reversal of the judgment, they recommended remanding the case to the district court "with instructions to quash the indictment and [to] discharge the defendant."[92]

On remand to the district court, the case of United States v. Sorrells came to an inauspicious end. No jury ever determined whether Sorrells was a rum runner or an ordinary citizen who procured some whiskey for a man he thought was his friend. On May 16, 1933, the district judge, apparently on the motion of the United States attorney, nol prossed the case, and the charges against Sorrells were dropped.[93]

After a brief flurry of case comments on the Supreme Court decision,[94] the entrapment issue, like the Sorrells case, slipped rapidly into obscurity. Only eleven appellate cases discussed the doctrine in the seven years between the Sorrells opinion and the start of World War 2, and only two of them reversed convictions on entrapment grounds.[95] Less than ten years after the Sorrells decision, the author of the leading law review article on entrapment argued that the defense was properly limited to the Volstead Act and should, therefore, have passed into oblivion when the Twenty-first Amendment repealed the Eighteenth.[96]

The Significance of the Entrapment Cases

The entrapment defense is one of the enduring doctrinal legacies of the prohibition era. In the 1950s, the Supreme Court interpreted Sorrells as establishing a general rule of statutory construction that applied to crimes other than violations of the Volstead Act.[97] That decision also adhered to the subjective approach embraced in the prohibition cases. More recent decisions have reaffirmed that position,[98] although legislative reform proposals have generally preferred the "objective" approach advocated by the dissenters in Sorrells.[99]

The prohibition backdrop offers a particularly valuable perspective for understanding the emergence of the entrapment defense as a legal doctrine. One can cite pre-prohibition precedents allowing the defense of entrapment, but the doctrine was largely undeveloped prior to the adoption of the Eighteenth Amendment. Prohibition greatly increased the number of entrapment claims and the sympathy with which they were received. In response federal judges accepted and delineated the entrapment defense. Not surprisingly, they shaped the defense so that it was responsive to the prohibition-related problems it was designed to solve.

In *Woo Wai* and other early decisions, the federal courts had recognized—at least tentatively—the defense of entrapment before the start of the era of national prohibition. To a large extent, these early cases fashioned an equitable defense drawn from the Anglo-American legal precept that the law should brand only a morally blameworthy individual as a criminal. In all of them, the appellate opinions bristle with indignation at police officials concocting illegal schemes and then enticing individuals who the police suspected, but could not prove, were criminals to join the conspiracy. Whether or not they prove the maxim that hard cases make bad law, the early cases made new law because the courts that decided them were willing to strain existing precedent to achieve just results.

Although national prohibition did not create the defense of entrapment, the evidence that efforts to enforce the noble experiment significantly influenced the development of the doctrine is convincing. Over one-half of all the reported federal entrapment decisions prior to 1933 involved offenses related to national prohibition. The number of cases dealing with entrapment rose dramatically after 1920, the year the Eighteenth Amendment went into effect, and the percentage of prohibition cases in the total rose even more dramatically. After 1924 all but two of the appellate cases that actually reversed convictions involved violations of the liquor laws. Moreover, repeal of the Eighteenth Amendment in 1933 again reduced the number of entrapment opinions to an insignificant total.

Judicial acceptance of the entrapment defense increased as public opposition to prohibition rose and as entrapment was more commonly invoked in the cases of the prohibition era. During the early years of national prohibition when the new amendment enjoyed widespread public support, the lower federal courts remained reluctant to recognize the defense. Not until significant public dissatisfaction with the amendment emerged during the middle years of prohibition was the defense generally accepted in prohibition cases. By the 1930s, all of the federal circuits had acknowledged a definition of the doctrine that emphasized the issue of the origin of the accused's criminal intent. If the intent to violate the law originated with the defendant, the defendant was guilty. If the officers of the law were responsible for the criminal intent, the defendant was entitled to an acquittal.

The entrapment cases were an understandable, but not inevitable, response to the difficulties of enforcing prohibition. Congress never authorized a federal enforcement effort large enough to make prohibition effective throughout the country.[100] Faced with widespread violations, federal efforts to detect and to deter violations often included efforts that seemed excessive to opponents.

One widely publicized incident involved the use of poisonous denaturants in industrial alcohol. The Volstead Act required that "denaturing materials" used by industrial alcohol plants "render the alcohol, or any compound in which it is authorized to be used, unfit for use as an intoxicating beverage." To implement the statutory mandate, regulations of the Prohibition Bureau required the use of poisonous denaturing elements. An outbreak of alcohol poisoning in the mid-1920s led to charges that the bureau regulations were responsible for the deaths that resulted.[101]

A 1926 report to the Senate documented several occasions when federal enforcement authorities were willing to participate in commercialized violations of the Volstead Act. For example, the Prohibition Bureau imported liquor from Canada for sale to retail bootleggers and set itself up in the retail liquor business on at least two occasions. Perhaps the most notorious example involved the Bridge Whist Club in New York City. For six months, the Bureau operated a speakeasy that openly sold illegal liquor to anyone who came through the doors.[102]

These incidents produced occasional public outrage, particularly in New York City. They were insufficient, however, to prompt a major backlash against prohibition itself. Throughout the 1920s, the Anti-Saloon League and its allies dominated the political process.

On a more individualized level, deception was frequently an important element in apprehending prohibition violators. In fact, two flamboyant undercover agents in New York City attracted so much publicity that they were forced to retire in 1925. Izzy Einstein and Moe Smith were perhaps the nation's most enterprising prohibition agents. Disguising themselves as automobile cleaners, milk drivers, gravediggers, streetcar conductors, and even visiting cowboys, they arrested hundreds of violators in New York City until they were dismissed in 1925.[103]

In large measure, the entrapment cases appear to reflect a judicial response to individual excesses in enforcement zeal. The difficulty of enforcing prohibition resulted in the widespread use of informers and undercover agents and made entrapment a common defense in prohibition cases. The entrapment doctrine that emerged in the lower federal courts in the 1920s allowed judges to respond to particular cases of injustice without directly challenging prohibition.

At least two elements of the federal entrapment doctrine made it particularly useful in prohibition cases. For one thing, the courts ruled that evidence of a defendant's prior criminal record and reputation was admissible when entrapment was raised as a defense. Admitting reputation evidence helped to limit the defense to "innocent" violators of the law; that is, those without prior criminal records. In addition, the generally accepted formulation of the entrapment defense also submitted the question to the jury and allowed the jury to determine the validity of the entrapment defense. Coupled with the liberal admission of evidence about the defendant's past, the entrapment defense, in effect, submitted the general worth of the defendant to a community evaluation with the jury serving as the representative of public opinion.

The courts apparently felt that innocent citizens would be safe in the hands of a cross section of the citizenry if they could prove their allegations of entrapment. Courts could then feel confident that they had adequately protected defendants in prohibition cases from overzealous law enforcement because community opinion no longer condemned private usage. At the same time, they avoided the necessity of committing the federal judiciary to the protection of defendants whose crimes were less socially respectable.

An interesting aspect of the emergence of the entrapment doctrine is the way it illustrates the interaction between preexisting legal thought and the social forces that transformed it. Having recognized the new defense of entrapment, lawyers and judges were required to define its boundaries and to incorporate it into the existing doctrinal framework. In that process, the doctrinal framework affected the legal adaptation without controlling its basic direction. Increasingly the opinions of lower federal courts focused their attention on "technical" questions such as allocating the burden of proof and determining what evidence was admissible. In these decisions, the prior legal tradition exerted its influence by shaping the new doctrine to fit within the existing legal framework.[104]

Finally, the Supreme Court's role in the development of the federal entrapment defense is an apt illustration of the Court's unique role in American legal institutions and, specifically, in the growth of federal legal doctrines. By exercising its discretionary control over the cases it wished to hear, the Court ignored the creative ferment that had spread throughout the federal judiciary. It declined to take a definite position on the doctrine, despite numerous opportunities to consider the issue, until the Fourth Circuit broke the relative uniformity of federal decisions in *Sorrells*.

When the Supreme Court eventually considered the question, it ratified the defense. The High Court, however, converted the doctrine from its original broad equitable base to a narrow question of statutory construction. National prohibition did not create the defense of entrapment in the Supreme Court any more than it had created the defense in the circuit courts, but the Court did choose a prohibition case to consider the defense. Moreover, as the lower federal courts had done, the Supreme Court formulated a doctrine that was peculiarly appropriate for prohibition cases. The Court affirmed the practices of submitting the question to the jury and allowing the prosecution to submit evidence of the defendant's prior character and criminal record. Furthermore, Chief Justice Hughes also tried to prescribe a narrow scope for the new doctrine. At a time when the Eighteenth Amendment was already well on its way to repeal, he grounded his opinion in principles of statutory construction as they applied to the Volstead Act.[105]

In short, the emergence of the entrapment defense is a paradigm of judicial enlargement of the law—the lawmaking process the United States inherited from the common law of England. A cynical observer might argue that the gradual development of the defense confirms Mr. Dooley's aphorism that the Supreme Court follows the election returns.[106] The opinions, however, reflect no conscious subservience to the increasing evidence that national prohibition was unenforceable. A more realistic assessment is that the development of the doctrine demonstrates the historicity of law as an intellectual discipline and the relativity of all legal doctrine. More significantly, the emergence of the entrapment defense shows how the historical forces that shape political and social affairs affect legal issues of which the public is largely unaware as well as legal doctrines of constitutional importance. It confirms that abstract ideals of "neutral principles" cannot, despite the best efforts of many able legal scholars, explain the way that courts will act because principles—legal or otherwise—are shaped by the realities of historical circumstance.[107]

The emergence of the defense of entrapment furnishes a vivid example of how doctrines of federal criminal law expanded during the prohibition era. With respect to entrapment, the judges of the federal courts of appeals were primarily responsible for the change. The next two chapters describe doctrinal growth in another area that changed dramatically during the prohibition era: the meaning of the Fourth Amendment's prohibition of unreasonable searches and seizures. Here the Supreme Court itself transformed the existing doctrine.

3 / The Fourth Amendment, 1920–1929:
A Doctrinal Explosion

In retrospect, the law relating to search and seizure appears poised for development at the beginning of the prohibition era. The Supreme Court had recently embraced the exclusionary rule, but relatively few decisions existed to define the rule's scope.

In 1914 the Court definitively established the importance of the Fourth Amendment[1] for federal criminal prosecutions. Over Dean Wigmore's vociferous objections,[2] *Weeks v. United States*[3] carved a Fourth Amendment exception to the principle that illegality in obtaining evidence does not preclude introduction of the evidence at trial. *Weeks* forbade the use of evidence seized in violation of the Fourth Amendment's prohibition against unreasonable searches and seizures in a subsequent criminal prosecution. To admit the evidence would, the Court declared, make the Fourth Amendment of "no value" to those who had been the victims of such searches.[4]

Other Supreme Court decisions prior to 1920 had solidified a few details of the law relating to the constitutional protection against unreasonable searches and seizures. Most importantly, the Court declared that the rights protected by the Fourth Amendment were to be liberally construed.[5] Individual opinions implemented this rule of liberal construction by extending the protection of the amendment to papers in the mail, refusing to allow the government to use the results of one illegal search as the basis for obtaining a subsequent search warrant, and permitting corporations to claim the protection against unreasonable searches.[6]

Of course, the Supreme Court decisions did not always favor the criminal defendant. *Weeks* itself had recognized an exception to the normal warrant requirement for searches conducted incident to the lawful arrest of a suspect, and it also limited the exclusionary rule to evidence obtained in searches conducted by federal officials. Nonetheless, the rule of liberal construction captures the general tenor of the early opinions.

Close examination of the cases that arose prior to prohibition uncovers some common themes that cross specific doctrinal categories. In establishing the exclusionary rule, *Weeks* protected two values that were deeply rooted in the Anglo-American property tradition: the sanctity of an individual's home as a sanctuary from government intrusion and the personal character of an individual's papers.[7] Most of the cases that evoked the Court's sympathetic approach to Fourth Amendment claims concerned the "papers" aspect of the property tradition. The opinions in those cases often produced ringing endorsements of the virtues of Fourth Amendment values.[8]

Occasionally particular cases forced the Court to move beyond the core concepts of home and papers. In those situations, qualifications began to creep into the protections provided by the Fourth Amendment. Long before *Weeks* established the exclusionary rule, the Court treated customs cases involving the seizure of contraband as exceptional.[9] In addition, by recognizing an exception to the normal warrant requirement for searches conducted incident to arrests, *Weeks* itself limited the potential reach of the amendment when the defendant seeking protection was a criminal who could lawfully be arrested. But perhaps the most perplexing problem of the pre-prohibition cases concerned how to fit corporations into a provision protecting "the people." In a series of decisions handed down in the two decades before the prohibition cases began to arise, the Court reached an accommodation. It granted corporations protection from "unreasonable" searches, but allowed the government to use its "visitatorial" powers to inspect corporate records without a warrant so long as the government's request was reasonable.[10]

Without a doubt, major alterations in the doctrinal landscape of the Fourth Amendment occurred during the prohibition era. The expansion of the scope of this branch of federal criminal law under the Volstead Act produced hundreds of appellate decisions discussing search and seizure issues.[11] The Supreme Court alone issued twenty opinions addressing Fourth Amendment questions between 1920 and 1933. In those cases, the Court established the conceptual framework that has continued to guide the development of Fourth Amendment doctrine down to the present. Those Supreme Court decisions affected a number of subtopics including the definition of the terms in the amendment, exceptions to the establishment of the normal warrant requirement, cooperation with nonfederal investigators, and the probable cause requirement as well as miscellaneous warrant-related issues.

The opinions handed down by the Supreme Court reflect the impact of the prohibition backdrop in the development of Fourth Amendment doctrine. Decisions in nonprohibition cases in the early years of the 1920s continued the liberal construction of Fourth Amendment rights. However, the first prohibition decisions reversed that pattern and upheld searches against Fourth Amendment challenges. That strong support for the government continued in the second half of the 1920s, although one can identify incipient doubts about enforcement techniques. Then, after 1930, the Court rediscovered the rule of liberal construction of Fourth Amendment rights and consistently ruled against the government.

The most dramatic doctrinal changes, and those that were most widely noted, occurred during the first decade of the prohibition experiment. Those decisions from the 1920s are the subject of this chapter. Chapter 4 completes the Fourth Amendment picture by focusing on the less obvious developments of the 1930s.

Supreme Court Decisions before 1925

Nonprohibition Cases

In 1921 the Supreme Court rendered its first three Fourth Amendment decisions of the prohibition era. None of the cases involved a prohibition violation, but they did complete the Fourth Amendment backdrop for the later decisions that arose under the Volstead Act.

Two of the 1921 decisions concerned aspects of Fourth Amendment protection from governmental intrusion to which the Court had traditionally been sympathetic. One defendant objected to the seizure of his papers, and the other protested an intrusion into his home. In each case, Justice William Clarke, a Wilson appointee who resigned a year later,[12] authored the Court's opinion. Both decisions ruled the searches unconstitutional.

The first of the 1921 decisions involved a prosecution for fraud and conspiracy. The government relied on documents that federal officers had secreted from the defendant's office while the defendant was absent. The case was a complicated one involving a number of important constitutional issues, but two holdings were particularly significant for the development of Fourth Amendment doctrine during the prohibition era. First, the Court ruled that the amendment covers searches conducted by stealth as well was those relying on direct governmental authority. Second, the opinion unequivocally declared that the Fourth Amendment did not authorize the issuance of search warrants for papers having mere "evidential value" as to crimes committed by the owner of the papers. To the contrary, search warrants were proper only when

> a primary right to [the] search and seizure may be found in the interest which the public or the complainant may have in the property to be seized, or in the right to the possession of it, or when a valid exercise of the police power renders possession of the property by the accused unlawful, and provides that it may be taken.

The Court justified both holdings by an appeal to the rule of liberal construction applicable to the Fourth and Fifth Amendments. That rule demanded that the amendments be construed "so as to prevent stealthy encroachment upon or 'gradual depreciation' of the rights secured by them, by imperceptible practice of courts, or by well-intentioned but mistakenly overzealous executive officers."[13]

The second Fourth Amendment decision rendered in 1921 involved pre-prohibition bootlegging. The basis for the prosecution was the seizure of slightly more than two quarts of whiskey from a bed in the defendant's home during a search for which the government agents had no warrant. When the agents arrived, the defendant was absent. They told the defendant's wife that they had come to search the premises, and she admitted them.[14]

Declaring that the government's own evidence "show[ed] clearly the unconstitutional character of the seizure," Justice Clarke summarily rejected the two justifications for the search offered by the government. He first ruled that the defendant's motion to exclude the evidence was timely. Because the "facts essential to the motion were literally thrust upon the court" by the testimony of the government's own witnesses, the motion did not inject any collateral issue into the trial. He also rebuffed the government's attempt to characterize the wife's admission of the agents as a waiver of Fourth Amendment protections. According to Justice Clarke, the agents' demand for entry "was implied coercion" that negated the possibility of finding a waiver.[15]

The third decision of 1921 raised a new issue: the applicability of the amendment to evidence obtained in illegal searches by private individuals. Former business associates had stolen personal papers of the defendant and turned them over to the Department of Justice. The district court ordered the papers returned and restrained the department from using the papers in any criminal prosecution of the defendant, but a divided Supreme Court reversed the lower court's decision. The basis for the majority's reversal was the principle that the Fourth Amendment restrained only "the activities of sovereign authority"; it "was not intended to be a limitation upon other than governmental agencies." Because "no official of the Federal government had anything to do with the wrongful seizure of the [defendant's] property," no violation of the Fourth Amendment had occurred. Thus, nothing in the Constitution forbade the government's use of the papers that had been given to federal prosecutors.[16]

The First Prohibition Case

The Supreme Court first addressed Fourth Amendment issues in a prohibition opinion in 1924. That opinion was considerably less generous than pre-prohibition decisions in interpreting the scope of the constitutional protection. More specifically *Hester v. United States*[17] circumscribed the Fourth Amendment's reach in two respects—by distinguishing the lawful observations of enforcement authorities from searches and by excluding "open fields" surrounding a house from the areas protected by the amendment.

The facts in *Hester* were relatively simple. "In consequence of information," revenue agents hid themselves approximately one hundred yards from the house where Hester lived. They were standing on land they "supposed" belonged to Hester's father who owned the house under observation. The agents observed a man drive near the house, and they saw Hester come out and give the visitor a quart bottle. After sounding an alarm, the agents arrested Hester and examined the residue in the bottle as well as the contents of both a jug Hester extracted from a nearby car and a jar lying on the ground near the house. According to the testimony of the experienced agents, all three containers had whiskey in them.[18]

Justice Holmes's opinion for a unanimous Supreme Court was characteristically brief. In the *Hester* opinion, Holmes rejected the idea that the agents had committed an illegal search or seizure. He first distinguished searches covered by the amendment from permissible police surveillance. Even if the agents had committed a trespass, he concluded, their testimony "was not obtained by an illegal search or seizure," for Hester's "own acts, and those of his associates disclosed the jug, the jar, and the bottle." Moreover, "there was no seizure in the sense of the law when the officers examined the contents" of the containers because they had been thrown aside when the officers sounded the alarm.[19]

Nor did the examination of the containers on the land outside the house owned by Hester's father amount to a search covered by the amendment. Although Justice Holmes declared this point to be "[t]he only shadow of a ground for bringing up the cases," he quickly dismissed it, citing Blackstone's *Commentaries* as his sole authority. The Fourth Amendment, he noted, afforded protection to the people only in their "persons, houses, papers, and effects." That protection did not extend to "open fields," for "[t]he distinction between the open fields and the house is as old as the common law."[20]

Decisions from the Second Half of the 1920s

Almost half of the Supreme Court's Fourth Amendment decisions during the prohibition era came during the period from 1925 to 1929. They are a transitional group. Most continued to favor the government, and several significantly expanded the government's enforcement powers. Others, however, reflect incipient doubts about prohibition enforcement techniques. Two actually reversed convictions; in another, the Court rejected an important theory advanced by the government; and dissents appeared in the two most famous cases.

The 1925 Decisions

In 1925 the Court decided five separate cases involving Fourth Amendment issues. Four of the five involved prohibition violations, and Chief Justice Taft authored the Court's opinion in three of the prohibition cases. As a group, the five decisions continued the pattern that the Court had established in the early years of the prohibition era. They narrowly construed the restraints that the Fourth Amendment placed on prohibition enforcement.

The first of the 1925 decisions is the one that continues to exert the greatest influence on contemporary law in the United States. *Carroll*

v. *United States*[21] carved a special exception to the Fourth Amendment's warrant requirement for automobile searches.

For reasons not disclosed in the Supreme Court record, a prohibition agent regarded the *Carroll* defendants and a third individual as bootleggers. He apparently invited them to his apartment where he introduced them to his supervisor. The supervisor represented himself as an employee of the Michigan Chair Company and said he wanted to buy three cases of whiskey. The three visitors agreed to supply the liquor. They said they would have to go to Grand Rapids to get it and left the apartment. A short while later, they returned empty handed and announced that their supplier was unavailable. The visitors promised to deliver the liquor on the next day but again failed to do so. A few days after the apartment visit, the supervisor observed the *Carroll* defendants traveling toward Detroit in the roadster they had used the night of the aborted sale. He and the agent who had arranged the original meeting followed the suspects to East Lansing where they lost them.

Two months later, the supervisor and the agent were patrolling the road from Detroit to Grand Rapids along with two other officials. They again spotted the *Carroll* defendants in the same roadster; this time they were traveling from the direction of Detroit toward Grand Rapids. The prohibition agents reversed direction and began to pursue the roadster. When they caught up with it, the supervisor ordered the driver to stop, and he inspected the vehicle. He failed to discover anything after raising up the back part of the roadster, but he noticed that the "lazy part" of the seat was hard. The supervisor began to tear back the seat cushion and found sixty-eight cases of liquor behind it. He then arrested the defendants and seized the liquor.[22]

A jury convicted both defendants of illegally possessing and transporting intoxicating liquors. Despite the amount of liquor that was being transported, the trial judge only imposed a $500 fine on each defendant. On appeal the Supreme Court affirmed the convictions. In upholding the seizure of the whiskey, the *Carroll* opinion limited the Fourth Amendment warrant requirement in two respects. It sanctioned a broad exception for vehicular searches, and it expanded the traditional doctrine concerning a police officer's authority to arrest without a warrant.

The first aim of Chief Justice Taft's majority opinion was to establish the validity of a special exception to the warrant requirement in automobile cases. The text and legislative history of the Volstead Act convinced him that Congress intended to distinguish "between the necessity for a search warrant in the searching of private dwelling and that of automobiles and other road vehicles." Thus, the issue before the Court was whether "such a distinction [was] consistent with the Fourth Amendment." The chief justice concluded the distinction was permissible because the Fourth Amendment "does not denounce all searches or seizures, but only such as are unreasonable."[23]

This premise of the Fourth Amendment's scope led the chief justice directly to his conclusion. None of the leading decisions that held searches unreasonable under the Fourth Amendment had involved "a seizure without a warrant of contraband goods in the course of transportation, and subject to forfeiture or destruction." Then, in the very next sentence, he leaped to the formulation of the "true rule" governing such seizures:

> [I]f the search and seizure without a warrant are made upon probable cause, that is upon a belief reasonably arising out of the circumstances known to the seizing officer, that an automobile . . . contains that which by law is subject to seizure . . . , the search and seizure are valid.[24]

To support his conclusion, the chief justice cited statutes allowing warrantless searches by customs officials, Indian agents, and revenue collectors in the territory of Alaska. According to the chief justice, his "somewhat extended reference to these statutes" demonstrated that the Fourth Amendment guarantee incorporated the rule he had postulated. The statutes showed the amendment had long been construed to recognize "a necessary difference between a search of a store, dwelling house, or other structure in respect of which a proper official warrant may be obtained, and a search of a ship, motor boat, or wagon for contraband goods where it is not practicable to secure a warrant because the vehicle can be quickly moved."[25]

Of course, the chief justice acknowledged, this practical distinction did not allow "a prohibition agent . . . to stop every automobile on the chance of finding liquor, and thus [to] subject all persons lawfully using the highways to the indignity and inconvenience of such a search." The "line of distinction between legal and illegal searches of liquor" was to be found in the "reasonable distinction" of the statute protecting a prohibition agent from personal liability: The seizing officer must "have reasonable or probable cause for believing that the automobile has contraband liquor therein which is being illegally transported."[26]

Judging the *Carroll* seizure by this test, the Court upheld it citing six factors justifying the search:

1. The *Carroll* automobile was proceeding from the direction of Detroit, which was "one of the most active centers for introducing illegally into this country spiritous liquors."

2. The prohibition agents were conducting a "regular patrol" along one of the main highways between Detroit and Grand Rapids.

3. The agents "had convincing evidence to make them believe" that the *Carroll* defendants were "bootleggers" in Grand Rapids.

4. The agents had attempted to follow the defendants from Grand Rapids to Detroit two months earlier.

5. The defendants were traveling "in the same automobile they had been in the night when they tried to furnish the whiskey to the officers."

6. The defendants "were coming from the direction of the great source of supply for their stock to the place . . . where they plied their trade."

On the basis of these facts, "the officers when they saw the defendants believed they were carrying liquor," and they "had reasonable cause for thinking so."[27]

Because the *Carroll* search occurred before the defendants were arrested, the Court took considerable pains to distinguish the automobile exception to the warrant requirement from the incident-to-arrest exception. In the course of articulating this distinction, the majority expanded the common law of arrest by allowing an officer to make warrantless arrests for misdemeanors committed in the officer's presence. The traditional common law rule, which the Court quoted in its opinion, allowed warrantless arrests only when a misdemeanor amounting to a breach of peace was committed in the officer's presence, but *Carroll* dropped the breach of peace element.[28] On the basis of the reformulated rule, the *Carroll* majority justified the arrest of the defendants once the liquor had been discovered. Since the defendants were committing the misdemeanor of illegally transporting intoxicating liquors in the presence of the prohibition agents, the agents could arrest them without seeking a warrant.

The *Carroll* decision prompted a dissenting opinion by Justice

McReynolds that Justice Sutherland joined. The dissenting opinion denied the existence of any special exception to the warrant requirement for automobiles. Thus, the seizure could be justified only if it fell within the incident-to-arrest exception, and that exception was inapplicable since "[t]he facts known when the arrest occurred were wholly insufficient to engender reasonable belief that [the defendants] were committing a misdemeanor and the legality of the arrest cannot be supported by facts ascertained through the search which followed."[29]

Chief Justice Taft also authored two other Fourth Amendment opinions that followed the *Carroll* decision by only six weeks. The two opinions came in companion cases involving a single defendant as well as the two most famous prohibition agents—Izzie Einstein and Moe Smith.[30] Although the new cases raised different issues, both continued the approach of *Hester* and *Carroll* by limiting the restrictions that the Fourth Amendment placed on prohibition enforcement authorities.

The companion cases differed from *Hester* and *Carroll* because the enforcement authorities had obtained a warrant authorizing the search. Nonetheless, the defendants challenged the validity of the search on a variety of grounds. In the first case, they argued that the warrant was improperly issued because the prohibition agents lacked the probable cause necessary to justify its issuance and that the warrant failed to satisfy the constitutional requirement that it particularly describe the place to be searched. In the second, the defendants argued that prohibition agents were not authorized to execute warrants under the Volstead Act.

The claim that the prohibition agents lacked probable cause was not a substantial one. Before obtaining the warrant, a prohibition agent had observed cases with the word "whiskey" on the side being unloaded in front of the building that was searched. In light of this testimony, the Supreme Court dismissed the probable cause issue rather curtly: "What the [prohibition agent] saw and ascertained was quite sufficient to warrant a man of prudence, caution, and his experience in believing that the offense had been committed of possessing illegally whiskey and intoxicating liquor and that it was in the building he described."[31]

The principal issue in the first case was the adequacy of the warrant's description of the place to be searched. The warrant authorized the search of a building described as "the garage at 611 West 46th

Street," together with "any building or rooms connected or used in connection with said garage." The building searched was "a four-story building in New York City on the south side of West 46th Street, with a sign on it 'Indian Head Auto Truck Service—Indian Head Storage Warehouse, No. 609 and 611.'" The building contained three entrances: "one on the 609 side, which [was] used, and which [lead] to a staircase running up to the four floors;" a similar staircase on the 611 side, which was closed; and, in the middle of the building, "an automobile entrance . . . into a garage and opposite to the entrance . . . an elevator reaching to the four stories." According to the Supreme Court's summary of the evidence presented to the commissioner on the petition to vacate the warrant, "the garage business covering the whole first floor and the storage business above were of such character and so related to the elevator that there was no real division in fact or in use of the building into separate halves."[32]

In executing the warrant, the prohibition agents searched the entire building and seized a large quantity of liquor. From the third floor on the 609 side of the building, they seized "150 cases of whiskey, 92 bags of whiskey, and one five gallon can of alcohol"; and from the second floor of that side, "33 cases of gin." On the second floor of the 611 side, they seized "six 5-gallon jugs of whiskey, 33 cases of gin, 102 quarts of whiskey, . . . two 50-gallon barrels of whiskey, and a corking machine."[33]

Chief Justice Taft's opinion for a unanimous Court summarily dismissed the suggestion that the description in the warrant was inadequate to justify the search. The chief justice found that the warrant's description of the place to be searched "as a garage and for business purposes clearly indicated the whole building as the place to be searched." All that was required, the chief justice emphasized, was a sufficient description so "that the officer with the search warrant can, with reasonable effort, ascertain and identify the place intended."[34]

Nor did the chief justice perceive any merit in the suggestion that the search went "too far." The affidavit for the warrant asked for permission to search any building or rooms connected with or used in connection with the garage. Thus, the search was justified because "the elevator in the garage connected it with every floor and room in the building and was intended to be used with it."[35] The opinion did not even address the question of whether the "connected or used in connection with" language of the warrant satisfied the amendment's requirement for a particular description.

The issue raised in the second of the companion cases involved statutory construction, and the defendants presented a strong linguistic argument. Under the Volstead Act, a magistrate could issue a search warrant "to a civil officer of the United States."[36] A similar phrase, "officer of the United States," is also used in the Constitution in a manner that did not include prohibition agents.[37] Moreover, earlier Supreme Court decisions had indicated that, "when employed in the statutes of the United States," the phrase is "usually [taken] to have the limited constitutional meaning." Notwithstanding the superficial appeal of this linguistic argument, Chief Justice Taft encountered little difficulty in concluding that a prohibition agent was a person to whom warrants could properly be directed under the statute. He insisted that the Court had occasionally "given [the phrase] an enlarged meaning," and he found such an enlarged construction justified in the warrant context because the purpose of the statutory phrase was to require "that the person designated shall be a civil and not a military agent of the government."[38]

A fourth prohibition decision in 1925 also raised search and seizure issues.[39] In this case, Justice Stone replaced the chief justice as the author of the Court's opinion, but he followed Taft's approach. His opinion rejected another claim that the evidence was insufficient to establish the probable cause necessary to justify issuance of a warrant.

The defendants owned a winery that had a permit to produce wine for nonbeverage purposes, as well as a grocery store that was located in a building adjoining the winery. On two separate occasions, prohibition agents purchased wine in the grocery store: In one instance, they saw the wine carried from the winery; in the other, they observed it being brought from the direction of the winery. After advising the commissioner about the purchases but neglecting to mention that the winery had a valid wine permit, the agents secured a warrant authorizing a search of the grocery store and the winery as well as the seizure of any intoxicating liquor possessed in violation of the Volstead Act.

As in the earlier case, the Supreme Court emphatically rejected the contention that the agents lacked probable cause, even as to the seizures from the winery. The facts submitted to the magistrate, Justice Stone's opinion for a unanimous Court declared, "lead to the inference that the suspected premises were the source of supply" and thus "gave rise to a reasonable belief that the liquors . . . [in the winery] were possessed for the purpose and with the intention of selling them unlawfully to casual purchasers." Indeed, according to Justice Stone, "the absence of such a well-grounded belief could be ascribed only to a lack of intelligence or singular lack of practical experience on the part of the officer."[40]

The final search and seizure decision of 1925 involved not a prohibition offense but a violation of the Harrison Anti-Narcotic Drug Act. Even though the Court reversed one of the convictions it was reviewing, its approach to the Fourth Amendment question was nonetheless a rather restrictive one analogous to that taken in the early prohibition cases. Without equivocation the decision sanctioned searches of persons arrested and of the premises on which an arrest was made. The Court did, however, refuse to allow use of an arrest as justification for searching a dwelling "several blocks distant" from the place where the arrest occurred. By the time the second search occurred, the Court ruled, "the conspiracy was ended and the defendants were under arrest and in custody elsewhere."[41]

In making this distinction, Justice Butler's opinion for a unanimous Court displayed a reluctance to approve warrantless searches of private dwellings. Conceding that the Supreme Court had never "directly decided" the point, he emphasized that "it has always been assumed that one's house cannot lawfully be searched without a search warrant, except as incident to an arrest." Later in the opinion, he repeated the assumption (in only slightly less dogmatic form) as a rule, and he emphatically denied the existence of any general probable cause exception to the rule: "Belief, however well founded, that an article sought is concealed in a dwelling house, furnishes no justification for a search of that place without a warrant. And such searches are held unlawful notwithstanding facts unquestionably showing probable cause."[42]

The Opinions of 1927

The next group of search and seizure decisions came in 1927. In that year, the Court issued four opinions addressing Fourth Amendment issues. This time, however, Chief Justice Taft authored none of the opinions, and in them exceptions to the pattern of supporting enforcement authorities began to emerge.

The most obvious shift in the Supreme Court's approach occurred in two cases involving searches by state officials. In these cases, the

Court limited the rule that the Fourth Amendment applied only to searches by federal officials, a rule that had been recognized in pre-prohibition decisions.[43] This so-called "silver platter" doctrine allowed federal prosecutors to use—in federal criminal trials—evidence obtained by nonfederal investigators in searches that would have violated the Fourth Amendment if conducted by federal officials. *Weeks* itself applied this "silver platter" doctrine to evidence obtained by state officials in a search conducted before the federal search that *Weeks* declared invalid. In addition the Court had extended the rule to evidence obtained in an illegal search by private citizens in one of the non-prohibition decisions of 1921.[44]

Of course, mere participation of state officials or private citizens did not make nonfederal a search conducted by federal officials, and several lower court decisions early in the prohibition era applied the Fourth Amendment's exclusionary rule to evidence obtained in searches conducted jointly by federal prohibition agents and state (or local) officers.[45] Yet none of these cases challenged the basic rule that evidence obtained by nonfederal investigators was admissible regardless of the means by which it was obtained. Moreover, in 1925 the Supreme Court had summarily confirmed the rule in a one-sentence per curiam.[46]

Two opinions issued in 1927 made important modifications to the cooperation rule. Both reflected increased willingness to find that the federal involvement in searches by state officials was sufficient to make the Fourth Amendment applicable.

In the first of the 1927 decisions, a state court issued a search warrant authorizing police officers to search the defendant's home "for intoxicating liquors and instruments and materials used in the manufacture of such liquors." As the officer in charge of the search was preparing to execute the warrant, he asked a federal prohibition agent whom he encountered in the police station to assist in the search. The prohibition agent agreed to help, and he searched one of the four rooms of the residence. The search uncovered no intoxicating liquors. The only pieces of incriminating evidence the search disclosed were "counterfeit strip stamps of the kind used on whiskey bottled in bond." The prohibition agent found some of these stamps, and the local police discovered some of them. The federal agent took control of all the stamps, and they formed the basis for the prosecution and conviction of the defendant.[47]

Without differentiating between the evidence seized by the prohibition agent and that seized by the police officers, the Supreme Court reversed the conviction in a unanimous opinion by Justice Sutherland. The most important element in prompting the reversal seems to have been the conclusion "that the federal prohibition agent was not invited to join the state squad as a private person but was asked to participate and did participate as a federal enforcement officer, upon the chance, which was subsequently realized, that something would be disclosed of official interest to him as such an agent." That conclusion was grounded on two essential facts: The police officer specifically asked the federal official, whom he knew to be a prohibition agent, to accompany him; and all of the stamps, "which were not within the purview of the state search warrant, . . . were surrendered to the exclusive possession of the federal agent—a practical concession that he was there in his federal capacity." Because the federal official thus participated "under color of his federal office," the search assumed the character of "a joint operation of the local and federal officers."

Notwithstanding its willingness to find joint participation, the Court's opinion included two important qualifications. First, the Court emphasized "that the mere participation in a state search by one who is a federal officer does not render it a federal undertaking." Second, the opinion reaffirmed the basic silver-platter doctrine recognized by Weeks. The Court refused to "question the right of the federal government to avail itself of evidence improperly seized by state officers operating entirely upon their own account."[48]

After concluding that the Fourth Amendment was applicable, the Court also ruled that the warrant pursuant to which the search had been conducted was invalid. The state warrant involved in the case authorized seizure of "instruments and materials used in the manufacture of [intoxicating] liquor." The items seized were counterfeit bonding stamps, the most obvious use for which was to give bootleg whiskey the appearance of a reputable brand. Without explicitly addressing the issue, Justice Sutherland's opinion simply dismissed the warrant with the dogmatic assertion that it was "bad if tested by the Fourth Amendment."[49]

The Supreme Court returned to the task of establishing the line distinguishing state and federal searches at the beginning of the following term. The new decision applied the exclusionary rule to evidence seized in a search by state officials without the active assistance of any federal officers because the state officials conducted the search "solely" for the benefit of the federal government.

To understand this second decision requires an appreciation of the atypical situation in New York where opposition to prohibition was always strong. New York initially passed a state enforcement statute after the Eighteenth Amendment was ratified, but the legislature repealed the state law just two years later.[50] Governor Smith signed the repeal measure, however, only after he formally advised the legislature that the state police would continue to cooperate in enforcing the Volstead Act in New York. As a result of this policy of cooperation, New York police authorities regularly apprehended violators of the Volstead Act and conducted searches as part of their enforcement efforts.[51]

The case before the Supreme Court in 1927 involved a search of the defendant's automobile by two New York state troopers. Justice Brandeis's opinion for a unanimous Court held the Fourth Amendment applicable even though "[n]o Federal official was present at the search and seizure" and the defendants offered no evidence indicating "that the particular search and seizure were made in cooperation with federal officials." The Court based this application of the Fourth Amendment standard on the conclusion "that the state troopers believed that they were required by law to aid in enforcing the [Volstead] Act," and "in the performance of that supposed duty" they conducted the search "solely for the purpose of aiding in the federal prosecution." According to Justice Brandeis, the subsequent federal prosecution was, "in effect, a ratification of the arrest, search and seizure made by the troopers on behalf of the United States"; and this ratification sufficiently involved the federal government to bring the Fourth Amendment into play.[52]

The decision in the New York case also showed a significant modification in the application of the probable cause standard in cases involving automobile searches. Having decided that the Fourth Amendment applied to the search conducted by state police officers, the Court also ruled that the search of the defendant's automobile violated the Constitution.

Formally, the 1927 opinion adhered to the *Carroll* standard for a warrantless search of an automobile.[53] On the merits, however, the Court ruled that the officers lacked probable cause. The opinion is an enigmatic one because the Court merely announced its conclusion without explaining why the facts known to the investigating officers were insufficient. Nonetheless, anyone who looks beyond the rhetoric to the record can discern that the Court was applying the *Carroll* standard in a more stringent fashion.

The record in the 1927 case reveals that the officers had the following information when they made the search. Two experienced prohibition agents observed the defendants' car about eleven miles from the border traveling away from Canada on a road that was frequently used by bootleggers. The rear end of the defendants' car "hung pretty low," suggesting to the officers that "[t]here was a load of booze." The officers followed the defendants to a nearby village, where the defendants stopped the car and got out to go into a garage owned by an individual who had "a reputation of being a bootlegger." After a brief conversation with the defendants, the officers searched the automobile and discovered fourteen cases of ale.[54]

The other two decisions from 1927 reflect the Court's continuing willingness to support prohibition enforcement efforts against substantial violators. In each the Court relied on the incident-to-arrest exception to the warrant requirement to sustain a search.

United States v. Lee[55] involved the seizure of a motorboat containing seventy-one cases of grain alcohol "in a region commonly spoken of as Rum Row, at a point 24 miles from land." The principal issue concerned the authority of customs officials to search American vessels beyond the twelve-mile boundary. The Court held that the Coast Guard had such authority "when there is probable cause to believe [the vessel] to be subject to seizure for violation of revenue laws."[56]

Almost as an afterthought, Justice Brandeis offered the incident-to-arrest exception as an alternate justification for the search. In explaining this incident-to-arrest exception, *Lee* implicitly treated the motorboat as the "premises" on which the search occurred. Search of the boat was thus permissible, especially since the trial had produced no evidence of "any exploration below decks or under hatches" and "[f]or aught that appears, the cases of liquor were on deck and, like the defendants, were discovered before the motorboat was boarded." The person making the arrest had scanned the boat with a searchlight when making the arrest, but that action did not violate the Constitution because "[s]uch use of a searchlight is comparable to the use of a marine glass or a field glass."[57]

Six months later, *United States v. Marron*[58] provided the first detailed consideration of the incident-to-arrest exception in a prohibition case. The *Marron* opinion exemplifies the approach characteristic of the prohibition cases in the second half of the 1920s—an ambivalent Court beginning to perceive dangers in prohibition enforcement but unwilling to let serious offenders go free. The unanimous opinion by Justice Butler refused to allow agents to use a search warrant to justify seizure of items not named in the warrant. But ultimately Justice Butler upheld the challenged seizures by broadly defining the "premises" that could be searched pursuant to an arrest and the things that could be seized as instruments of the crime for which the arrest was made.

A United States Commissioner had issued a warrant authorizing the search of the premises leased by Marron. The warrant described the things to be seized as "intoxicating liquors and articles for their manufacture." Prohibition agents went to the premises the next day and, after securing admission by ringing the doorbell, observed about a dozen persons in the place, "some of [whom] were being furnished intoxicating liquors." The agents handed the warrant to the individual in charge and placed him under arrest; they then "searched for and found large quantities of liquor, some of which were found in a closet." The agents also found and seized certain items not expressly named in the warrant. In the closet they uncovered "a ledger showing inventories of liquors, receipts, expenses, including gifts to police officers, and other things relating to the business." Beside the cash register, they discovered "a number of bills against petitioner for gas, electric light, water, and telephone service furnished on the premises."[59]

The Court refused to develop an exception for seizures incidental to execution of a valid search warrant. "General searches," Justice Butler emphasized, "have long been deemed to violate fundamental rights" and the Fourth Amendment forbade them. To make general searches impossible, the amendment required "that warrants shall particularly describe the things to be seized."[60] This requirement, reiterated by Congress in the provisions of the *United States Code* authorizing the issuance of search warrants,[61] also prevented "the seizure of one thing under a warrant describing another." The warrant described "what was to be taken," and "nothing [was] left to the discretion of the officer." Since the search warrant issued in *Marron* had not mentioned the ledger or the bills, it did not authorize the agents' seizure of them.[62]

Notwithstanding this strict rule limiting what could be seized when executing a search warrant, the Court affirmed Marron's conviction. When the agents arrived at the premises, they immediately arrested the individual in charge. That individual "was actually engaged in a conspiracy to maintain, and was actually in charge of, the premises where intoxicating liquors were being unlawfully sold." Thus, the arrest was lawful as one for a "crime committed in [the agents'] presence," and the agents "had a right without a warrant contemporaneously to search the place in order to find and seize the things used to carry on the criminal enterprise." Pursuant to this authority, the agents could seize both the ledger and the bills, the ledger because "it was . . . a part of the outfit or equipment actually used to commit the offense," and the bills because "they were convenient, if not in fact necessary, for the keeping of accounts" and "so closely related to the business" that it was "not unreasonable to consider them as used to carry it on." Moreover, the Court emphasized, the seizure of the ledger was valid even though it was found in a closet. The area that officers could search incident to a valid arrest "extended to all parts of the premises used for the illegal purpose." The closet where the ledger was found "was used as a part of the saloon"; thus, it was part of the area in the "immediate possession and control" of the person arrested.[63]

Olmstead: The Final Decision from the 1920s

In 1928 the Court issued its final Fourth Amendment opinion from the 1920s and its most famous prohibition decision. Chief Justice Taft again wrote for the majority, and the majority again favored the government. However, a four-member minority now protested the narrow construction of the Fourth Amendment that had emerged in the prior prohibition cases.

Olmstead v. United States[64] required the Court to explain the relationship between the Fourth Amendment and new techniques of electronic surveillance. More specifically the Court had to decide if evidence obtained by surreptitious "tapping" of an individual's telephone could be introduced into evidence when the person whose conversation was being tapped was criminally prosecuted.

The story leading up to the Olmstead decision began in 1920, when a highly regarded young police lieutenant was attracted by the financial opportunities associated with bootlegging in Seattle, Washington.

Early in his new endeavor, the lieutenant was apprehended by prohibition agents and fined $500. This escapade led to his dismissal from the police force, and so he turned his full attention to a new career in smuggling liquor from Canada. Supported by eleven investors who contributed $1,000 each, Olmstead soon established a highly successful smuggling operation. By the simple device of clearing the ships on which he carried his Canadian liquor for Mexico rather than the United States, he avoided Canada's heavy export tax on liquor cleared for the United States. He also secured cash discounts for his large volume purchases and developed an efficient distribution system. The net result of these innovations was commercial success: Olmstead succeeded in underselling his competition by as much as 30 percent.

Olmstead soon established a virtual monopoly of the Seattle bootlegging business. His close contacts within the local political structure and police force allowed him to operate with near impunity. He was a well-known and, apparently, respected citizen of Seattle. The definitive history of prohibition in Washington even credits him with stabilizing the price of liquor so "that good whiskey in Seattle cost only two dollars more than a bottle did in the government stores of British Columbia."[65]

Not surprisingly, the federal prohibition office did not share this high regard for Olmstead and his work. In 1924 William Whitney, the chief assistant in the Seattle office, hired a freelance wiretapper as a prohibition agent and had him insert taps on the phones at Olmstead's office and several other locations.[66] Olmstead was aware of the taps, but he did not significantly alter his operations. He apparently remained confident that a Washington statute forbidding wiretaps[67] would make evidence obtained against him inadmissible in any criminal prosecution.

Following the seizure of his boat on a customs charge and a raid on his home, the federal government indicted Olmstead and a host of coconspirators. In the widely publicized trial, the government agents testified regarding the conversations, and they were allowed to refresh their memories by consulting the transcripts. After objections to this testimony were overruled, a jury convicted Olmstead, and the district judge sentenced him to a four-year term of imprisonment.[68]

Olmstead appealed, but a divided panel of the Ninth Circuit affirmed his conviction.[69] Along with his codefendants,[70] Olmstead then sought review in the Supreme Court. The Court first denied the petitions for certiorari but then later granted requests for reconsideration.[71]

On the merits, the Supreme Court decided in favor of the prosecution, but this time it did so by the narrowest of margins. Writing for the five members of the majority, Chief Justice Taft began his analysis of the constitutional issue with a lengthy survey of the Court's previous Fourth Amendment decisions. After completing this survey, he declared that "[t]he reasonable view is that one who installs in his house a telephone instrument with connecting wires intends to project his voice to those quite outside, and that the wires beyond his house and messages while passing over them are not within the protection of the Fourth Amendment." According to the chief justice, none of the Court's earlier decisions had found a violation of the Fourth Amendment except in situations involving "an official search and seizure of [an individual's] person or such a seizure of his papers or his tangible material effects or an actual physical invasion of his house 'or curtilage' for the purpose of making a seizure." From this definition of the underlying principle of the earlier cases, he drew his conclusion without further elaboration: "The wire tapping here disclosed did not amount to a search or seizure within the meaning of the Fourth Amendment."[72]

One can discern the implicit link between the definition and conclusion in some of the distinctions and analogies the chief justice drew in his survey of prior cases. On the one hand, he carefully distinguished earlier decisions applying the Fourth Amendment to searches conducted by stealth and to mail that had been entrusted to the Post Office. The case prohibiting searches conducted by stealth, he argued, "carried the inhibition against unreasonable searches and seizures to the extreme limit," and its authority would not be "enlarged" by implication. When thus confined to its facts, it was distinguishable because a government agent actually entered "into the private quarters of the defendant and . . . [took away] something tangible." By contrast the *Olmstead* testimony only concerned "voluntary conversations secretly overheard." The decision regarding mail was also easily distinguishable according to the chief justice. Since a "letter is a paper, an effect, and in the custody of a government that forbids carriage except under its protection," it fell "plainly within the words of the Amendment to say that the unlawful rifling by a government agent of a sealed letter is a search and seizure of the sender's papers or effects." By contrast, the amendment could not naturally apply to the government's actions in *Olmstead*. The federal government did not take "such care of telegraph and telephone messages as of mailed sealed letters." Even more importantly, the wiretapping case involved neither a "searching" nor a "seizure." The agents secured the evidence "by the use of the sense of hearing and that only," without any "entry of the houses or offices of the defendants." On the other hand, the chief justice found the narrow approach of *Hester* a particularly persuasive precedent. Even though the officers in *Hester* were guilty of a trespass, the Court nonetheless found that they had not engaged in any search of the defendant's person, house, papers, or effects.[73]

Justice Brandeis's dissenting opinion, the most comprehensive of the four prepared in *Olmstead*,[74] appealed to the spirit of the Court's own precedents in objecting to the majority's handling of the constitutional issue. "Time, and time again," he asserted, these precedents had rejected "an unduly literal construction" of the Fourth Amendment. Thus, he argued that the Court should now construe the Fourth Amendment, along with the Fifth, to confer "the right to be left alone—the most comprehensive of rights and the right most valued by civilized men." To enforce that right, the Court should declare "every unjustifiable intrusion by the Government upon the privacy of the individual, whatever the means employed" a violation of the Fourth Amendment.[75] Judged by this standard, the defendant's objections to the evidence obtained by wiretapping had to be sustained, and the factors emphasized by the majority, the place where the physical connection occurred and the law-enforcement motive that prompted the wiretapping, were irrelevant.

An Analysis of the Changes

The prohibition cases of the 1920s reflected a sharp break with earlier decisions interpreting the Fourth Amendment. Most conspicuously, the Court abandoned the rule of liberal construction of the protections afforded by the Fourth Amendment. Instead, it interpreted the amendment to permit a variety of intrusive enforcement actions by prohibition authorities.

The most obvious result of the Supreme Court decisions was to limit the occasions when enforcement agents had to obtain warrants. The Fourth Amendment contains no explicit requirement mandating that officials obtain a warrant before conducting a search, but the

warrant requirement is a natural implication of the amendment's jux-
taposition of its prohibition of unreasonable searches next to the requirement for obtaining warrants. The implication is one that the
Supreme Court has generally accepted, although it has always recognized exceptions to the requirement. In three of the decisions from the
1920s, the Court developed exceptions that have remained important
in Fourth Amendment doctrine. It permitted warrantless searches of
open fields and automobiles and expanded the exception that allowed
warrantless searches that were conducted incident to an arrest.

Hester, the Supreme Court's first Fourth Amendment case involving a prohibition violation, recognized the "open fields" exception to
the warrant requirement. As a practical matter, the significance of
Hester was limited in prohibition cases. Because most bootlegging
activity occurred in urban areas, violators were unlikely to have large
parcels of property surrounding the location of their illicit activities. Nonetheless, the decision is an important one because it shows
the strength of the Court's sympathy to prohibition enforcement in the
first half of the 1920s. In *Hester* the Court refused to construe the
amendment to respect even the traditional property rights of land-
owners.

A year after *Hester*, the Court decided *Carroll*, and the 1925
decision was equally favorable to those charged with enforcing prohibition. Indeed, the *Carroll* opinion expanded the authority of prohibition agents in three important respects. First, it created an "automobile" exception to the Fourth Amendment's normal requirement
for a search warrant. Second, it dramatically expanded the traditional
rule regarding warrantless arrests. Third, it reflected a willingness to
find "probable cause" on very sketchy facts.

The automobile had begun to exert its enormous influence on
American life in the decades before the Eighteenth Amendment was
adopted, and the growth of the automotive industry accelerated during the 1920s. Automobile registrations rose from eight thousand in
1900 to more than 9 million in 1920 and then to 26.5 million in 1929.
By the 1920s, the automotive industry was the largest in the country.
Two million automobiles were manufactured in 1920, and this figure
grew to 5.5 million by 1929. The development of techniques of mass
production and consumer credit helped to reshape American life as
well as to stimulate a variety of associated industries like highway
construction and steel manufacturing.[76]

The automobile's impact on American legal institutions is easily discernible in a variety of statutory and judicial developments.[77] Thus, it is hardly surprising that automobiles also required special treatment in the law of search and seizure. The increased availability of automobiles during the 1920s was an obvious boon to bootleggers. Not only did it greatly enhance their transportation capabilities, but the mobility of automobiles also made use of search warrants difficult because the automobile might move to another location or the bootlegger might finish delivering the vehicle's illicit cargo while agents were seeking the warrant. In *Carroll* the Supreme Court granted its imprimatur to a new exception to the warrant requirement that had previously been developed in lower federal courts.[78]

Carroll made a second significant change in federal criminal law. It allowed officers to make arrests for misdemeanors that did not involve a breach of the peace. When the American Law Institute published its *Commentaries on Torts* in 1927, the *Commentaries* acknowledged the novelty of the Supreme Court's new approach. The *Commentaries* observed that until the Supreme Court decision in *Carroll* "the statement both of judicial decisions and textbooks were substantially unanimous to the effect that there was no privilege to arrest without warrant for a misdemeanor other than breach of peace."[79] What the *Commentaries* did not note was that the *Carroll* reformulation was particularly useful in Volstead Act cases because transportation of intoxicating liquors was a misdemeanor until the passage of the Jones Act in 1929, and transportation would not, by itself, amount to a breach of the peace.[80]

In *Carroll* the Court was also willing to find probable cause on extremely thin evidence. The weakness of the government's showing at the trial is immediately apparent. At most, the government's evidence showed that prohibition agents reasonably believed the agents were bootleggers, that the suspected bootleggers were traveling in an automobile they had used in an earlier unsuccessful attempt to obtain whiskey, and that the suspects were driving from a potential source of supply of whiskey to the city where they normally conducted their business. What was missing was any evidence indicating that the defendants had whiskey at the time they were searched. In short, the evidence would have existed anytime the defendants drove the automobile in the Detroit area.[81]

The Court continued to create exceptions to the warrant requirement as late as 1928. In *Olmstead* Chief Justice Taft's opinion altered the approach of *Hester*, but reached a similar result. *Hester* refused to rely on property law to expand the reach of the Fourth Amendment. By contrast, in *Olmstead*, the Court declined to apply the amendment to the new technology that permitted electronic eavesdropping precisely because the wiretapping did not involve an invasion of traditional property rights.

In its 1925 decisions, the Supreme Court also limited the constitutional and statutory requirements applicable when prohibition agents did obtain search warrants. It generously construed a warrant authorizing the search of a building at a named address to permit a search of a connected building with a different street address. Similarly, it expansively interpreted the provision in the Volstead Act allowing warrants to be issued to any "civil officer of the United States."

These changes in legal doctrine did not completely escape scholarly notice. Indeed, scholarly analyses of Fourth Amendment doctrine during the prohibition era routinely acknowledged "the rapid development of the subject under prohibition."[82]

A student commentator even tried to quantify the explosion that prohibition had produced in the number of reported cases. According to the student's count of cases in the *American Digest*, "more than 700 cases involving the admissibility of illegally obtained evidence [had been] reported" since the Volstead Act went into effect, and approximately 575 of the cases had involved prosecutions for violations of liquor laws. Moreover, the number of cases was still growing when the student published the account in the *Yale Law Journal* in 1927. On an annual basis, "the number of liquor cases turning upon the rule ha[d] increased from four, during the first year, to more than 220 during the past year."[83]

Even before the first major group of Supreme Court opinions, an article in the *Central Law Journal* encouraged the Court to construe the Eighteenth Amendment as implicitly repealing the Fourth Amendment for liquor cases. The author conceded that this approach would lessen protection in the prohibition context. Nonetheless, he argued that the decreased protection for the individual in that context was necessary to avoid the even greater danger that "the host of decisions constantly arising under the Volstead Act will serve as precedents by which the guarantees in question will be permanently undermined for all purposes."[84]

The federal courts never formally embraced the implied repeal argument.[85] Nor did most commentators even discuss prohibition's possible role as a factor in influencing the course of doctrinal development.[86] However, a few observers did detect the changing emphasis of the early prohibition cases. In 1927 a student commentary noted that courts had often found "[t]he purpose of the [exclusionary rule] as an auxiliary to the Constitution incompatible with the task of enforcing [prohibition] laws." Faced with this dilemma, they elected to forego constitutional protection to accomplish the enforcement goal. "As a result of this tendency, many exceptions and limitations of the federal rule ha[d] arisen which ha[d] greatly narrowed the scope that the rule was originally thought to have."[87]

The most outspoken advocate of the view that judicial decisions in the prohibition era had restricted American liberties was Forrest Revere Black, a law professor at the University of Kentucky. In 1930 he published a book of essays entitled *Ill-Starred Prohibition Cases*, and three of the book's nine essays attacked decisions that he regarded as restricting the individual liberty protected under the Fourth Amendment. The existence of a casual link between prohibition and the decline in liberties is the implicit assumption of the entire work, but Black never defined the exact relationship with any precision. Perhaps the best summary of his argument is the following excerpt from the introduction to his essay on the *Carroll* case:

> In the last decade, the American Government has been engaged in "the noble experiment" of enforcing constitutional prohibition. As the direct result of this effort, it is being discovered that Bills of Rights, federal and state, are being denaturized; certain old landmarks in the law are crumbling and the relation between the nation and the states is being altered.[88]

Commentators who called attention to the impact of prohibition generally failed to notice the doubts about enforcement that were creeping into Fourth Amendment doctrine by the end of the decade. Not only did the leading prohibition decisions produce dissents, but defendants even won occasional victories during the second half of the 1920s. Although the Court continued to uphold searches conducted in connection with arrests for prohibition violations, it refused to let prohibition agents rely on a search warrant to seize items not described in the warrant. Moreover, the decisions of 1927 even reversed two convictions as they limited the federal government's ability to use the fruits of searches initiated by state enforcement officials.

Although they passed unnoticed by contemporary observers, the ambiguity of the decisions from the second half of the 1920s are fully consistent with the general trend of decisions during the prohibition era. By the time *Olmstead* was decided in 1928, opposition to prohibition had increased substantially, and enforcement excesses achieved wide publicity. Nonetheless, most observers considered repeal an impossible dream. Thus, it is hardly surprising to find the Supreme Court divided over controversial enforcement practices but still willing to tolerate the intrusive practices necessary to catch serious violators.

The commentators of the 1920s understandably failed to predict the rapid fall of prohibition in the 1930s. The general pattern of Supreme Court decisions suggests that the changing attitudes toward prohibition would also find reflection in Fourth Amendment doctrine. Chapter 4 explores that hypothesis to complete the survey of Fourth Amendment doctrine during the prohibition era.

4 / The Fourth Amendment, 1930–1933:
Refinement and Rediscovery

One historian has termed *Olmstead*, "the last major Supreme Court decision concerning prohibition enforcement."[1] In reality, it was not even the Court's last important decision involving the Fourth Amendment. Between 1930 and 1933, the Supreme Court decided seven other cases that raised Fourth Amendment issues. All involved prohibition violations.

The decisions from the 1930s provide a distinct contrast to the earlier prohibition cases. Not only did the Court significantly refine and modify prior doctrine, but it rediscovered the principle calling for liberal construction of Fourth Amendment rights. The outcomes of the cases also changed dramatically. The defendants won at least partial victories in all seven cases.

The primary architects of the new approach to Fourth Amendment rights were Justices Butler and McReynolds. They authored five of the seven opinions, and all five reversed the convictions that were being appealed.

The decisions from the 1930s offer additional confirmation of the utility of using the prohibition backdrop to understand the development of federal criminal law doctrine. In these cases, the Supreme Court again altered course in fashioning search and seizure doctrine. As public opposition to prohibition grew, the Court increasingly construed the Fourth Amendment to impose strict limits on those charged with enforcing the Eighteenth Amendment.

The Supreme Court Decisions

1931: The New Direction

Two 1931 decisions began the new series of Fourth Amendment decisions. Justice Butler authored the opinion in the first of them. In it, he returned to the problem that he had first addressed in 1927 in *Marron*: the constitutionality of a seizure of business property incident to an arrest of the person who was operating the business. In contrast to *Marron*, the 1931 decision ruled the seizure invalid.

Not surprisingly, the new decision claimed doctrinal continuity with earlier cases. Nonetheless, the shift in focus is dramatic. Illustrative of the shift was the renewed emphasis on the need for a broad construction of the Fourth Amendment to protect all individuals—innocent and guilty alike—from arbitrary governmental power.[2]

In June 1929, prohibition agents went to the New York office of an importing company and arrested the president and the secretary-treasurer of the company for conspiracy to sell intoxicating liquor. Falsely claiming to have warrants authorizing a search, the agents then searched the three-room office and forced the persons they had arrested to open locked desks in the office. In the course of the search, they seized "approximately a dozen bottles of assorted intoxicating liquor, a large number of memoranda, books of account, records, filing cases, and other papers all of which pertained to unlawful dealings by [company officers] in intoxicating liquors."[3]

"Without pausing to consider the matter," the Court treated "the arrests as lawful and valid." It nonetheless ruled that the Fourth Amendment had been violated and required the seized papers to be returned to the company.

Justice Butler's opinion began its analysis by emphasizing the Fourth Amendment's "general" prohibition of "unreasonable searches and seizures." Because of the generality of this prohibition, the amendment provided "no formula for the determination of reasonableness" and required each case to "be decided on its own facts and circumstances." Judged by this individualized standard, the search of the company's office "was a lawless invasion of the premises and a general exploratory search in the hope that evidence of crime might be found." Without specifying precisely which facts were crucial in reaching this conclusion, the opinion enumerated four factors: the lack of any evidence that a crime was being committed at the time the arrests were made; the failure to obtain a search warrant even though the special agent in charge "had an abundance of information and time to swear out a valid warrant"; the "pretension of right and threat of force" used in the search; and "the general and apparently unlimited [nature of the] search, ransacking the desk, safe, filing cases and other parts of the office."[4]

Justice Butler was equally vague in distinguishing Marron. He vehemently asserted that "[p]lainly" the two cases were "essentially different." He did not, however, specify the essence of the difference. Instead, he was content merely to catalog these factual distinctions:

the person arrested in *Marron* was one "who in pursuance of a conspiracy was actually engaged in running a saloon"; the things seized in *Marron* were "visible and accessible and in the offender's immediate custody"; and the agents who made the *Marron* seizure did so "without threat of force" and without engaging in a "general search or rummaging of the place."[5]

Justice Stone was the author of the other 1931 opinion, the only one from the 1930s in which the Supreme Court affirmed a defendant's conviction.[6] Even here, however, the government did not achieve a total victory because the Court remanded the case for sentencing reconsideration.

The case involved a warrantless search of an automobile. Without reconsidering the issue, Justice Stone's opinion reaffirmed the *Carroll* rule allowing warrantless searches of automobiles when the enforcement authorities had probable cause. Moreover, the Court also held that the facts in the particular case were sufficient to establish probable cause.

The evidence to support the probable cause finding was substantial if not overwhelming. One of the prohibition agents involved in the search "testified that he had known [the defendant] to be a 'bootlegger' for a number of years," that he had arrested the defendant on two earlier occasions for violating the Volstead Act, and that both arrests had resulted in convictions. On the day the search occurred, an informant advised the agent that the defendant "had two loads of liquor in automobiles of a particular make and description, parked in particular places on named streets." The prohibition officer had known the informant "for about eight years," and on prior occasions, the informant had given the officers "similar information" that had proved reliable. When the officers proceeded to one of the locations the informant had named, they found one of the described automobiles unattended. They later observed the defendant get into the car. After he started the car, the agents stopped him and conducted the search that uncovered eighteen cases of whiskey.[7]

Although the Court affirmed the convictions of the defendants, Justice Stone managed to remand the case for resentencing. After the arrest of the defendants but before their convictions, Congress passed the Jones Act,[8] which increased the maximum penalties for prohibition violations. Relying on the new statute, the trial court had sentenced the defendants to substantial terms of imprisonment. On appeal, Justice Stone's opinion stopped short of expressly holding the Jones Act inapplicable. The Court did, however, remand the case for resentencing "in view of the confusion which has arisen with respect to the propriety of the sentences."[9]

The Decisions of 1932

The Supreme Court decided four more cases involving search and seizure issues in 1932. Those decisions continued the liberal construction of Fourth Amendment rights that had begun to emerge the preceding year.

The first of the 1932 decisions returned to the issue of the permissible scope of a search of business premises incident to an arrest. Justice Butler again authored the Court's opinion, and he reiterated the narrowness of the incident-to-arrest exception to the Fourth Amendment's warrant requirement.[10]

As in the decision from the preceding term, the precise basis of the 1932 decision is difficult to isolate, but the impact of the decision is clear: to limit the scope of searches and seizures permissible under the incident-to-arrest exception. In effect the case resurrected the distinction between things wanted only for their "evidential value" and items that may properly be the object of a search warrant by government officials. The Court then applied the distinction to a warrantless search conducted in connection with a valid arrest.

A prohibition agent filed a complaint before a United States Commissioner charging that the defendants, "commencing June 21, 1930, and continuing to the time of making the complaint," had engaged in a conspiracy "to sell, possess, transport, furnish, deliver and take orders for intoxicating liquors" in violation of the Volstead Act. According to the complaint, the defendants solicited orders from a certain room identified by its address; they then arranged for orders to be delivered by common carriers and collected the proceeds of the sale. Since "[t]he allegations of the complaint show[ed] that the complaining witness had knowledge and information of facts amply sufficient to justify the accusation," the commissioner issued the warrant, and a group that included several prohibition agents proceeded to the room specified in the complaint. They arrested one of the defendants and searched the room, which was "about ten feet wide and twenty feet long and was divided by a partition." The "outer portion" of the room contained an unlocked "stenographer's desk . . . , a towel cabinet and a waste basket"; the "inner part," another unlocked desk and a basket. In searching the room,

> [t]he agents opened all the drawers of both desks, examined their contents, took away books, papers and other articles. They also searched the towel cabinet and took papers from it. . . . They also took the contents of the baskets and later pasted together pieces of paper found therein.[11]

Echoing the "reasonableness" emphasis of his opinion from the previous year, Justice Butler declared that the "only question presented" in the 1932 case was "whether the searches of the desks, cabinet and baskets and the seizures of the things taken from them were reasonable as an incident of the . . . valid arrests under the warrant." He concluded that they were unreasonable. The conduct of the agents "was unrestrained" as shown by the number and variety of things taken. Moreover, the officers wanted the papers "solely for use as evidence of crime of which [the defendants] were accused or suspected." Searches for, and seizures of, such papers were impermissible "even under a search warrant issued upon ample evidence and precisely describing such things and disclosing exactly where they were," and the incident-to-arrest exception "certainly" did not confer greater search authority "than that conferred by a search warrant issued upon adequate proof and sufficiently describing the things to be obtained."[12]

As in the earlier case, Justice Butler distinguished *Marron* in some detail. Once again, the distinction amounted to the cataloging of a number of factual differences. In *Marron* "prohibition officers . . . arrested the bartender for a crime openly committed in their presence"; the officers did not search for the ledger and bills seized but merely picked up items "in plain view"; and the ledger and bills seized were being used "to carry on the criminal enterprise" for which the defendants were convicted. By contrast the record in the 1932 case failed "to support the claim that, at the time of the arrest, . . . any crime was being committed in the presence of the officers"; the searches conducted by the agents "were exploratory and general and made solely to find evidence of [the defendants'] guilt of the alleged conspiracy or some other crime"; and "the papers and other articles found and taken were in themselves unoffending," although they were "intended to be used to solicit orders for liquor in violation of the Act." The Court indicated that the last difference was the crucial one, but it made no further effort to elaborate how the character of the items differed from those seized in *Marron*. Instead, the opinion chose to conclude with an appeal to more recent authority: "This case does not differ materially from the [the decision from 1931] and is ruled by it."[13]

The second of the 1932 decisions rebuffed an attempt to expand the exceptions to the warrant requirement to allow a search of a garage. The case involved the nocturnal search of a garage adjacent to, and on the same lot as, the building where the defendant lived. Having received complaints "over a period of about a year," a group of prohibition agents decided to investigate the premises. As they approached the garage, they detected the "odor of whiskey coming from within." Looking through "a small opening," they saw a number of cardboard boxes "which they thought probably contained jars of whiskey." After breaking the door fastening, they entered the garage and found the 122 cases of whiskey that formed the basis for the defendant's indictment.[14]

The Supreme Court opinion by Justice McReynolds was a brief one that reversed the convictions. Without attempting to decide whether the garage constituted part of the private dwelling, Justice McReynolds declared that "the action of the agents was inexcusable and the seizure unreasonable." Thus, "the evidence was obtained unlawfully and should have been suppressed."[15]

The opinion appeared to concede that the agents had sufficient evidence to obtain a search warrant. Nonetheless, it emphasized that the availability of such evidence did not allow officials to search a building without obtaining a warrant. The mere presence of "a distinctive odor" indicating a "possible crime" could "not strip the owner of a building of constitutional guaranties against unreasonable search," especially in a situation where the agents could easily have secured a warrant "even after odor had emphasized their suspicions."[16]

The remaining decisions from 1932 involved searches for which warrants had been issued. Nonetheless, the Court found the searches invalid in both cases by construing constitutional and statutory opinions to impose strict limits on the availability of warrants.

Grau v. United States[17] was the more important of these last two decisions from 1932. Not only did the Court impose a new evidentiary requirement applicable to all search warrants, it also sympathetically applied the special restrictions that the Volstead Act imposed on searches of private homes.

The new evidentiary requirement mandated that the evidence presented to a magistrate to obtain a warrant had to be legally admissible in a criminal trial. Although the requirement was a procedural limit of considerable import, the Court adopted it with little explanation or analysis. In almost offhand dictum, Justice Roberts's opinion for a unanimous Court declared that a warrant must be supported by "evidence which would be competent in the trial of the offense before a jury."[18]

The primary issue in *Grau* involved one of the political compromises of the Volstead Act, the decision to grant special protection from searches of private dwellings. Under the act, a magistrate could issue search warrants for private dwellings only when prohibition agents had probable cause to believe that intoxicating liquor was being sold on the premises or when the residence was "in part used for some business purpose such as a store, shop, saloon, restaurant, hotel, or boarding house." For any other type of building, probable cause to believe that any offense under the act was being committed was sufficient to authorize issuance of the warrant.[19]

The precise question in *Grau* was whether evidence that intoxicating liquor was being manufactured in a dwelling in large quantities could constitute probable cause to infer a selling operation. According to the affidavit on which the warrant was based, the affiant "went around and about the premises"; in doing so, he "saw persons haul cans, commonly used in hauling whiskey, and what appeared to be corn sugar, up to and into the place and saw the same car or truck haul similar cans, apparently heavily loaded, away from there." He also "smelled odors and fumes of cooking mash coming from the place," from which he concluded that "there [was] a still and whiskey mash on the premises."[20] On the basis of this affidavit (which did not describe the place to be searched as a residence), the United States Commissioner issued a warrant, and the agents seized a still as well as 350 gallons of whiskey.

The district court refused to suppress the evidence obtained in the search that the warrant authorized, and the Sixth Circuit affirmed the conviction that the evidence was used to support.[21] Because the Sixth Circuit's holding arguably conflicted with decisions of other circuits, the Supreme Court granted certiorari so that it could resolve the conflict.[22]

The Supreme Court reversed. Justice Roberts's opinion criticized the Sixth Circuit's "broad construction" of the act, which allowed it to hold these allegations adequate to warrant a belief that the dwelling was being used as the headquarters for a merchandising effort. According to Justice Roberts, such a construction "unduly narrow[ed] the guaranties of the Fourth Amendment, in consonance with which the statute was passed." It thereby conflicted with the rule that Fourth Amendment protections were themselves to be liberally construed. To the contrary, the Court asserted, the act should be more narrowly construed to effect the congressional intention "not to encroach upon the citizen's right to be immune from unreasonable searches and seizures."[23]

After stating this justification for a restrictive approach to the act when Fourth Amendment values were implicated, Justice Roberts declared that the *Grau* warrant should be judged by the reasonableness standard. He then proceeded directly to his conclusion without any further discussion or explanation:

> While a dwelling used as a manufactory or headquarters for merchandising may well be and doubtless often is the place of sale, its use for those purposes is not alone probable cause for believing that actual sales are made there.[24]

The fourth decision from 1932 concerned the procedures governing the issuance of search warrants. In it, the Court refused to allow a magistrate to "reissue" a warrant after the ten-day period for which it remained valid under the statute. Emphasizing that the "proceeding by search warrant" was "a drastic one," Justice McReynolds's majority opinion again specifically invoked the liberal rule of construction for Fourth Amendment rights that had been announced in the preprohibition cases involving Fourth Amendment issues. The statutes imposed certain conditions that had to be satisfied, the Court declared, and a magistrate could not escape those conditions "by describing his action as a reissue" of an earlier warrant. "If the warrant is an old one, sought to be revived, the proceeding is a nullity, and if it is a new warrant the commissioner must act accordingly."[25]

The Last of the Prohibition Cases

The Supreme Court issued its final Fourth Amendment decision in 1933, the year prohibition was repealed. Like the last of the 1932 decisions, the Court again increased the procedures necessary to obtain a warrant. In it Justice McReynolds established one of the procedural rules of the Volstead Act as an implied mandate of the Fourth Amendment applicable to all search warrants directed to federal officials. Specifically the Court held that the affidavit presented to the magistrate had to be based on "fact or circumstances" within the affiant's knowledge. "[M]ere affirmance of belief or suspicion," the Court asserted, was "not enough."[26]

Fourth Amendment Doctrine at the End of the Prohibition Era

If one takes a panoramic view of the Fourth Amendment cases as of the repeal of prohibition, dramatic changes from pre-prohibition doctrine are evident in at least two contexts. On the one hand, the complexity of Fourth Amendment doctrine had greatly increased. On the other, the background situations of the prohibition cases had shifted noticeably from those of the early cases. Tracing these changes through the doctrinal subcategories that emerged re-emphasizes the extent to which they paralleled changing attitudes toward prohibition.

Doctrinal Complexity

The most obvious change is the increased doctrinal complexity. By the end of the prohibition era, new exceptions, qualifications, and refinements abound. In effect, the Court had molded a rather limited group of precedents into a detailed body of doctrine that has retained its basic structure down to the present.

Two principal forms of doctrinal development occurred during the prohibition era. In some cases, the Court created new doctrinal categories by holding that the Fourth Amendment's protection of the home did not extend to "open fields," that the amendment did not apply to the tapping of telephone conversations, and that the warrant requirement did not apply to automobile searches. But even more commonly, the Court refined subcategories developed only marginally in the earlier cases. It expanded the common law of arrest and struggled to prescribe the scope of warrantless searches conducted incident to arrests. It also tried to define the degree of federal involvement that would make the Fourth Amendment applicable to searches conducted in whole or in part by state or local officers, explained and applied the probable cause standard in a variety of circumstances, and gave content to statutory and constitutional provisions governing the issuance of search warrants.

Although they do not limit themselves to the Supreme Court cases, various secondary sources nevertheless confirm the extent to which the content of Fourth Amendment doctrine expanded during the prohibition era. The first treatise on the subject appeared in 1926 when Asher Cornelius published his 925-page *Law of Search and Seizure*. Just four years later, he published a second edition of 1,265 pages. In explaining the need for the new edition, he called attention to the "[h]undreds of new questions [that] have been presented to the courts for solution" since the preparation of the manuscript for the first edition.[27]

The growth of the indexing system of the National Reporter System offers additional evidence of the increasing complexity of Fourth Amendment doctrine. As originally presented in the *Century Edition of the American Digest* in 1893, the category "Searches and Seizures" was divided into seven "key" numbers. In the first two decennial digests, the number of key numbers remained constant even though their content was altered slightly. But when the *Third Decennial Digest* (covering cases decided in the period 1916–1926) was published in 1929, it added thirty-nine subtopics.[28] Thus, the new digest contained more than six times as many indexing categories as its predecessors.

One can glean still further evidence of the growing complexity of Fourth Amendment doctrine during the prohibition era by examining the treatment given the subject in legal encyclopedias. In 1919 Lawyers Cooperative Publishing Company published the volume of *Ruling Case Law* that contained the topic "Searches and Seizures." The topic consisted of thirty-four sections and covered twenty-nine pages. By the time *American Jurisprudence* replaced *Ruling Case Law* in 1943, the number of sections had grown to seventy-four and the number of pages to fifty.[29] Similarly the *Cyclopedia of Law and Practice*, which was published in 1910, assigned only forty-two sections to the topic "Searches and Seizures," and the topic covered fifteen pages. When the *Cyclopedia* was replaced by *Corpus Juris* in 1932, the number of topics had expanded to 220 and the number of pages to 114.[30] Although no encyclopedia was published in new versions precisely at the beginning and end of prohibition, cumulating the evidence from these encyclopedias issued by the two leading publishers points to the prohibition era as the decisive time of development. The relatively sparse coverage in the 1919 *Ruling Case Law* indicates the limited refinement of Fourth Amendment doctrine prior to the onset of prohibition, and the exceptionally detailed coverage in the 1932 edition of *Corpus Juris* suggests that the time of growth was the period during which the Eighteenth Amendment was part of the Constitution.

The preceding discussion documents the changing trends that one can observe in the various doctrinal categories discussed in the Supreme Court decisions rendered during the prohibition era. Since no single trend continued throughout the period, no simple characterization of the body of doctrine extant in 1934 as progovernment or prodefendant is possible. Different doctrinal subcategories reflect restrictive, ambivalent, or sympathetic approaches to the Fourth Amendment depending on when the decisions giving content to the subcategory were rendered.

New Situations

Increasing doctrinal complexity is not the only change that one can observe in the search and seizure cases decided during the prohibition era. A significantly greater variety of background situations also appeared in the cases.

As noted in chapter 3, the Fourth Amendment cases prior to prohibition primarily concerned two types of problems: protecting an individual's home as a sanctuary and maintaining the secrecy of papers that related to the personal or business affairs of individuals. Historically[31] and linguistically,[32] these concepts formed the core of the Fourth Amendment, and the Supreme Court rather zealously protected both interests in the early-twentieth-century cases.

In certain boundary cases, the Court was more tolerant of governmental searches. It carved an early exception in customs (i.e., smuggling) cases, when the government was looking for contraband; and it also recognized an incident-to-arrest exception to the customary warrant requirement when the individual seeking protection was a person whom the government could lawfully arrest. The Court also struggled, in a series of cases that provided the bulk of the before prohibition cases, with a vexing problem—how to fit corporations into a provision designed to make "the people" secure.

Naturally, cases involving the core concepts of house and papers continued to arise during the prohibition era. In cases challenging searches of places that would obviously fall within the definition of "houses," the Supreme Court was relatively consistent in continuing the pre-prohibition protection of the defendant. From 1921 to 1932 the Court adopted a strict approach when reviewing searches of buildings in which individuals lived.[33]

One should not overemphasize this theme of consistency, however. Dictum in the one drug case of the period approved searches of houses where arrests took place,[34] and considerably less consistency is apparent in cases concerning seizures of papers. They can be better summarized by reference to the general pattern of prohibition decisions.[35]

Even more important, the central tendency of the prohibition decisions when they are considered as a whole was not the refinement of doctrine within the core area but relentless expansion of the boundary class of cases. The new cases demanded more precise definition of the places and things protected by the amendment. Did "houses" include open fields surrounding them or garages located near them? Did telephone conversations fall within the protection afforded to "papers and effects"? Did the "effects" protected by the amendment include liquor that the Volstead Act declared was contraband to which no property rights attached; that is, should one appeal to the narrower approach of the smuggling cases or the broader one of the papers cases?

The boundary became most obscure in the cases involving automobiles. The warrant clause of the Fourth Amendment required particular descriptions of "the place to be searched" and "the things to be seized." Unfortunately, that language simply did not fit automobile searches, for the search of an automobile involved a search (not merely a seizure) of a "thing" rather than a "place." In the face of such linguistic ambiguity, the Court's response was understandable if not predictable. It improvised dramatically by jettisoning the normal warrant requirement and applying a watered-down version of the usual Fourth Amendment protection.

Seen in this light, *Carroll* represents an important step in the evolution of Fourth Amendment doctrine. In a particular and individualized context, it adopted the very approach that a majority would later reject emphatically in *Olmstead*. It dislodged Fourth Amendment doctrine from its property moorings, which protected the house as sanctuary and papers as things free from government scrutiny, and reconceived the interest sought to be protected by the Fourth Amendment. The reconceived right was narrower than the traditional concept because the defendant lost the procedural protection afforded by the customary warrant requirement. At the same time, the reconceived right was broader than the traditional concept because what was being protected was not a particular place or thing but the desire of "persons lawfully using the highways" to avoid "the indignity and inconvenience" of having their automobiles searched for no particular reason.

In *Carroll's* redefinition of Fourth Amendment rights, one can discern a noticeable shift in emphasis from the pre-prohibition cases. Rather than protecting property rights, the Court was beginning to recognize a more generalized (and less absolute) right to privacy as the interest deserving protection. A few other Fourth Amendment decisions[36] as well as some scholarly literature of the prohibition era[37] described Fourth Amendment interests in privacy terms, and the new approach obviously provided the seed for the emphasis in modern Fourth Amendment doctrine on reasonable expectations of privacy.[38]

One should not attach excessive importance to this analytical shift, however. The property aspects of Fourth Amendment doctrine remained important in a number of cases that were decided after *Carroll*. Moreover, the analytical shift does not explain the trend of the prohibition cases as a whole any better than does an attempt to view them as an uninterrupted continuation of themes established in the pre-prohibition cases. As the preceding section shows, all of the boundary cases decided during the prohibition era tend to follow a zigzag pattern that crosses analytical categories or background circumstances. The early ones take a fairly restrictive view of the Fourth Amendment; as the middle years of the era passed, the decisions reflect divided sentiments; and the opinions rendered in the final years of prohibition revive the rule of liberal construction.

Survey of Doctrinal Subcategories

Definitional Issues.—One problem inevitably associated with the articulation of a new legal doctrine is the need to establish its limits by defining its constituent terms. Not surprisingly the problem is one that the Supreme Court faced in the 1920s with respect to the Fourth Amendment. In *Weeks* the Court had conclusively established the exclusionary rule for evidence obtained by illegal searches. Now it had to define the types of activities covered by the amendment; that is, to decide what constituted a "search" and when a search invaded the protected area of "persons, houses, papers, and effects."

The Supreme Court addressed these definitional issues in two cases during the 1920s, and both decisions adopted narrow definitions of the scope of the Fourth Amendment. *Hester* ruled the amendment inapplicable to "open fields," and in *Olmstead* a divided Court held that the amendment did not cover telephone wiretaps. In both results and approaches, the two decisions show that changing attitudes toward prohibition exerted an important influence on the development of Fourth Amendment doctrine.

Relatively few reported opinions of the lower federal courts during the prohibition era dealt with the definitional problems addressed in these Supreme Court cases. This paucity of decisions suggests that *Hester* and *Olmstead* involved techniques that were relative aberrations in prohibition enforcement, and a little reflection and research strengthens this inference. The Court's willingness in *Hester* to exclude "open fields" from the scope of the Fourth Amendment's protection would prove useful only rarely in urban areas where prohibition enforcement encountered its most serious difficulties and where few urban dwellings would contain a large yard in which agents could conceal themselves while observing the dwelling. Moreover, the "open fields" exception would not aid prohibition authorities in apprehending careful suspects who kept their supplies and transactions inside. Even in the prohibition era, the Court (and the Volstead Act) normally required warrants to justify intrusions into a dwelling.[39]

Initially one might think that *Olmstead* presented great opportunities for official exploitation, but that conclusion ignores the political reality of the times. By the time *Olmstead* was decided, the federal government itself had disavowed the use of wiretaps as an enforcement device.[40] Indeed, the internal opposition to wiretapping within the government was so significant that the assistant attorney general originally assigned to handle the appeal for the government asked to be relieved of the assignment after the Supreme Court granted certiorari.[41] In the remaining years of prohibition after the *Olmstead* decision in 1928, opposition to the Eighteenth Amendment grew substantially. Consequently, it is not surprising that the officials in charge of prohibition enforcement failed to exploit an investigatory technique that was likely to strengthen and to crystallize opposition to their work.

Even though the open fields and wiretapping problems were relatively isolated and episodic ones, the Supreme Court's handling of them was important for the development of the conceptual framework of the Fourth Amendment. In effect, close examination reiterates what initial observation suggested, for the definitional decisions also follow the changing public mood about prohibition.

As one of the early prohibition cases, *Hester* fit in nicely with the political mood that was still generally satisfied with prohibition and had developed few doubts about techniques of prohibition enforcement. The decision was unanimous and brief, and it accepted surreptitious trespass on the property of private citizens as a natural incident of effective enforcement of the Eighteenth Amendment. Moreover, this narrow construction of the reach of the amendment was not dictated by some ineluctable logic of existing precedents. The opinion does not cite any of the Court's earlier decisions as authority for its decision. Indeed, if one examines the small group of arguably relevant precedents carefully, *Hester* reflects more of a break than a continuation of tradition, for those earlier decisions manifest an approach to the Fourth Amendment that is far less literalistic than the one taken in *Hester*.

By the time *Olmstead* was decided in 1928, doubts about the value of prohibition and about its effects on American life were widespread, but the supporters of prohibition remained in charge of the political scene. Similarly the dissenters in *Olmstead* perceived significant dangers in unbridled prohibition enforcement, but the majority refused to endorse an approach that would let a defendant whose violations of the law were serious and pervasive go free.

Olmstead was, after all, no ordinary case. The majority opinion described the operation that formed the basis of the defendant's convictions as "a conspiracy of amazing magnitude to import, possess, and sell liquor unlawfully" with aggregate yearly sales of liquor exceeding $2,000,000. In this conspiracy, *Olmstead*'s role was preeminent; he "was the leading conspirator and general manager of the business," contributing almost half of the venture capital used to start the project and taking one-half of the profits. Conversations overheard on the challenged wiretaps "disclosed the conspiracy charged in the indictment" and "revealed the large business transactions of the partners and their subordinates."[42] Nor was the Court guilty of hyperbole in its description of Olmstead's activities. In an article written two years later, the New York Times described Olmstead's Seattle operation as "one of the most gigantic rumrunning conspiracies in the country."[43]

Exceptions to the Warrant Requirement.—The next major subcategory of prohibition cases involved warrantless searches. One of the most universally recognized exceptions has been the rule allowing police officers to search persons whom they have arrested. Dicta in Weeks itself confirmed this "incident-to-arrest" exception,[44] but Weeks did not clearly define the precise scope of the search that was permissible when a search was conducted "incident" to an arrest. Determining the limit to the exception proved to be a continuing problem in the decisions rendered after the Eighteenth Amendment was adopted. Indeed, the problem was such a vexing one that the Supreme Court issued no less than five separate opinions addressing the subject during the prohibition era.[45]

The incident-to-arrest exception was not the only circumstance in which the Supreme Court permitted warrantless searches during the prohibition era. A second major exception developed for automobile searches, and this contribution of the prohibition era has proved to be one of the most enduring legacies of the Taft Court.

Looking at the warrantless search cases as a group, one can see in them further evidence of the general pattern that was characteristic of the prohibition cases as a whole. The willingness in Carroll to support the practical needs of enforcement is typical of the prohibition cases from the mid-1920s. The sympathetic Carroll opinion aided prohibition officials in two distinct ways, and both were significant aids to enforcement if the number of reported decisions is a reliable guide.[46] First, Carroll granted a general dispensation from the search warrant requirement in automobile cases. This dispensation obviously saved time, and Carroll's willingness to find probable cause on very skimpy facts also suggested that courts should avoid second-guessing the judgment of officials whose suspicions about contraband proved to be

correct. Second, *Carroll* allowed officers to make arrests (and implicitly to conduct searches incident to those arrests) for misdemeanors
that did not involve a breach of the peace. As noted above, the *Carroll*
rule was particularly useful in Volstead Act cases. Until the passage of
the Jones Act in 1929, transportation of intoxicating liquors was a
misdemeanor that would not ordinarily amount to a breach of the
peace.

Yet even in the *Carroll* decision, one can see an emerging ambiguity
in the presence of two dissenting justices. That early appearance of
dissent is probably best explained by the extremely sketchy set of
facts that the majority was willing to accept as adequate to demonstrate probable cause.[47]

The other cases decided in the second half of the 1920s display the
common ambivalence of the cases in that period even more clearly.
Two of the decisions manifest a continued willingness to uphold
convictions in struggles against violators of the law who operated on a
relatively large scale, while the third reflects greater sympathy for
more casual offenders. The shipboard search involved an arrest in the
notorious "Rum Row" that was the center of the smuggling trade,[48]
and *Marron* challenged a raid on a saloon-type operation that seems to
have operated quite openly.[49] By contrast the New York case that
found insufficient evidence to establish probable cause involved seizure of fourteen cases of ale being transported in a private automobile,[50] a less substantial violation (albeit not a trivial one).

Even in *Marron*, one can detect an increasing awareness of potential
enforcement abuses. The greater part of Justice Butler's opinion in
Marron is devoted not to the acceptance of the government's incident-
to-arrest justification but to the rejection of the alternate rationale that
the seizures could be sustained as incidental to the execution of a
valid search warrant naming other things. The Court's own explanation for this "advisory opinion" approach relies on the assertion in
the government's brief "that the facts of this case present one of the
most frequent causes of appeals in current cases."[51] In light of this
explanation, it seems appropriate to describe the *Marron* opinion as
one that refused to let a serious offender go free while it also articulated some limits to increasingly obvious abuses in the enforcement of
the prohibition laws.

The last of the prohibition decisions involving searches incident to
an arrest, those coming in the decade of the 1930s, reflect a return to a
"liberal" construction of the Fourth Amendment even when that con-

struction resulted in freeing some relatively serious offenders.[52] In particular the Court emphatically reasserted the need for a warrant to search any building and rejected any lesser standard for structures that were not used as dwellings. Of course, the decision that produced that assertion was an easy case, for the solicitor general essentially asked for the reversal by advising the Court that, in his opinion, the search was illegal.[53]

The doctrinal shift within the Court itself is more apparent in the two decisions that limited *Marron's* rule allowing a search of business premises pursuant to an arrest of the person in charge of the business. Only one who had attained the "artificial perfection" of reason that Coke described as "the life of the law"[54] could detect a clear distinction between those cases and *Marron*. The Court's own confusion is apparent in the conflicting justifications it offered in the two cases. In the first, the Court emphasized the nature of the criminal activity that the officers discovered and the generality of the search conducted. The second understandably cited the prior decision as the controlling precedent, but it shifted the emphasis for distinguishing *Marron* to the nature of the items seized. Surely one does not have to be overly cynical to suggest a more likely distinction is a change in the Court's concern about the type of police activity that was being challenged.

These last incident-to-arrest cases may also reveal the limits of judicial creativity during the prohibition era, for neither makes any effort at express overruling of the *Marron* precedent. This reluctance to overrule was typical of the Taft and Hughes Courts,[55] and it also provides a link toward understanding the remaining decision from the 1930s. In that decision, the Court was concerned enough over the trial court's treatment of the defendants to demand that they be resentenced. But the opinion gives no consideration to whether *Carroll* should be overruled in light of changing attitudes toward prohibition. *Carroll* is accepted as stating the applicable rule, and the only search issue that receives any significant consideration is whether the officials had sufficient information to support a probable cause finding. Since the factual information known to the investigators was considerably greater than that in *Carroll*, the Court perceived no alternative to affirming the conviction.

Searches by State Officers.—A third important doctrinal subcategory concerned the degree of federal involvement that was necessary to make the Fourth Amendment applicable to a search conducted by state officials. A 1925 decision summarily affirmed the rule that the Fourth Amendment's exclusionary rule did not apply to evidence obtained by nonfederal investigators. But just two years later, the Court modified the rule considerably in two important decisions. One ruled that the ban on unreasonable searches applied to a search when the federal prohibition agent's involvement began after local police officers had secured a search warrant from a state court. The other held the amendment applicable to a search conducted by state officials "solely" for the benefit of the federal government.

The 1927 cases were the last Supreme Court decisions to address the cooperation issue during the prohibition era. Even though at least one contemporary commentator declared that "[i]t would be but a short step from the [second 1927] case to hold that the constitutional guarantees of [the Fourth and Fifth Amendments] restrict the activities of state agencies generally,"[56] the Supreme Court did not take that step until long after prohibition.[57] Nor do the lower courts seem to have substantially expanded the rules in subsequent prohibition cases. They occasionally applied the Fourth Amendment standards to searches in which the federal involvement was significant.[58] But when the federal involvement was minimal, they continued to apply the "silver platter" doctrine until the very end of the prohibition era.[59]

Once again, the doctrinal theme of the Supreme Court's decisions parallels the broader decisional pattern. The internal development of the doctrinal category reveals a shift in emphasis that is part of a changing emphasis in the trend of the decisions as a whole. Of course, the decisions in the cooperation cases reflect a more prodefendant impulse than most of the decisions in the doctrinal categories examined earlier. However, that apparent divergence is not surprising in view of the time frame in which they arose, for both Supreme Court decisions were rendered in the middle years of prohibition when a number of the Court's decisions began to reflect vague doubts about the direction prohibition was taking.

One could argue that the cooperation decisions are not entirely consistent with the general pattern of decisions because they are less ambivalent than other decisions of the middle years of the era. The 1927 decisions, for example, can easily be contrasted with *Olmstead* and *Marron*. The cooperation cases actually reversed convictions and did not merely reflect some general misgivings. But that analysis ignores two crucial features of the cooperation cases.

First, the cooperation cases involved relatively modest seizures when compared with the "large quantities of liquor" seized in *Marron* or the conviction in *Olmstead* of one of the most notorious bootleggers in the country. The state warrant in the first of the cooperation cases indicated that the police were planning to raid a manufacturing establishment producing illicit liquor. When they searched the premises, they found neither intoxicating liquor nor any manufacturing equipment; all they discovered was a handful of counterfeited bonding stamps of the type used for bonded whiskey.[60] Similarly the search in the other cooperation case uncovered only fourteen cases of ale in the defendant's automobile.

Second, neither of the cooperation cases necessarily precluded prosecution of offenders who violated state laws. The second of the decisions was obviously a decision with limited applicability. Only six other states joined New York in repealing their state enforcement statutes,[61] and the Court's rationale simply did not apply to searches by state officials in states with their own prohibition enforcement laws. Furthermore, as far as the Supreme Court was concerned, states could still use evidence obtained in joint state-federal searches in state trials. When these nondoctrinal elements of the cooperation case are considered, the decisions seem fully consistent with the trend of decisions in the middle years of prohibition: Relatively minor offenders are released without completely eliminating the possibility of serious offenders being punished in the vast majority of states that maintained enforcement statutes.

The 1927 decisions produced the only Supreme Court opinions with respect to cooperation with nonfederal investigators. However, the problem proved a source of litigation throughout the prohibition era, and the lower court decisions are not confined to the middle years. A review of the decisions of the district courts and courts of appeals suggests a pattern of development similar to that observed in the Supreme Court decisions, although the evidence is far from conclusive. Not surprisingly the lower court decisions seem to reflect less of an innovative spirit than do the Supreme Court opinions inasmuch as the lower courts did not change the rule itself. Nonetheless, the lower court decisions do seem to evidence a greater willingness in the later years of prohibition to find sufficient federal involvement to treat the search as federal.[62] Moreover, the factual summaries in several of the post-1927 opinions holding the federal involvement insufficient indicate that the search would have satisfied Fourth Amendment standards had they been applicable.[63] One could hardly posit any firm conclusions on such a limited survey, but the decisions cited indicate that a detailed examination of the cases in the lower federal courts might reveal that the doctrinal response of the lower federal courts also reflected the impact of prohibition.

Probable Cause Standards.—The Fourth Amendment allows the issuance of search warrants only "upon probable cause." In *Carroll* the Supreme Court also established the probable cause requirement for warrantless searches of automobiles. The pervasiveness of the requirement coupled with the vagueness of the term made the existence of probable cause a commonly litigated issue, and it was an issue that the Supreme Court had to address in a number of prohibition cases.

One of John Marshall's opinions in the early nineteenth century held that a customs seizure was supported by probable cause when "made under circumstances which warrant suspicion."[64] Eventually, however, the Court abandoned that expansive definition except in smuggling cases.[65] In its place, the Court developed a reasonableness test that it applied in challenges to warrants and warrantless searches throughout the prohibition era. Almost invariably the Court invoked the *Carroll* formulation, which was itself extracted from a nineteenth-century decision: "If the facts and circumstances before the officer are such as to warrant a man of prudence and caution in believing that the offense has been committed, it is sufficient."[66]

Despite the formal consistency in the Supreme Court's definition of probable cause in all the decisions from the prohibition era, close analysis of the decisions reveals considerably less consistency in the application of the definition. As one might anticipate, the trend was to impose an increasingly stringent requirement as the years passed. The first decisions consistently found probable cause even in cases where the factual support for the finding was rather questionable.[67] But the middle years of the era produced tightening of the application of the standard in the New York case involving a warrantless automobile search that uncovered a relatively minor violation.[68] Finally, in the last years of prohibition, the Court extended the new restrictive application of the standard to search warrants in a case involving an operation of obviously commercial dimensions.[69] Yet despite the increasingly strict application of the reasonableness standard, the Court never abandoned the standard. Even in the 1930s, the Court remained willing to find probable cause when presented with a strong factual basis for such a finding.[70]

Search Warrants.—The final group of Fourth Amendment opinions dealt with requirements for search warrants. The language of the Fourth Amendment imposes two limits on the issuance of warrants— the requirements that the place to be searched and persons or things to be seized be particularly described and that the probable cause to issue the warrant be supported by oath or affirmation. In addition a host of statutory mandates applied to warrants issued under the Volstead Act.[71] The prohibition era produced a number of Supreme Court decisions construing and applying these constitutional and statutory restrictions.

The 1925 case allowing a search of an adjacent warehouse pursuant to a warrant authorizing the search of a garage[72] was the only Supreme Court decision that attempted to define the precision with which the premises to be searched had to be described. But two other cases also decided in the middle years of prohibition raised, at least implicitly, another aspect of the description issue—the need for a description of the items to be seized. Both were less sympathetic to enforcement authorities than the 1925 decision.

The issue surfaced most directly in *Marron* where agents executing a valid search warrant discovered incriminating evidence not specifically named in the warrant. The *Marron* opinion ultimately sustained the search as incident to a lawful arrest, but it refused to rely on the search warrant to uphold the seizures. More precisely, it refused to construe the warrant language, which covered "intoxicating liquors and articles for their manufacture," to include items associated with the sale of illegally manufactured liquor and thus to cover the ledger and bills that had been seized.

The first of the 1927 decisions invalidating a search initiated by state authorities reflected a similar antagonism toward state warrants, even though the Court never explicitly discussed the description issue. In that case, the Supreme Court summarily held that a warrant authorizing seizure of "instruments and materials used in the manufacture of such [intoxicating] liquor" did not cover counterfeit bonding stamps. Despite the utility of the stamps for giving bootleg whiskey the appearance of a reputable brand, the Court's opinion summarily dismissed the warrant as invalid under the Fourth Amendment.[73]

During the final years of prohibition, the Court strictly construed both statutory and constitutional provisions governing warrants. Dicta in a 1932 decision introduced a new procedural safeguard by requiring a warrant to be supported by "evidence, which would be competent in the trial of the offense before a jury."[74] Two other decisions displayed similarly strict attitudes toward procedural requirements. In one the Court refused to allow a magistrate to "reissue" a warrant when the warrant's ten-day period of validity had expired.[75] The second held that the Fourth Amendment requires the affidavit presented to the magistrate to be based on "facts or circumstances" within the affiant's knowledge, not mere "belief or suspicion."[76]

Even though the warrant cases address less of a single doctrinal theme than the other doctrinal subcategories, they nonetheless repeat the familiar pattern when considered as a group. The earliest decisions uniformly favored the government. The decisions of the middle years took a more critical perspective, but in cases where the violations were fairly insignificant. Finally, during the last years of national prohibition, the rule calling for liberal construction of the Fourth Amendment was resurrected from the pre-prohibition opinions and supplied the rationale for a strict application of constitutional and statutory limits governing search warrants.

An Assessment of the Fourth Amendment Developments

The Temporal Influence of Prohibition

Undoubtedly prohibition provided the occasion for the elaboration of enduring concepts underlying Fourth Amendment doctrine. The volume of prohibition cases and the accompanying growth in doctrinal complexity are surely sufficient to document so modest a claim. Indeed, scholarly analyses of Fourth Amendment doctrine during the prohibition era routinely acknowledged "the rapid development of the subject under prohibition."[77]

Even this weak description of the relationship between prohibition and Fourth Amendment doctrine serves to clarify the historical development of federal criminal law. For one thing, explaining when and why the federal courts created a unified body of Fourth Amendment doctrine helps one to understand the federalization of the law of search and seizure in modern times.

The very act of developing the federal doctrine seems to have encouraged the process of federalization. Initially federalization proceeded because state courts voluntarily copied the Supreme Court's example. In fact, the number of states applying the exclusionary rule during the 1920s jumped dramatically.[78]

The Supreme Court did not complete the federalization process until it imposed the exclusionary rule on the states long after prohibition had been repealed.[79] Nonetheless, the prohibition developments were an important preparatory step to imposing the exclusionary rule as a requirement of federal constitutional law. By establishing and refining many of the modern categories in federal doctrine, they provided a benchmark against which state rules could be measured. Without such a development, the ultimate federalization almost surely would have been delayed. The Supreme Court would probably have hesitated to impose a requirement that had never been defined in federal litigation. Even if a general requirement had been imposed, state courts unsympathetic to the federal rule would have found it comparatively easy to frustrate implementation until the Supreme Court had the opportunity to refine the general concepts.

The Causative Influence of Prohibition

One can reasonably go beyond the temporal link between prohibition and the development of Fourth Amendment doctrine and assign the prohibition experience a significant causative influence as well. This claim argues that changing attitudes toward prohibition and prohibition enforcement decisively influenced the direction of Fourth Amendment doctrine.

The preceding sections have marshaled the evidence to support this causal claim. In brief, that evidence demonstrates that the trend of the prohibition decisions closely mirrors changing public attitudes toward prohibition. The first prohibition cases strongly supported those who were enforcing the prohibition laws by upholding searches against Fourth Amendment challenges.[80] The decisions in the middle years of prohibition reflected incipient doubts about some of the techniques of prohibition enforcement, but most affirmed convictions of serious violators.[81] Finally, after 1930, the Court rediscovered the need for a liberal construction of the Fourth Amendment rights and became increasingly strict in applying Fourth Amendment rules.[82]

Significantly, the growth of the new doctrine was not haphazard whether the cases are viewed as a whole or within the newly created doctrinal subcategories. From either perspective, the developments in the prohibition era mirror changing public attitudes toward prohibition. The chronological portions of the last two chapters provide an overview that describes the shifting pattern for the Fourth Amendment cases as a whole. Even closer examination in the analysis above shows that the trend of mirroring prohibition attitudes also manifests itself within the various doctrinal subcategories established during the prohibition era.

No commentator of the prohibition era sketched this process in full, although—as noted in chapter 3—some perceived the influence of prohibition in the initial abandonment of the rule of liberal construction of Fourth Amendment rights. But even those contemporary observers who suggested that prohibition exerted an influence on the direction of the Fourth Amendment decisions noticed only part of the process, the retreat from the rule of liberal construction in the early cases. The obvious reason for this inattention to later developments is the date of the writings, for the commentaries stressing the link between prohibition and the trend of judicial opinions appeared before the second shift of the cases in the last years of prohibition. That answer, however, merely begs the question because it does not account for the lack of a critical literature with respect to the later cases.

Perhaps a partial explanation for this void lies in the nature of the later decisions. They seem less drastic. Rather than carving out new subcategories, they tend to refine, to limit, and to apply qualifications that had been created in the earlier cases. Thus, these developments might have seemed to contemporaries to lie more completely within an autonomous zone of legal concepts than did the early prohibition cases that boldly created new doctrinal categories.

The repeal of prohibition within a very few years after the new trend definitely appeared offers an even more likely explanation for the lack of scholarly attention to the later cases. If search and seizure problems were merely symptoms of a broader "prohibition" problem, one should not find it surprising that scholars ignored the symptoms once the underlying problem had been replaced by the the pressing economic concerns associated with the Great Depression.

Perhaps the strongest support for the claim that the prohibition experience was decisive in shaping the course of Fourth Amendment doctrines derives from the inadequacy of alternate explanations. As noted in the introductory chapter, the general stability of the Court's personnel and the lack of a consistently divided Court on Fourth Amendment issues render an emphasis on judicial personality inadequate. Likewise, it is impossible to regard the Fourth Amendment decisions as the product of "legal reasoning" or as responsive to economic or similar forces.

The lack of consistency in the Fourth Amendment decisions virtually requires one to reject the possibility that the course of the decisions was primarily the product of an autonomous world of legal reasoning. On too many occasions, the Supreme Court reached different results in similar cases. Sometimes, it achieved its objective by expanding doctrinal categories and exceptions. *Weeks*, for example, allowed the use of evidence seized by state officials in a search conducted immediately before the search in which the evidence seized by the federal officials was ruled inadmissible, but a 1927 prohibition decision excluded all evidence seized in a search where the federal official participated in his federal capacity. *Marron* allowed the introduction of a ledger and bills as instrumentalities of a crime, while a decision from the 1930s applied the ban on the seizure of "mere" evidence to exclude very similar records. On other occasions, the application of rules shifted noticeably even when the rules themselves remained constant. Comparison of the facts known to the officers in *Carroll* and the 1927 case from New York offers the most obvious example of this form of indeterminacy within the system of legal concepts.

One must also reject a variant of the legal reasoning argument, the suggestion that the changing pattern of decisions was produced by a change in the Court's analytic approach.[83] As the preceding summary of Fourth Amendment doctrine at the conclusion of the prohibition era indicates, the prohibition cases did tend to de-emphasize the property element of Fourth Amendment doctrine. But this shift in the interests seeking protection does not provide a reliable guide to the trend of the decisions. The most obvious inadequacy is the argument's inability to account for more than one change in direction when, in fact, the initial shift to a restrictive interpretation is reversed in the decisions rendered at the end of the prohibition era. Furthermore, although the prohibition cases relentlessly pushed at the property moorings of Fourth Amendment doctrine, the Court vigorously reiterated the property aspects in several opinions handed down in the middle or later years of prohibition.

Finally, one must acknowledge the lack of any obvious economic or behavioral justification for the decisions of the prohibition era. It almost strains credulity even to suggest that the myriad exceptions and qualifications to the *Weeks* exclusionary rule were designed to maximize the efficiency of enforcement techniques. At any rate, contemporary enforcement officials vigorously protested that they were hampered by the restrictions under which they operated.[84] Nor are the decisions better explained as serving any simple behavioral objective such as controlling police conduct or protecting innocent citizens from official intrusion into their lives. Indeed, a student commentator who attempted to prepare a realist-style analysis of the decisions from the admittedly scanty database available concluded that they did not accomplish either of those objectives in practice.[85]

Needless to say, the prohibition experience and the Fourth Amendment did not interact in a vacuum. Other factors also influenced the Fourth Amendment opinions of the prohibition era.

In the first place, one can identify other substantive values that appear to have had an impact on the Fourth Amendment decisions. The relative consistency of the Court's application of the ban against warrantless searches of private dwellings mirrors the Court's general willingness to protect property rights in other areas. In addition, the Fourth Amendment decisions of 1921 were basically unrelated to the prohibition experience. None involved either the Eighteenth Amendment or the Volstead Act, and the Court's opinions contain no indication that they were drafted with an eye toward the problems of enforcing prohibition. The first, which involved bootleg whiskey on which the federal tax had not been paid, continued the pre-prohibition cases protecting private dwellings in a case that arose before prohibition. The second involved government access to business papers, and its broad interpretation of the Fourth Amendment is a continuation of the Court's decisions prior to 1920. By contrast the third comes from the patriotic excesses associated with World War 1, and its tolerance for "private" searches is typical of the "Red Scare" decisions of the early 1920s.[86] Finally, the remaining case that did not involve prohibition enforcement involved narcotic drugs rather than intoxicating liquors. Apparently, however, the Court's support of enforcement authorities in the 1920s extended to the enforcement of drug laws as well.[87]

A second influence that affected the Fourth Amendment rulings was the Supreme Court's reluctance to overrule its own decisions. This common theme of the Court under both Taft and Hughes[88] frequently dictated the form of the Supreme Court opinion, although it did not alter the general trend of the decisions. None of the Court's opinions expressly overruled an existing precedent. Instead, the Court achieved its divergent results by manipulating doctrinal categories or by more stringent application of formally consistent rules.

The importance of individual cases was a third factor that appears to have impacted the Fourth Amendment decisions. In the middle years of prohibition that provide a transition from the restrictive approach of the early cases to the liberal construction of the last years, the Supreme Court was more willing to protect Fourth Amendment rights in cases involving minor rather than serious violations. But the severity of the violation is a much less reliable guide after 1930 when many of the decisions involved violations of the prohibition laws that cannot fairly be dismissed as minor.[89]

A final factor with explanatory power in the Fourth Amendment cases is Charles Evans Hughes's replacement of William Howard Taft as chief justice in 1930. Certainly Taft was the author of some of the most restrictive of opinions of the middle years of the era,[90] and the revival of liberal construction of Fourth Amendment rights occurred after Hughes became chief justice. But Hughes did not author any of the liberal construction opinions.[91] Moreover, he later exerted little influence on Justices Butler and McReynolds, the leaders of the revival of Fourth Amendment rights, during the New Deal crisis that followed the repeal of prohibition. Thus, it is difficult to give him complete credit for the shift that occurred. To view the new chief justice's hostility to prohibition as an aid to the revival of the rule of liberal construction seems reasonable. To postulate his appointment as the decisive force in shaping the course of doctrinal development stretches thin evidence too far.

The Importance of Prohibition

Recognition of the significance of these other factors in affecting the outcomes of the prohibition decisions does not require abandonment of the view that the prohibition experience was the primary or (to use the legal idiom) proximate cause of the Fourth Amendment decisions.

Simply put, none of the other factors should be regarded as important as prohibition because none of them is as useful in explaining the general trend of the decisions. The power of an explanation that gives primacy to the influence of prohibition inheres in its ability to account for the triple shift in the trend of Supreme Court opinions from liberal construction of Fourth Amendment rights in the pre-prohibition era to the strict construction of the early prohibition cases followed by the ambivalence of the following years and, finally, by the rediscovery of the rule of liberal construction at the end of the prohibition era. The triple shift supports the recognition of the decisive importance of the relationship between prohibition enforcement and Fourth Amendment doctrine in two respects. For one thing, the multiple levels of correlation between changing public attitudes toward prohibition and the trend of the Fourth Amendment decisions decrease the likelihood that it can be dismissed as mere coincidence. In addition, the erratic course of the Fourth Amendment decisions makes them difficult to explain by reference to other factors that do not display a similarly erratic course.

Close study of the Fourth Amendment cases thus demonstrates that prohibition was as important in transforming existing doctrine as it was in creating the new defense of entrapment. In short, that study confirms the value of focusing on changing public attitudes toward prohibition to understand doctrinal developments relating to search and seizure. It shows that the course of doctrinal growth is not primarily controlled by some internal logic or some special "legal reasoning" that is the exclusive domain of professionals. To the contrary, it suggests that the direction of doctrinal growth is primarily determined by the views with respect to substantive issues external to the doctrine itself. To state the matter in a crude and reductionist way, judges who were convinced that prohibition was a noble reform and should be strictly enforced tended to contract the reach of the Fourth Amendment's exclusionary rule. Once judges became convinced that prohibition was a terrible mistake that should be repealed, they were more likely to advocate liberal construction of Fourth Amendment rights.

Of course, that crude summary does not tell a complete story. No decisions are ever the product of any single influence, especially decisions, like those of the Supreme Court, that require collegial agreement. Moreover, the existence of search and seizure precedents and the very existence of the amendment itself operated to limit the range of choices that were entertained by, or even suggested to, the Court. But the degree of restraint imposed by these traditions and precedents was indeterminate; that is, their influence tended to expand or contract not as the result of an internal dynamic but in response to external stimuli. And the primary external stimulant to which they were responding was the changing public attitude toward prohibition enforcement.

5 / Double Jeopardy: Crystallization of an Enduring Exception

The enactment of the Eighteenth Amendment and the Volstead Act expanded federal regulatory authority and increased the number of federal crimes. Many of the acts that violated the new federal statutes also violated state criminal laws. As a result, defendants increasingly faced the possibility of prosecutions by both governments, and the Supreme Court had to decide whether the Double Jeopardy Clause of the Fifth Amendment[1] permitted both governments to prosecute an individual for a single act.

In an early prohibition decision, the Court allowed successive prosecutions by state and federal governments on the ground that the double jeopardy guarantee does not apply when the two prosecutions are initiated by separate sovereigns. This doctrine not only endured for the remainder of the prohibition, but it has remained part of federal jurisprudence down to the present.[2] Tracing the crystallization and retention of this dual sovereignty exception to double jeopardy during the prohibition era is the object of this chapter.

Once again, a review of the developments of the prohibition era illustrates the value of focusing on the prohibition backdrop to understand the growth of criminal law doctrines. As with entrapment and the Fourth Amendment, changing attitudes toward the Eighteenth Amendment appear to have been the dominant influence. However, the double jeopardy cases also illustrate the importance of other factors.

Supreme Court Decisions prior to the Prohibition Era

Nearly all of the Supreme Court's double jeopardy decisions prior to prohibition involved multiple prosecutions by the federal government.[3] Not surprisingly they provided relatively little guidance for determining whether the Double Jeopardy Clause applied when the federal government initiated one of the prosecutions and a state initiated the other.

Had the Court been inclined to disallow successive prosecutions, dicta in two pre-prohibition opinions could have furnished a conceptual basis for such an approach. Neither of the cases actually involved successive prosecutions. Nontheless, language in both opinions suggested that the prohibition against double jeopardy, and the common law concepts on which it was based, applied when two different governments each had authority to proscribe a single criminal act.

The earlier of the precedents was an 1820 case involving federal prosecutions for robbery and murder on the high seas. In defining the scope of federal power to punish extraterritorial crimes, the Court tied its definition to the defendant's protections against successive prosecutions.[4]

Because "[r]obbery on the seas is considered as an offense within the criminal jurisdiction of all nations," it fell within Congress's legislative jurisdiction even when the robbery was committed by a foreigner on a foreign victim on a foreign ship. But one incident of this "universal jurisdiction" was the preclusion of successive prosecutions in different nations. "[T]here can be no doubt, the Court asserted, that the plea of *autre fois acquit* would be good in any civilized state, though resting on a prosecution instituted in the courts of any other civilized state."[5]

By contrast, murder did not come within the universal jurisdiction principle or its *autre fois acquit* corollary. A nation did, however, have authority to punish a murder when the murder was committed by its citizen or within its territorial boundaries. Thus, successive prosecutions were possible when an American citizen committed a murder on a foreign vessel. In such situations, the Constitution protected defendants "from being twice put in jeopardy" in American courts, and their potential liability to subsequent trials in another country was justifiable because it stemmed from "their own act in subjecting themselves to those laws."[6]

Eighty-nine years later, the Court used similar language when it construed a statute that designated the Columbia River as the common boundary of Oregon and Washington and gave both states "concurrent jurisdiction on the waters of that river."[7] The Court's actual ruling held that the jurisdiction conferred by the statute did not allow one state to punish conduct committed within the territorial waters of the other when the other state's law expressly permitted the conduct. The opinion, however, also indicated that successive prosecutions would be impermissible in situations where an act violated the criminal laws of both states. According to the Supreme Court "one purpose, perhaps the primary purpose, in the grant of concurrent jurisdiction, was to avoid any nice question as to whether a criminal act sought to be prosecuted was committed on one side or the other of the exact boundary of the channel." When an act violated the criminal laws of both states, "the one first acquiring jurisdiction of the person" of the offender could "prosecute the offense." Moreover, its judgment would be "a finality in both states, so that one convicted or acquitted in the courts of the one state [could not] be prosecuted for the same offense in the courts of the other."[8]

The Supreme Court ignored these precedents when cases in the prohibition era forced it to decide whether the constitutional prohibition against double jeopardy applied when the federal government initiated one prosecution and a state initiated the other. Instead, the Court derived the conceptual framework for its prohibition cases from nineteenth-century decisions defining the appropriate spheres of federal and state legislative power. More specifically, the Court turned to decisions that explained when states and the federal government had concurrent power to regulate or to punish a particular act.

The term "concurrent power" did not appear in the Constitution prior to the adoption of the Eighteenth Amendment. Nonetheless, the term had surfaced in a number of Supreme Court opinions, including the decision involving the Columbia River boundary. Most of the cases in which the phrase appeared involved the issue of whether the positive delegations of congressional power in Article I, Section 8 of the Constitution carried a negative implication denying state authority to enact legislation affecting these matters. In 1922 a constitutional authority as renowned as Noel Dowling concluded that the nineteenth-century decisions had failed to give the term concurrent power "an established meaning by judicial usage."[9] The decisions did, however, indicate that granting power to Congress could operate in some situations to displace a state's power to legislate under the police power.

The Commerce Clause offered the preeminent example of how granting power to Congress could limit a state's legislative power. Dicta in one of John Marshall's opinions suggested that granting Congress the power to regulate interstate commerce precluded state regulation of that commerce even in areas that Congress had not chosen to regulate.[10] By the late nineteenth century, this doctrine of an implied denial of state authority to regulate interstate commerce had passed from dicta to holding[11] and had even temporarily limited the application of state prohibition laws to liquors imported from outside the state.[12] The ban was never absolute, and its exact parameters remained uncertain.[13] Nevertheless, the Commerce Clause cases of the nineteenth century did confirm that granting regulatory authority to Congress could operate to displace the regulatory power that the states would otherwise enjoy.

Relying on the Supremacy Clause,[14] the Supreme Court also invalidated state laws that conflicted with federal statutes regulating interstate commerce. For example, the Marshall Court declared the New York statute granting a ferry monopoly invalid because it conflicted with the federal statute governing the licensing of coastal vessels.[15] Similarly, a 1915 decision[16] held that Indiana could not apply its statute punishing a railroad's failure to use certain safety equipment on its trains to a railroad covered by the Federal Safety Appliance Act.[17]

Of course, the Supremacy Clause objection only applied when the Court found some conflict between the federal and state statutes. On this ground, the Court rejected the argument that federal statutes that forbade obstructing the mail and interfering with interstate commerce precluded a state murder prosecution when a train derailment resulted in the death of the train's engineer. Noting that no statute authorized a federal murder prosecution for the defendant, the Court invoked the "settled law that the same act may constitute an offense against the United States and against a state, subjecting the guilty party to punishment under the laws of each government."[18] Likewise, the Court held that federal statutes governing national banks did not evidence an intent to forbid a state forgery conviction when the forged notes were payable to a national bank and were used in a scheme that violated federal law.[19]

When state laws were challenged because they conflicted with other congressional powers, the Supreme Court was even more tolerant of state authority, whether or not Congress had exercised the power conferred on it. For example, Fox v. Ohio[20] held that a state retained authority to punish the offense of circulating counterfeit coins, despite the Constitution's grant to Congress of the powers to coin money and to provide for the punishment of counterfeiting the coin of the United States.[21] Similarly a decision at the beginning of the prohibition era[22] upheld a state's authority to punish acts that deterred military enlistments or that discouraged aiding in the war effort against a claim that the state law conflicted with the Constitution's grant of the war-making power to Congress.[23]

None of the pre-prohibition cases defining the scope of state and federal legislative authority involved an actual case of successive prosecutions by both state and federal governments. Nonetheless, dicta in several decisions indicated that successive prosecutions would not violate the Fifth Amendment's Double Jeopardy Clause because the prosecutions involved offenses against two different sovereigns. The counterfeiting cases furnish an apt illustration of this dicta, especially since they were later expressly invoked by supporters of the "concurrent power" language that was added to the Eighteenth Amendment. As indicated above, Fox upheld the state's power to punish the circulation of counterfeit coins. Some language in Fox suggested that the grant of power to Congress to punish "counterfeiting" might not include the power to punish the circulation of those coins. But the Court also indicated that the Fifth Amendment would not forbid multiple prosecutions if the same act fell within the "competency" of both state and federal governments. According to the Fox majority, protection for the individual in such a case would come not from the judiciary but from "the benignant spirit in which the institutions both of the state and federal systems are administered."[24]

A few years later, the Supreme Court affirmed a federal conviction for uttering counterfeit currency against the claim that Congress did not have the power to punish the crime of uttering.[25] The Court upheld the validity of the federal criminal statute on the ground that the power to coin money included "the correspondent and necessary power and obligation to protect and to preserve in its purity this constitutional currency for the benefit of the nation." In dicta the Court again admitted that, in view of the prior holding of Fox, an individual could be subjected to both federal and state prosecutions for the single act of uttering counterfeit coins. The result was proper because the act would, "as to its character and tendencies, and the consequences it involved, constitute an offense against both the State and federal governments, and might draw to its commission the penalties denounced by either as appropriate to its character in reference to each."[26]

To summarize, the Supreme Court decisions prior to the prohibition era suggested two approaches to the problem of successive prosecutions. Dicta in two cases indicated that successive prosecutions could be proscribed in cases where two different governments had legislative authority to make the same conduct criminal. In addition, a few decisions—primarily involving the Commerce Clause— had held that a constitutional grant of power could operate by itself to displace state authority to regulate activities that fell within the scope of congressional power. Furthermore, other decisions had invalidated state laws that conflicted with valid exercises of congressional power. On the other hand, a number of decisions had allowed both state and federal regulation of certain activities. Although none of these decisions had involved successive federal and state prosecutions, dicta in several opinions (including the counterfeit cases) indicated that the Constitution permitted such multiple prosecutions as to activities that fell within the regulatory authority of both governments.

These decisions constituted the doctrinal legacy available to the Supreme Court regarding successive prosecutions by different governments. From them the Court established the dual sovereignty exception to double jeopardy. In contrast to the Fourth Amendment decisions described in the preceding chapters, the dual sovereignty exception remained unaltered throughout the prohibition era.

Prohibition Reforms:
The Eighteenth Amendment and the Volstead Act

The Eighteenth Amendment originated as Senate Joint Resolution 17 of the Sixty-fifth Congress. As initially introduced by Senator Sheppard of Texas,[27] the resolution included two sections. Section 1 contained a substantive ban on the manufacture, sale, transportation, importation, or exportation of intoxicating liquors for beverage purposes. Section 2 gave Congress the power to enforce the amendment by appropriate legislation. In addition, the enforcement section also contained an express disavowal of any intent to "deprive the several states of their power to enact and to enforce laws prohibiting the traffic in intoxicating liquors."

The prohibition resolution was referred to the Senate Judiciary Committee, and the committee reported the resolution favorably after amending it to delete the language preserving state power to prohibit traffic in intoxicating liquor.[28] Although this deletion might suggest an intent to displace state authority to prohibit traffic in intoxicating liquor,[29] language in the Senate Report[30] as well as statements by the resolution's sponsor during the floor debate[31] indicated that the committee had no such intention.

The Senate passed the amended version[32] and sent it to the House of Representatives where it was referred to the House Judiciary Committee.[33] The House committee altered the enforcement section again; the new version granted both Congress and the states "concurrent power" to enforce the amendment.[34] The committee report offered no explanation for the change,[35] but during the floor debate the chairman of the Judiciary Committee discussed the new language. He explained that the concurrent power language was added to forestall any argument that the enforcement section might implicitly deny "the various states the right to enforce the prohibition laws of those states."[36]

Several members questioned the chairman as to the meaning of the "concurrent power" language, but his responses were less than clear. Initially, he invoked the precedent of the counterfeiting cases. The "crime of counterfeiting" was, he asserted, "peculiarly a national offense" but was also punished by "nearly all the states." Later, however, he distinguished the counterfeiting cases because "Congress [had] passed a statute giving the States power to enforce the criminal law against these various acts" whereas the prohibition amendment "propose[d] to give concurrent power by the Constitution itself."[37]

Despite this confusion over the meaning of concurrent power, the chairman was clear with respect to one point: *The committee language was not designed to permit both federal and state governments to prosecute offenders for a single act!* Representative Denison specifically asked the chairman whether the concurrent jurisdiction language would permit successive prosecutions by state and federal authorities for the same act. The chairman replied that he did "not think the punishment of the offense by the state government would be followed by the punishment of the same offense by the federal government or vice versa." An earlier proposal that "provided that the State and Federal Governments might jointly or separately exercise jurisdiction and punish" would, he declared, have allowed federal and state prosecutions "for the same offense." By contrast he interpreted the concurrent power language as meaning that "the Federal Government cannot do it if the State government does it, and vice versa."[38]

Following this exchange, Representative Denison indicated his agreement with the chairman's construction of the "concurrent power" language. Then he posed the following question:

[I]f one of the States should provide very small penalties for the violation of the law, and had jurisdiction first, would not that practically defeat the operation of the law in that State?

When the chairman acknowledged that such a situation could occur "to a limited extent for a little while," Representative Denison asked him to comment on "the wisdom" of giving states that power. The chairman responded by professing confidence that the states would not abuse the trust placed in them:

> I think it is all right. I am not afraid to trust the States about that. The gentleman need not worry about the States. I never saw one that went counter to the United States Constitution or whose law officers failed to enforce the law.[39]

The House eventually approved its committee's amendment to the enforcement section,[40] and the Senate concurred in the House amendment.[41] When the states ratified the proposal thirteen months later, the "concurrent power" language became part of the Eighteenth Amendment.

Once the amendment had been ratified, Congress adopted the Volstead Act as the federal enforcement legislation. Despite the earlier debate over the possibility of successive state and federal prosecutions, the Volstead Act made no attempt to address the issue. The statute did not preclude federal prosecution if a defendant had previously been prosecuted in state court, nor did it forbid state prosecution following a federal prosecution for violating the Volstead Act.

The legislative history of the Volstead Act also ignored the successive prosecution issue. Neither the House nor the Senate committee reports discussed the issue, and the floor debates were likewise silent with respect to the question.[42] The only discussion of the "concurrent power" language was a belated argument by Volstead Act opponents to the effect that the phrase required state approval before any federal enforcement statute applied within the state's boundaries.[43]

The Judicial Response during the Prohibition Era

Acceptance of the Dual Sovereignty Doctrine

The Supreme Court's first construction of the "concurrent power" language of the Eighteenth Amendment came less than six months after the amendment became effective in January 1920, while Edward White was still chief justice. As in the earlier cases from the nineteenth century, the issue arose not in the double jeopardy context but in an attempt to define the scope of legislative power. In the *National Prohibition Cases*, the Court consolidated "seven cases involving the validity of the [Eighteenth] Amendment and of certain general features of the National Prohibition Law, known as the Volstead Act."[44]

The decision in the *National Prohibition Cases* was an unusual one. Although a seven-to-two majority of the Court upheld both the amendment and the act, it did not prepare a typical opinion. Instead, Justice Van Devanter announced the "conclusions of the court." These conclusions consisted of eleven numbered paragraphs that briefly summarized the majority's rejection of the arguments advanced by those challenging the prohibition amendment and the statute that enforced it.

Five of the "conclusions" concerned the scope of the enforcement powers conferred by Section 2 of the amendment. Conclusion 7 emphasized that both Congress and the states were only authorized to enforce the prohibition announced in Section 1, not to "defeat or [to] thwart" it. Conclusions 8 and 9 rejected arguments that would have limited congressional enforcement power, and conclusion 10 confirmed the validity of enforcing the amendment against liquor that was manufactured before prohibition became effective. Finally, conclusion 11 upheld the validity of the statutory provision that defined as intoxicating any liquor that contained as much as one-half of 1 percent of alcohol by volume.[45]

In rejecting the narrow constructions of congressional power, the Court treated Section 2 of the Eighteenth Amendment as conferring a power that was independent of the states and unrestrained by traditional notions of federal power. Thus, conclusion 8 declared that the federal power conferred by Section 2 was independent and plenary. It was not a "joint power" requiring state approval or sanction for the federal statute to be valid. Nor was the enforcement power divided between the states and the federal government "along the lines which separate or distinguish foreign and interstate commerce from intrastate affairs." Conclusion 9 reiterated the plenary character of the federal power under Section 2. "[W]hile not exclusive," federal power to enforce prohibition was "territorially coextensive with the prohibition of the first section, embrace[d] manufacture and other intrastate transactions as well as importation, exportation, and interstate traffic, and [was] in no wise dependent on or affected by action or inaction on the part of the several states or any of them."[46]

Although the issue did not reach the Supreme Court as rapidly as the legislative power questions, the possibility of successive prosecutions quickly surfaced in prosecutions initiated after the Eighteenth Amendment became effective. Within two years, at least seven federal cases, in addition to several analogous state decisions, had considered the argument that the Double Jeopardy Clause of the Fifth Amendment forbade a federal prosecution under the Volstead Act for an act that had previously been the basis for a prosecution under a state prohibition law.

Two early decisions, one state[47] and the other federal,[48] held that successive prosecutions by two levels of government were impermissible, but the remainder of the federal[49] and state[50] decisions permitted successive prosecutions. Interestingly, none of the early decisions referred to the congressional debate that occurred on the issue when the Eighteenth Amendment was proposed, even though briefs filed in one early prohibition case indicated that prohibition supporters, at least, were aware of the legislative history.[51]

The lone federal decision precluding successive prosecutions also provided the vehicle for the Supreme Court to resolve the issue. Federal prosecutors charged defendants in a case from the state of Washington with violating the Volstead Act on April 12, 1920, by manufacturing, transporting, and possessing intoxicating liquor and by having in their possession a still and material for the manufacture of intoxicating liquor. The defendants filed a special plea claiming that they had previously been convicted in the state court of manufacturing, transporting, and possessing the same liquor in violation of Washington's prohibition statute. The district court sustained the plea on the ground that "[i]t seems manifest that it was not the intent that a person should be punished by the state and [by] federal law for the same offense." The court did not analyze the legislative history or attempt to explain its ruling in any detail. It simply announced the conclusion quoted above and dismissed the indictment.[52]

Although the Washington case produced the first decision on the dual sovereignty issue, it did not establish a trend. The government prevailed in the other federal cases where the issue was raised. Similarly, state prosecutors prevailed in all cases except one when state prosecutions were challenged as prohibited by prior federal prosecutions for the same conduct.

The government appealed the district court's dismissal of the Washington indictment, and the Supreme Court reversed the lower court in *United States v. Lanza*.[53] Chief Justice Taft authored the opinion for a unanimous Court. He rejected the defendants' argument "that two punishments for the same act, one under the Volstead Act and the other under a state law, constitute double jeopardy." The chief justice rejected the argument because he rejected the premise on which the argument was based: "that both laws derive their force from the same authority—the [second] section of the [Prohibition] Amendment—and therefore, that in principle, it is as if both punishments were in prosecutions by the United States in its courts." According to the chief justice, "[t]o regard the Eighteenth Amendment as the source of the power of the states to adopt and enforce prohibition [was] to take a partial and erroneous view of the matter." State prohibition laws, he insisted, "derive their force . . . not from this Amendment, but from power originally belonging to the states, preserved to them by the Tenth Amendment."[54]

After determining that state authority to enact prohibitory laws was not dependent on the enforcement clause of the Eighteenth Amendment, the chief justice had little difficulty concluding that the Fifth Amendment's ban on double jeopardy did not forbid successive state and federal prosecutions. Without referring to the arguably contrary precedents from the nineteenth century, he declared that the prohibition against double jeopardy only applied to "a second prosecution under authority of the Federal government after a first trial for the same offense under the same authority." But in *Lanza*, "the same act" was an offense under both state and federal laws, and "[t]he defendants thus committed two different offenses by the same act." Citing the dicta from legislative power decisions of the nineteenth-century decisions as well as the lower federal courts that had allowed successive prosecutions, he held that "a conviction by the court of Washington of the offense against that state is not a conviction of the different offense against the United States." As a result, the Double Jeopardy Clause "did not bar the subsequent federal prosecution."[55]

Before concluding, the chief justice inserted a paragraph that expressly recognized congressional power "to bar prosecution by the Federal courts for any act when punishment for violation of state prohibition has been imposed . . . by a proper legislative enactment." But, he asserted, Congress "ha[d] not done so." He explained the likely reason for the lack of a legislative provision by invoking the very hypothetical that had troubled Representative Denison (but not the Chairman of the House Judiciary Committee) in the congressional debate on the Eighteenth Amendment:

> If a state were to punish the manufacture, transportation, and sale of intoxicating liquor by small or nominal fines, the race of offenders to the courts of that state to plead guilty and secure immunity from Federal prosecution for such acts would not make for respect for the Federal statute, or for its deterrent effect.

After raising the issue, the chief justice quickly avoided answering it with the declaration that "it is not for us to discuss the wisdom of legislation." Instead, he contented himself with the holding

> that, in the absence of special provision by Congress, conviction and punishment in a state court, under a state law, for making, transporting, and selling intoxicating liquors, is not a bar to a prosecution in a court of the United States, under the Federal law, for the same acts.[56]

With few exceptions,[57] analyses of *Lanza* accepted the conceptual framework that undergirded the Supreme Court decision. Typical of the legal reviews[58] was a short article that appeared in *Law Notes*.[59] In it the author denied that any "valid ground" existed for attacking *Lanza* as "unsound in law." Nonetheless, he recognized "the decision, if acted on and carried out to its permissible limits, would obviously result in gross injustice." As a result, he seized on the paragraphs of Chief Justice Taft's opinion that recognized congressional power to prohibit multiple prosecutions by passing appropriate legislation as "suggest[ing] the remedy" for the possible divergence between law and justice.[60]

An editorial in the nation's leading newspaper sounded a similar theme. The *New York Times* quoted the Supreme Court opinion at length and with obvious approbation. However, it too ended by quoting the concluding paragraphs of the chief justice's opinion as providing a useful guide for legislative action.[61]

Reaffirmation in the Middle Years of the Prohibition Era

Congress never adopted the suggestions that it abrogate or modify the dual sovereignty exception legislatively. As a result, the issue resurfaced in the Supromo Court a few years later in a slightly different form. Emphatically reaffirming the principles underlying the exception, *Hebert v. Louisiana*[62] held that a pending federal charge for violating the Volstead Act did not preclude a prosecution for violating a state prohibition statute based on the same act.

The United States initially indicted the *Hebert* defendants for manufacturing intoxicating liquor for beverage purposes in violation of the Volstead Act. After the defendants had been released on bail and while they were awaiting trial in the federal district court, the state relied on the same acts to charge them with violating the Louisiana prohibition statute. The defendants argued that the state court lacked authority to try them because the acts alleged in the state prosecution constituted an offense against the United States and that the Federal Judicial Code gave the federal district court exclusive authority to try such an offense.[63] Relying on *Lanza*, the Louisiana Supreme Court summarily rejected the objection,[64] and the United States Supreme Court affirmed the state court judgment.[65]

The Court was again unanimous, and Justice Van Devanter was the author of the Court's opinion. He began from the premise that the Eighteenth Amendment "contemplates that the manufacture of intoxicating liquor for beverage purposes may be denounced as a criminal offense both by the federal law and by the state law; and that these laws may . . . be given full operation, each independently of the other." From this premise, he deduced the nonapplicability of the Double Jeopardy Clause. Since "manufacture is thus doubly denounced one who engages therein commits two offenses." Thus, multiple prosecutions do not violate "the constitutional rule against double jeopardy, it being limited to repeated prosecutions 'for the same offense.'"[66] The Van Devanter opinion also rejected the contention that the Federal Judicial Code's provision granting federal district court's exclusive jurisdiction to try offenses "cognizable under the authority of the United States" amounted to a statutory bar to state court jurisdiction. That provision, the Court ruled, had "no bearing" on the state court's authority to try the defendants. It only applied to "offenses against the laws of the United States," and the defendants were charged with "offense[s] against state law."[67]

Perhaps because it merely reaffirmed the *Lanza* principles, *Hebert* attracted relatively little attention in legal periodicals. But only one[68] of the four articles discussing the case[69] praised the decision. Two student commentators sternly opposed the *Hebert* result,[70] although they still accepted the conceptual framework that dictated the result.

A student commentary in the *Boston University Law Review* criticized the result through rhetorical questions that asked: "But is it 'just punishment'? Does it not shock one's sense of 'justice' to permit a man to be twice punished for *substantially* the same offense, as in the principal case?"[71] In a similar vein, a student note in the *Cornell Law Quarterly* argued that even though *Hebert* was "not constitutionally wrong, it [was] manifestly unjust, to prosecute an accused in two jurisdictions for substantially the same offense."[72]

The student commentator writing in the *Boston University Law Review* also referred without citation, to the "various newspaper comments made on the present cases" in which "[t]he doctrine was denounced as unfair."[73] If intended as general overview of newspaper commentary, that summary represented somewhat of an exaggeration, for a number of newspapers praised *Hebert*.[74] Nonetheless, the case did attract significant newspaper coverage, and increased criticism definitely appeared in a number of urban dailies.[75]

Comparing the *New York Times* editorials on *Lanza* and *Hebert* illustrates the more hostile tenor of much newspaper coverage of the later case. Whereas the *Lanza* editorial had praised Chief Justice Taft's opinion even while it proposed legislative relief, the analysis of *Hebert* criticized Van Devanter's legal reasoning as well. The editorial acknowledged that "ancient doctrine, founded on a long line of decisions," limited the protection of the Double Jeopardy Clause "solely to proceedings under the federal government." However, it argued that "application of the doctrine to infringements of the Volstead [A]ct in states that have availed themselves of 'concurrent power' . . . seems new"; and "[t]o believers in the Bill of Rights," this new application "seems abhorrent." The editorial concluded by coupling a renewed appeal for federal legislation prohibiting multiple prosecutions with the suggestion that "each fresh reminder of how much liberty has been thrown away in an attempt to repeal custom and to enact the morality of the Anti-Saloon League" was "helpful for the return of common sense and something at least of earlier freedom."[76]

The Disappearance of the Problem

Hebert provided the Supreme Court's final discussion of the dual sovereignty doctrine during the prohibition era. Moreover, the problem virtually disappeared from the reported decisions of the lower federal courts[77] and of state courts[78] as well. As a result, the *Lanza* holding survived the prohibition era unchallenged and unchanged.

No irrefutable logic dictated this adherence to the *Lanza* doctrine. When other double jeopardy issues reached the Supreme Court in the 1930s, the Court's decisions showed an increased sensitivity to individual rights. Furthermore, the final years of prohibition produced a major scholarly attack on the dual sovereignty exception to double jeopardy. This attack offered the Court a conceptual framework on which it could have relied if it had faced the dual sovereignty issue in another prohibition case.

During the 1930 term, the Supreme Court rendered two important double jeopardy decisions involving multiple federal actions against a single defendant. Justice Sutherland authored both opinions, and the results reached in those cases reflect a willingness to protect individual, but not institutional, violators of the Volstead Act from overly aggressive prosecutors. On the one hand, the Court broadly construed the Willis-Campbell Act's ban[79] on successive prosecutions under the tax laws and the Volstead Act to bar the collection of civil tax penalties from an individual who had previously been convicted of violating the Volstead Act with respect to the same acts that gave rise to the tax penalties.[80] On the other hand, the Court was considerably more tolerant of postconviction forfeitures when the property being forfeited was a distillery. It held that since "[t]he forfeiture [was] no part of the punishment for the criminal offense," the Double Jeopardy Clause of the Fifth Amendment "did not apply."[81]

An article published in the 1932 volume of the *Columbia Law Review*[82] provided the scholarly attack on the dual sovereignty exception. In it, Professor J. A. C. Grant sketched a conceptual framework that the Supreme Court could have used to revise the *Lanza* doctrine if it had faced the dual sovereignty issue during the final years of the prohibition. Professor Grant's article argued that, notwithstanding the nineteenth-century dicta endorsing the dual sovereignty exception to double jeopardy, the *Lanza* result was a novel one. *Lanza*, he noted, was the first case "in which the Supreme Court, faced with an actual instance of double prosecution, failed to find some remedy, consistent with the law, to avoid it." Moreover, he challenged the *Lanza* reasoning as well as its result. A reexamination of the dual sovereignty question was appropriate, he argued, because *Lanza* was inconsistent "with the views of the author of the 'concurrent power' clause of the

Eighteenth Amendment, and of leaders of the dry lobbies, as to the legal consequences of that clause."[83] This reexamination convinced him that continental jurisprudence, English common law doctrine, and leading American treatises had all rejected a dual sovereignty exception to double jeopardy.[84] Thus, it led him to conclude that the *Lanza* rule was "unsound" "as a matter of legal analysis" and should be abandoned to avoid "fritter[ing] away our liberties upon a metaphysical subtlety, two sovereignties."[85]

Of course, the Supreme Court never made use of Professor Grant's reexamination because it did not face the dual sovereignty issue in any prohibition case after *Hebert*. The result was to leave *Lanza* as an enduring precedent that remained as authoritative when the Eighteenth Amendment was repealed in 1933 as it had been when it was initially rendered in 1922.

The Significance of the Double Jeopardy Developments

The most obvious significance of the developments described above is their documentation of the prohibition origins of the dual sovereignty exception to double jeopardy. *Lanza* presented a novel problem because it was the first occasion when the Court faced successive prosecutions as an actual rather than a potential problem. Once it was forced to address the issue of successive prosecutions directly, the Court chose to establish the dual sovereignty exception, an ironic result because the exception restricts individual liberty. Thus, the dual sovereignty exception to double jeopardy contradicts the original purpose of the very federalism concept from which it is purportedly derived.[86]

More important for the present study, the developments affecting double jeopardy clarify the pattern of development in the doctrines of federal criminal law during the prohibition era. Not only do the double jeopardy cases re-emphasize the importance of the prohibition backdrop in shaping the doctrines, they also highlight other influences that were important. More specifically, they show the impact of other ideological concerns, the importance of prior doctrinal precedents, and the significance of litigation in prompting doctrinal changes.

A careful review of the historical development of the dual sovereignty exception confirms that the *Lanza* result was not dictated by logic. As Professor Grant's historical research documented, Chief Justice Taft ignored precedents in the pre-prohibition heritage that the Court could have used to forbid successive prosecutions. Furthermore, Grant's *Columbia Law Review* article shows that those authorities could easily have been combined into a conceptual framework forbidding successive prosecutions.

Not only did the Supreme Court's *Lanza* opinion ignore some precedents that would have tended in an opposite direction, it also reached a result diametrically opposed to the one that the *Congressional Record* indicates was anticipated by influential supporters of prohibition in the Congress that proposed the Eighteenth Amendment.[87] *Lanza's* brief cited portions of that legislative history,[88] and briefs filed in the *National Prohibition Cases* indicated that dry leaders themselves—including Wayne Wheeler, the general counsel of the Anti-Saloon League—were aware of the legislative history and accepted it as a correct statement of the respective authority of the state and federal governments under the Eighteenth Amendment.[89] Nonetheless, the Supreme Court ignored that legislative history when *Lanza* created the dual sovereignty exception.

How then does one account for the ignoring of relevant legislative history? To some degree, the question is anachronistic; the contemporary focus on the intention of framers of constitutional and statutory materials as the criterion for judicial construction is itself a modern development of law in the United States.[90] Nevertheless, the tradition of ignoring legislative debates cannot serve as a completely satisfactory response. For one thing, legislative history was not completely ignored when *Lanza* was decided.[91] The Supreme Court had used legislative reports to aid in construing a statute as early as 1892.[92] Justice Holmes relied on legislative materials in a case decision that was decided during the prohibition era,[93] and Justice Stone made a limited reference to legislative history in one of the forfeiture cases discussed in the next chapter.[94] Furthermore, explaining why the Court did not use legislative history falls short of a positive explanation of why the Court acted as it did.

A close analysis of *Lanza* in its historical context suggests that at least three ideological factors were significant in producing the Supreme Court's decision: the Court's general tendency to favor governmental enforcement authorities in its early prohibition cases, the availability of nineteenth-century dicta endorsing the dual sovereignty concept, and an acceptance of a pre–New Deal perspective on the proper roles of the state and federal governments in the American system.

Viewed in light of the general prohibition experience and the other decisions of the era, the dual sovereignty cases provide yet another example of prohibition's impact on an important twentieth-century doctrine. *Lanza* was not simply an unexceptional case in which the Supreme Court applied extant doctrine. Instead, it was a case in which the Court chose between competing authorities, and an important force influencing the choice was the inclination of the Court—and the public—to support enforcement authorities during the early years of prohibition.

The other double jeopardy decisions are also consistent with the general pattern of prohibition opinions. Like other decisions from the middle years of the prohibition era, *Hebert* was characteristic of an inclination to avoid an activist approach that would reshape existing doctrine to protect prohibition defendants. By contrast, the double jeopardy decisions of the final years of prohibition displayed a greater concern for individual defendants, and they manifested that concern in two ways commonly used in the final prohibition cases. First, the Court showed a preference for protecting individual violators rather than those involved in highly organized and commercialized disobedience of the law. Thus, the Court barred collection of civil tax penalties from an individual who had been convicted of violating the Volstead Act for the conduct giving rise to the tax penalties.[95] At the same time, the Court allowed the forfeiture of a distillery under the revenue laws even though its owner had previously been convicted of violating the Volstead Act by manufacturing intoxicating liquors at the distillery.[96] Second, the Court also relied on statutory construction in fashioning new protections for prohibition defendants and thereby limited the impact of its decisions in liquor cases. Since the civil penalty was based on the Court's construction of a prohibition statute (the Willis-Campbell Act), the Court could easily limit it to prohibition cases and allow the government to collect civil tax penalties from defendants convicted of other crimes.[97]

Of course, the foregoing analysis does not provide a complete explanation of the double jeopardy cases for two reasons. In the first place, *Lanza* itself shows the impact of influences other than public attitudes toward prohibition enforcement. In addition, the emphasis on the importance of prohibition does not account for the lack of any change in dual sovereignty doctrine during the final years of prohibition when the Supreme Court was so willing to reshape other areas of criminal law.

Neither of these objections requires rejection of the hypothesis that changing public attitudes toward prohibition was the significant force in shaping the content of federal criminal law decisions during the prohibition era. They do, however, require qualification of the hypothesis to recognize the impact of three other factors: pre-prohibition doctrine, ideological concerns not directly related to prohibition, and the importance of litigation as a catalyst to doctrinal development.

Lanza was not an inevitable decision; the Supreme Court had alternate precedents available to it. Nonetheless, both the dual sovereignty dicta in the nineteenth-century decisions and the *National Prohibition Cases* decision on the scope of congressional power under Section 2 of the Eighteenth Amendment undoubtedly influenced the Court to permit successive prosecutions. Although contrary authorities could be invoked, candor requires the acknowledgement that, in 1922, the most obvious of the existing precedents supported successive prosecutions. How else, for example, does one explain the nearly uniformly favorable reaction to *Lanza* among contemporary legal commentators? Thus, at least in part, the *Lanza* decision shows that prior precedents—what Dean Pound called the "taught tradition of law"[98]—can play an important role in structuring solutions to novel problems.

Yet another influence in shaping dual sovereignty doctrine was the Court's more general concern about the meaning of federalism. The basic issue of the dual sovereignty cases was the respective roles of state and federal governments in the American system of government, and that issue raised ideological questions that transcended the prohibition problem. Chief Justice Taft authored the *Lanza* opinion in the October 1922 term, his second as chief justice.[99] In his inaugural term, he had written a series of opinions that tried to define the nature of state-federal relations, and the *Lanza* result is consistent with the general theme of those decisions. In them, Taft fashioned a framework that combined a broad federal power to control matters closely connected with interstate commerce[100] with a determination to preserve an area of state authority free from federal control.[101] As the rhetorical basis for defining the parameters of that area, he invoked the "reserved powers" of the states under the Tenth Amendment,[102] the very same concept that provided the analytical underpinning for his *Lanza* opinion.

When subjected to this more searching analysis, *Lanza* indicates that existing doctrinal concepts and ideological concerns not directly related to prohibition both played influential roles in directing the course of doctrinal growth during the prohibition era. Other prohibition decisions—for example, those involving entrapment and the Fourth Amendment—demonstrate that the power of these other influences was not absolute, that an existing framework did not prevent antagonistic doctrinal developments that were consistent with the Court's changing attitudes toward prohibition enforcement. But the dual sovereignty cases illustrate how prior doctrine can be a powerful force when it pushes in the same direction as the general thrust of the prohibition cases and the Court's non-prohibition ideological agenda. In *Lanza* it persuaded the Court to ignore contrary authority and even to override contemporary expressions of legislative intent expressed in what would be regarded as authoritative sources today. Similarly, in *Hebert* clarity in existing doctrine may well have discouraged an ambivalent Court from innovation even though it did not mandate adherence to precedent.

Even more striking than the roles precedent and non-prohibition concerns seem to have played in *Lanza* and *Hebert* is the lack of any doctrinal development regarding dual sovereignty during the last years of the prohibition era. The absence of change contrasts sharply with the general pattern of prohibition decisions, with the specific trend with respect to a variety of individual areas including entrapment and the Fourth Amendment, and with the ability of legal scholars to reshape the conceptual framework on which *Lanza* and *Hebert* rested.

The reason for the lack of doctrinal development regarding dual sovereignty is obvious. The Supreme Court never reconsidered *Lanza* during the prohibition era because no case decided after *Hebert* presented the dual sovereignty issue. Furthermore, the likely reason for the disappearance of the legal issue is also straightforward: By the 1930s, multiple prosecutions for liquor violations were almost certainly rare.

Almost no decisions reported during the last years of prohibition discuss the dual sovereignty issue, and reasons for the paucity of decisions are not difficult to discover. In several states, successive prosecutions by federal and state authorities were impossible because no state prohibition statute existed;[103] and a number of other states had enacted laws barring state prosecutions following a federal prosecution for the same act.[104] Even in those states where successive prosecutions were possible, both federal and state prosecutors faced more prohibition cases than they could handle effectively.[105] They were thus unlikely to risk adverse publicity by prosecuting persons already convicted by another government when large numbers of defendants had never been prosecuted by anyone.

Hebert itself offers an illuminating illustration of this tendency to avoid successive prosecutions. *Hebert* is frequently cited as a double jeopardy case, but no evidence exists to suggest that the defendant was prosecuted more than once. Although a federal prosecution following the Supreme Court's affirmance of his state conviction was possible, the records of the United States District Court for the Western District of Louisiana show that the court dismissed the charges against Hebert on the motion of the assistant United States Attorney.[106] Moreover, the district court entered its order of dismissal on December 7, 1925, slightly more than a year and a half after the Louisiana Supreme Court affirmed the state charges but almost eleven months before the United States Supreme Court rendered its opinion in *Hebert*. Thus, the *Hebert* proceedings suggest that the reason for disappearance of appellate opinions challenging state and federal prosecutions was the same across the country. The opinions disappeared because the multiple prosecutions themselves disappeared.

Viewed from this perspective, the dual sovereignty cases offer still another caveat to any reductionist attempt to draw a one-to-one correlation between the doctrinal developments of the prohibition era and changing public attitudes toward prohibition. Because judicial doctrine was established in litigated cases, new doctrines developed only when active litigation challenged current dogma. On the other hand, doctrine survived unchanged when the legal system developed methods to avoid the dogma without resorting to the courts.

A comparison of the dual sovereignty cases with the Fourth Amendment decisions of the prohibition era offers a dramatic illustration of this role that litigation plays in the formation of doctrine. Because state laws and prosecutorial discretion largely eliminated successive prosecutions by state and federal governments, the dual sovereignty issue almost never arose in litigation, and the *Lanza* rule survived the prohibition era intact. By contrast, litigation offered the only feasible means for resolving Fourth Amendment issues. As a result, all federal courts, including the Supreme Court, regularly addressed search questions; and many of the Court's early decisions were significantly altered by the end of the prohibition era.

The dual sovereignty cases thus warn that any explanation of the relationship between politics and legal thought that focuses on a single cause is too simplistic to capture the complex reality. As important as prohibition appears to have been in shaping American judicial decisions, the double jeopardy cases offer a reminder that prohibition was not the only political issue that had an impact on the legal system during the 1920s. Prescribing the appropriate scope of governmental power was also becoming increasingly important as all governments tended to increase their regulatory controls. As a result, defining the division of power between state and federal governments and protecting private economic interests were major ideological concerns of both the Taft and Hughes courts. Sometimes, as in *Lanza*, those ideological interests coincided with attitudes toward prohibition. When they did coincide, the Court was much bolder and innovative than in the later years of prohibition when attitudes toward prohibition tended to diverge from opinions about the proper scope of governmental power.

Perhaps even more importantly, the double jeopardy cases offer a qualification to a major premise of much modern legal history, the assumption that law is a reflection of the economic and political preferences of a particular society.[107] In the main, the double jeopardy decisions of the prohibition era are consistent with that premise, for they show the ability of legal thought to accommodate itself to the times of which it is a part. Nonetheless, the dual sovereignty subset of the double jeopardy decisions does suggest that the premise is valid only if one broadly defines the term "law" to include all of the ways a society solves legal problems. If one limits law to its intellectual manifestations, the reflection of society is only partial. The general trend or drift of judicial doctrine moves in harmony with general cultural forces, and the judicial doctrine that these forces produce is capable of radical transformation. Nonetheless, anomalies still remain; and the dual sovereignty cases explain one reason for these anomalies—the possibility that a particular problem might be solved in other ways than by revising formal law. When these alternate solutions solve the immediate problem, they eliminate the incentive for litigants to challenge the doctrine and the need for the courts to revise it. As a result, the unchallenged doctrines remain intact, and the attitudes they reflect may stand in sharp contrast to the attitudes reflected in most other doctrinal areas.

6 / Property Forfeitures: Interpreting the Language of the Volstead Act

Prohibition's most obvious influence on the law of the United States involved legislation rather than judicial doctrines. Both the Eighteenth Amendment and the Volstead Act were bold and innovative attempts to achieve reform through the legislative process. Thus, obtaining a complete picture of prohibition's impact on legal thought requires consideration of the judicial response to the new statutory provisions.

One of the most notable of the Volstead Act reforms was the provision for forfeiture of vehicles used to transport intoxicating liquors in violation of the act. This chapter analyzes the judicial interpretation of that forfeiture provision. Once again the analysis confirms the importance of the prohibition backdrop for understanding doctrinal developments.

Statutory Provisions for Forfeiture before Prohibition

By the end of the nineteenth century, statutory provisions authorizing forfeiture of property used in unlawful activities had become a well-established feature of federal revenue laws and statutes relating to customs and navigation.[1] A number of these forfeiture statutes applied to violations of taxes and customs requirements specifically relating to intoxicating liquor,[2] but the more important ones were generally applicable to all violations of revenue and customs laws.[3]

The primary forfeiture provision in the revenue statutes was R.S. § 3450. Section 3450 authorized forfeiture whenever goods or commodities on which a tax was due were "removed, or deposited or concealed in any place, with intent to defraud the United States." More specifically, it made the following items of property subject to forfeiture: the goods being removed, deposited, or concealed; "any materials, utensils, or vessels" intended to be used in making the goods; all "packages" containing the goods; and "every vessel, boat, carriage, or other conveyance whatsoever . . . used in the removal or for the deposit or concealment thereof."[4]

The general smuggling statute also contained a forfeiture provision.

It provided that a "vehicle" or "beast" was subject to forfeiture when used to convey merchandise that had been unlawfully introduced into the United States.[5]

In construing these statutes, the Supreme Court had occasionally upheld forfeitures where the government could not prove that the owner of the property was involved in the illegal activities. Most of the early opinions forfeiting property where the owner's fault was not proved involved shipowners.[6] However, an 1878 opinion involving a distillery expanded the concept to cover a normal lease relationship. In the 1878 decision, the lessee operated the distillery in violation of various provisions of the revenue laws. The Supreme Court ruled that forfeiture of the property was appropriate whether or not the owner knew that the lessee was using the property to defraud the public revenue: "If [the owner] knowingly suffers and permits his land to be used as a site for a distillery, the law places him on the same footing as if he were the distiller and the owner of the lot where the distillery is located; and, if fraud is shown in such a case, the land is forfeited just as if the distiller were the owner."[7]

The Forfeiture Provision of the Volstead Act

Many of the pre-prohibition decisions construing forfeiture statutes had involved the application of revenue and customs provisions to intoxicating liquor.[8] Not surprisingly, therefore, the architects of prohibition laws appropriated the forfeiture device in the statutes they drafted.

A number of states included forfeiture provisions in their state prohibition statutes,[9] and the Volstead Act followed this state lead[10] by authorizing forfeiture of vehicles used to transport intoxicating liquor illegally. When prohibition authorities discovered intoxicating liquor being transported in violation of the act, Section 26 of Title II[11] instructed them to do three things. First, they were to seize the liquor. Second, they were to take possession of any "vehicle and team or automobile, boat, air or water craft, or any other conveyance" used in the illegal transportation or possession. Third, they were to arrest the person in charge of the vehicle or conveyance. Upon conviction of the person arrested, the section provided for the destruction of the liquor and the sale of the property seized with the proceeds paid into the United States treasury.

Unlike the tax and customs statutes, Section 26 tempered its forfeiture requirement with protections for owners and lienors. First, conviction of the person in charge of the property was a prerequisite to
forfeiture.[12] Second, the owner could avoid an order mandating the
sale of the transporting vehicle by showing "good cause to the contrary."[13] Third, the owner could secure the return of the vehicle during the pendency of the forfeiture proceedings by executing a bond in
a sum double the value of the property.[14] Fourth, even when the
property was forfeited and sold, the officer selling the property had to
pay all liens that were created without the lienor having notice of the
planned illegal use.[15]

The legislative history offers little insight as to why Congress decided to add Section 26 to the Volstead Act. The House Report on the
bill that included the section contained no individualized discussion
of the section. Moreover, supporters of the committee proposal did
not even bother to speak in response to Representative Sanders's floor
amendment to delete the forfeiture provisions; they simply voted it
down.[16]

The only congressional document to discuss the forfeiture concept
directly was a memorandum incorporated in the Senate Report. It
asserted that the "necessity of [the] provision" was "manifest" because of the "carefully worked out system to evade the law" that "was
in actual operation." According to the memorandum, that system involved "alleged owners of automobiles" who gave mortgages to ac-
complices "and then when the automobile [was] seized" claimed the
vehicle, alleging "that it was used without their consent or knowledge." These owners were willing, the report declared, to employ
"every possible scheme to distribute liquor illegally and [to] use the
safeguards of property rights to insure their success."[17]

This justification for Section 26 is confusing because it is inconsistent with the Senate's acceptance of the protections for owners and
lienors that the House had previously incorporated into Section 26.
Nonetheless, the report is significant for gauging the basic purpose of
Section 26. It indicates that the section was designed to expand the
government's authority to reach bootleggers and gives no indication of
any intent to restrict the government's ability to resort to forfeiture
provisions found in other statutes.

Of course, the protections afforded to owners and lienors were
noticeable additions when Section 26 is compared to the forfeiture

provisions of the revenue and customs statutes. Moreover, they were additions of potential importance because of the widespread use of automobiles to transport intoxicating liquors.[18] A principal impetus to the automobile boom of the 1920s was the rise of the installment sale system that allowed the purchaser to advance a minimum cash down payment and to pay the remainder over an extended period.[19] Since a vast number of automobiles were financed in this fashion,[20] the protection that the Volstead Act offered innocent owners and lienors effectively allowed bootleggers to limit their forfeiture exposure to the small equity they were required to maintain in the car.

One question that the Volstead Act did not expressly resolve was whether those charged with enforcing prohibition could continue to rely on the forfeiture provisions of the revenue and customs statutes if the conduct charged fit under one of those statutes as well as under Section 26. Section 35 of Title II[21] repealed provisions of other laws inconsistent with the Volstead Act but "only to the extent of such inconsistency." It also provided that the Act's regulation of those engaged in the manufacture and trafficking of intoxicating liquor was to "be construed as in addition to existing laws" and that the act did "not relieve anyone from paying any taxes or other charges imposed on the manufacture or traffic in [intoxicating] liquor." The section did, however, forbid issuance "in advance" of any "revenue stamps or tax receipts for any illegal manufacture or sale" of liquor.

Section 35 also made persons responsible for illegal manufacture or sale of intoxicating liquor liable for a tax "in double the amount now provided by the law with an additional penalty of $500 on retail dealers and $1,000 on manufacturers." Moreover, the section also declared that payment of this tax and penalty gave "no right to engage in the manufacture and sale of [intoxicating] liquor," nor did it "relieve anyone of criminal liability." Indeed, the section provided that nothing in the Volstead Act "relieve[d] any person from any liability, civil or criminal, heretofore or hereafter incurred under existing laws."

Left unanswered by Section 35 was whether government prosecutors could use the harsher forfeiture provisions of the revenue and customs statutes in prohibition cases or whether Section 26 with its protections for innocent owners and lienors was the exclusive vehicle for all liquor forfeitures. Nothing in the legislative history indicated that Congress ever considered the possibility of a conflict.[22] As a result, the issue was left to the courts. It was the central doctrinal dilemma that the judiciary faced in prohibition forfeiture cases, and the Supreme Court struggled with it throughout the prohibition era.

The Supreme Court's Forfeiture Decisions

Encouragement at the Outset of Prohibition

The Supreme Court did not decide a forfeiture case arising under the Eighteenth Amendment during the first five years of constitutional prohibition, but a January 1921 decision in a case involving a seizure of intoxicating liquor upheld a forfeiture of the interest of an innocent property owner under R.S. § 3450. The effect of this holding was to encourage government prosecutors to use the general revenue statutes to avoid the restrictive provisions of Section 26 of the Volstead Act. However, another decision in the same term held that Section 35 of the act repealed the criminal provisions relating to the pre-prohibition liquor taxes. The result was confusion as to the availability of the general forfeiture provisions in liquor cases, and the confusion persisted throughout the first half decade of the prohibition era.

The 1921 forfeiture decision[23] involved a seizure in 1918 of an automobile being used to transport intoxicating liquor on which the tax had not been paid. The government moved to forfeit the automobile under R.S. § 3450, the revenue statute that authorized forfeitures of property used for removing, depositing, or concealing goods on which a tax was due. The owner of the vehicle intervened in the forfeiture action alleging that it held title to the automobile being forfeited and that it had no notice of the illegal use to which the automobile was being put.

The Supreme Court held that the tax statute could and did forfeit the interest of the innocent property owners. The primary basis for the holding was an appeal to authority. Nineteenth-century cases, the Court declared, fixed Section 3450 "too firmly . . . in the punitive and remedial jurisprudence of the country" for it to be displaced.[24]

The 1921 decision described the property owner's argument as "formidable" in the abstract. Nonetheless, at least three aspects of the opinion suggest that the Court regarded the forfeiture device as a reasonable restriction of property rights. First, the Court underscored the importance of the governmental interest served by forfeiture. In enacting revenue measures, Congress "was faced with the necessity of making provision against their violation, and the ways and means of violation or evasion." Since "some forms of property [were] facilities" for breaching revenue provisions, Congress sought to interpose "the care and responsibility of their owners in aid of the prohibitions of the law and its punitive provisions, by ascribing to the property a certain personality, a power of complicity and guilt in the wrong." Second, the opinion emphasized that the forfeiture concept was one that could be reasonably confined. The Court acknowledged that hypothetical examples of extreme injustice—like the forfeiture of a Pullman sleeper because a passenger takes a bottle of illicit liquor aboard— could be posited. However, the Court noted, no such applications had arisen in the half century of experience with the forfeiture law. This experience gave the Court confidence that the hypotheticals could be adequately resolved when situations raising them presented themselves. Third, the opinion noted the "adaptability" of the automobile being forfeited to the illegal uses the forfeiture statute was designed to prevent. The automobile was "a thing that can be used in the removal of 'goods and commodities' and the law [was] explicit in its condemnation of such things."[25]

From the viewpoint of federal prosecutors, the effect of the 1921 decision was to make R.S. § 3450 (and, implicitly, other pre-prohibition forfeiture statutes) a far preferable forfeiture provision to Section 26 of the act. By using the general revenue statute, prosecutors could avoid the greater protection that the act gave to innocent owners and lienors.[26] Unfortunately for the prosecutors, the 1921 decision left the crucial question unanswered: whether the government could still use the general forfeiture provisions for seizures occurring after the Eighteenth Amendment and the Volstead Act became effective in 1920.

The Supreme Court did not address this issue for five years. In the meantime, lower federal courts rendered conflicting decisions on the issue. At least part of the confusion in the lower court decisions stemmed from uncertainty on a related, but distinct, issue—the question of whether the stricter criminal provisions of the revenue laws[27] were inconsistent with the Volstead Act and thus repealed by Section 35 of the act insofar as they applied to intoxicating liquors. Although technically distinguishable from the forfeiture issue, a decision concerning criminal penalties was crucial with respect to forfeiture authority because the forfeiture provisions of the revenue and customs laws were generally found in the sections establishing criminal penalties for tax violations.[28]

In one of its earliest prohibition decisions, the Supreme Court resolved the inconsistency issue adversely to the government. The Court held that Congress "did not intend to preserve the old penalties [of the revenue laws] in addition to the specific provision for punishment made in the Volstead Act." The exact basis for the Court's holding is difficult to pinpoint, but Justice Day's opinion emphasized two factors: the Volstead Act's establishment of lesser penalties "practically covering the same acts" as those covered by the revenue laws and the "comprehensive" nature of the prohibitions found in the Eighteenth Amendment and the Volstead Act.[29]

The opinion on the inconsistency question stressed that the Court based its decision on principles of statutory construction rather than on constitutional limits to congressional power, and Congress acted quickly to indicate its disapproval of the Court's holding. Less than a month after the Court rendered its decision, a House Committee reported a bill designed to overrule it.[30] Congress passed the statute, the Willis-Campbell Act,[31] before the end of the year.

Section 5 of the new statute continued in force "as to both beverage and non-beverage liquor" all laws relating to the manufacture and taxation of intoxicating liquor "that were in force when the [Volstead] Act was enacted," except those that were "directly in conflict with the [Volstead] Act or this Act." It also made all taxes and penalties imposed by Section 35 of the Volstead Act collectible "in the same manner and by the same procedure as other taxes on the manufacture of or traffic in liquor." The Willis-Campbell Act did, however, require the government to choose whether to prosecute under the revenue laws or the Volstead Act. It provided that, when any act violated both the revenue laws and the prohibition laws, "a conviction for such act or offense under one [would] be a bar to prosecution therefor under the other."

Two years later, the Supreme Court held that Section 5 of the Willis-Campbell Act achieved its objective of overruling the 1921 decision on implied repeal.[32] As to violations committed after the passage of the new statute, reliance on the earlier decision was misplaced. The new legislation reestablished the criminal penalties of the revenue laws that were in effect when the Volstead Act was passed.

In view of this confusion over the continuing validity of revenue provisions relating to intoxicating liquor, it is hardly surprising that one can discern considerable confusion on the related forfeiture issue. Lower federal courts adopted a variety of rationales in deciding whether Section 26 was the sole procedure for forfeiting illicit liquor and the conveyances in which the liquor was transported or whether the government could also rely on the general forfeiture provisions of the revenue laws.[33]

The reported decisions of the district courts were sharply divided on the forfeiture question. A majority accepted the argument that the provisions of the general forfeiture statutes were not inconsistent with those of Section 26 and allowed recourse to the general statutes.[34] However, even some of those that permitted liquor forfeitures under the general statutes narrowly construed those statutes to distinguish them from Section 26.[35] Moreover, a substantial minority ruled that the government had to follow the Section 26 procedures, especially when the government had named that section as one basis for its forfeiture authority.[36]

By contrast, the decisions of the courts of appeals were virtually unanimous in result. Nearly all refused to allow prosecutors to use the general forfeiture provision as an alternative to Section 26.[37] But despite the uniformity of the result, the appellate courts applied a variety of rationales.[38] To clarify the scope of the government's forfeiture authority the Ninth Circuit certified to the Supreme Court a list of six questions regarding the government's forfeiture authority in liquor cases.[39] Together with the Court's grant of certiorari in a case arising in the Fifth Circuit,[40] the Ninth Circuit's certification provided the occasion for the Supreme Court's initial attempt, in the second half of the 1920s, to reconcile Section 26 with the general forfeiture provisions.

Equivocation in the Second Half of the Decade

The Supreme Court resolved a variety of forfeiture questions in November 1926 when it handed down a series of four opinions on the subject. Considered as a group, the thrust of these 1926 opinions was equivocal. Three favored the government: The Court confirmed the existence of a broad power to forfeit property used to carry intoxicating liquor, declined to allow a procedural irregularity to invalidate a prohibition forfeiture, and refused to require the federal government to initiate all prohibition forfeitures under Section 26 of the Volstead Act. At the same time, the final opinion of the group limited the government's ability to resort to the general forfeiture provisions. It imposed an election requirement that forced the government to proceed under Section 26 whenever it convicted the party in control of the property of violating the transportation provisions of the Volstead Act.

The first of the 1926 opinions involved a state prohibition statute rather than the Volstead Act. Nonetheless, the opinion is significant for the Court's emphatic reaffirmation of the constitutionality of forfeiting the property of an innocent owner.

Pursuant to the forfeiture provision of a Kansas prohibition statute, the defendant's automobile was forfeited even though he did not know the vehicle was being used illegally. The Court began its analysis noting that earlier decisions had settled that statutory forfeitures of the interest of innocent owners and lien holders under the revenue laws did not violate the Fifth Amendment's guarantee of due process. According to Justice Stone's opinion for the Court, these precedents required the Court to uphold the Kansas statute because no reason existed for holding that "the police power of the state in this field" was not as plenary as the federal government's taxing power. Acknowledging that the Kansas prohibition act offered the innocent property owner less protection than did the federal statute enforcing the Eighteenth Amendment, the Court declared that difference was insufficient to render the state law unconstitutional.[41]

In another opinion issued on the same day, a sharply divided court indicated that Section 26 was not the exclusive procedure for liquor-related forfeitures and that the government could rely on R.S. § 3450 in some situations. Reversing the Fifth Circuit, Justice Brandeis's comprehensive opinion in *United States v. One Ford Coupe Automobile*[42] first affirmed that the Volstead Act, as amended by the Willis-Campbell Act, imposed a tax on illicitly manufactured liquor. It then rejected the argument that this tax was actually a penalty and refused to accept a narrow construction of the revenue statute's forfeiture provision before turning to the central issue: whether Section 26 of the Volstead Act superseded R.S. § 3450 insofar as it applied to forfeitures involving intoxicating liquor.[43]

The majority concluded that Section 26 did not supersede Section 3450 because "[t]he two statutes cover different grounds" and "[d]ifferent purposes underlay their enactment." While many acts punishable under Section 3450 were also punishable under Section 26, "many [were] not." With respect to this point, the Court offered three examples. First, Section 3450 applied "to a vehicle, whether used for removal, deposit, or concealment, and even [though] the vehicle [was] not in motion and movement was never contemplated"; by contrast, Section 26 "applie[d] only to a vehicle used in transporting contrary to law." Second, Section 3450 might "apply although a permit was obtained to transport the liquor; [Section] 26 [could] not." Third, Section 3450 "as applied to liquor relate[d] only to that on which taxes have not been paid; [Section] 26 applie[d] whether taxes have been paid or not."[44]

Ultimately, however, the Court declined to decide the case on the record before it. According to the majority, the existing record was inadequate to resolve whether Section 26 required an election to proceed under the Volstead Act or under the revenue laws or whether the institution of criminal proceedings under Section 26 barred recourse to Section 3450. Section 26 applied "only if a person is discovered in the act of transporting intoxicating liquor in violation of law." But the libel before the Court contained no allegations "that the automobile had been so discovered or was being so used" or that the person in possession of the automobile had even been arrested.[45] Thus, the libel was adequate to withstand a motion to quash.

The Court also indicated a reluctance to avoid forfeitures for minor procedural irregularities in a decision rendered on the day following the decision in *One Ford Coupe*. Even though municipal police officers had made the initial seizure of the motor boat that was being forfeited and even though "when the vessel was handed over to the prohibition director, the liquor was no longer aboard and . . . the man arrested was not present," the Court nonetheless upheld a forfeiture under Section 26 of the Volstead Act. Justice Holmes's brief opinion applied the normal forfeiture rules: "[A]nyone may seize any property for forfeiture and . . . if the government adopts the act and proceeds to enforce the forfeiture by legal process, this is of no less validity than when the seizure is by authority originally given." The opinion emphasized that the owner suffered "nothing that he would not have suffered if the seizure had been authorized." However the seizure was effected, it brought "the object within the power of the court . . . and justice to the owner is as safe in the one as in the other."[46]

The fourth opinion in 1920 forced the Court to analyze the election of remedies issue that *One Ford Coupe* had declined to reach. *Port Gardner Investment Co. v. United States*[47] involved the Ninth Circuit's certification of six questions designed to clarify the government's forfeiture authority in prohibition cases.[48] The Supreme Court, however, declined the invitation to issue a comprehensive opinion explaining the relationship between Section 26 of the Volstead Act and R.S. § 3450. Although the Court did rule that the government had to proceed under Section 26 of the Volstead Act in *Port Gardner*, the opinion carefully confined itself to the issue necessary to resolve the specific case before the Court. As a result, the Supreme Court answered only one of the six questions propounded by the Ninth Circuit. Moreover, it answered even that one question in terms more restrictive than the question had been asked.[49]

The driver of the car involved in *Port Gardner* had pleaded guilty to unlawful possession and transportation of intoxicating liquor, and the Court seized on the conviction as the crucial factor requiring the government to use the forfeiture procedures of Section 26. Once the driver had been convicted of the transportation offense, the Court declared, Section 26 mandated forfeiture under its provisions. Since this disposition required by Section 26 was inconsistent with forfeiture under the R.S. § 3450, the government could not resort to the latter section.[50]

As one might have anticipated, the cautious response in *Port Gardner*—when combined with *One Ford Coupe's* ambiguous endorsement of the use of the general forfeiture statutes in some cases—tended to stimulate litigation to determine exactly when the government had to proceed under Section 26 rather than the general forfeiture statutes. To clarify the issue, the Court returned to the election issue two years later. The new decision expanded the *Port Gardner* rule slightly to make it applicable when the driver had been convicted of illegal possession of intoxicating liquor as well as when the driver had been convicted of illegal transportation.

The unanimous opinion in *Commercial Credit Co. v. United States*[51] continued to define the forfeiture issue narrowly. The parties tried to phrase the question in terms of whether prohibition officials had to use Section 26 "whenever an officer discover[ed] a person in the act of transporting intoxicating liquor in a vehicle." The Court, however, refused to reach that issue. Instead, it focused on the driver's conviction for unlawful possession of intoxicating liquor. Emphasizing that the conviction for unlawful possession followed the driver's "arrest when discovered in the act of transportation," the Court concluded that the conviction was sufficient to make the forfeiture provisions of Section 26 mandatory. According to the Court, Section 26—when read in its entirety—governed the disposition of any vehicle "when the person in charge of the vehicle is convicted of the unlawful possession incidental to the transportation, as well as where he is convicted of the transportation itself."[52] Thus, the *Port Gardner* rule applied once the driver had been convicted, and it required the government to use the forfeiture provisions of Section 26.

Commercial Credit was the last Supreme Court forfeiture decision of the 1920s. Along with the other decisions of the second half of the decade, it displayed the pattern typical of the Supreme Court's prohibition decisions in the middle years of prohibition: a willingness to temper the zeal of prosecutors by narrow construction but an unwillingness to articulate bold doctrines that would challenge the government's basic ability to enforce prohibition.[53] The ultimate result was to leave the law of forfeiture in an uncertain state that provided little guidance for lower federal courts.

Perhaps the best evidence of the Court's failure to offer clear guidance is the confusion among the lower federal courts on the issue the Supreme Court declined to reach in *Port Gardner* and *Commercial Credit*. The Fifth Circuit concluded that arresting the person in charge of a vehicle and charging that person with a violation of the Volstead Act was sufficient to make the Section 26 procedures mandatory.[54] By contrast, the Fourth and Ninth Circuits ruled that the government could proceed under the general forfeiture statute so long as the government did not prosecute the person in charge for violating the Volstead Act.[55] As a result of this split, the Supreme Court had to return again to the issue in the last years of the prohibition era.

The Final Years: Expanding and Limiting
the Election Doctrine

After 1930 the Supreme Court dramatically expanded the election doctrine announced in *Port Gardner* and *Commercial Credit*. It required all transportation cases to proceed under Section 26 of the Volstead Act rather than under R.S. § 3450. Yet even at this point in the history of prohibition, the Court continued to allow prosecutors to use general forfeiture statutes in two classes of cases: forfeitures of furnishings used in establishments selling intoxicating liquor, and forfeitures of vehicles and vessels violating customs and navigations laws.

The first of the decisions from the 1930s was *Richbourg Motor Co. v. United States*.[56] In *Richbourg* the Court reviewed the decisions of the Fourth and Ninth Circuits that allowed the government to proceed under the general forfeiture provision of the revenue laws even though the person in charge of the vehicle had been initially arrested for transporting intoxicating liquor in violation of the Volstead Act. Reversing both judgments before it, the Court broadened the election doctrine to encompass the rule the claimant in *Port Gardner* had originally urged: Arrest alone was sufficient to require the government to use the forfeiture provisions of Section 26.

The facts in each of the cases consolidated for review in *Richbourg* were similar to those of *Port Gardner* and *Commercial Credit*. In all three cases, a person driving an automobile belonging to another had been arrested and arraigned on a charge of illegal transportation of intoxicating liquor, and the officer making the arrest had seized the liquor and the automobile used to transport it. Nonetheless, the *Richbourg* cases were distinguishable from the earlier decisions because none of the *Richbourg* defendants had been convicted of violating the Volstead Act.

In the *Richbourg* case, federal prosecutors chose not to proceed with the original charges that were based on the Volstead Act. Instead, they invoked the 1921 precedent that had allowed the forfeiture of an automobile under R.S. § 3450.[57] The prosecutors indicted and convicted the drivers for removing and concealing spirits with intent to defraud the government of the tax due on the spirits. Following these convictions, the prosecutors moved to forfeit the vehicles under Section 3450.

The Supreme Court ruled that these forfeitures under R.S. § 3450 were impermissible. To support that conclusion, the *Richbourg* opinion emphasized the mandatory form of the language used throughout Section 26. Literal compliance with this language would "compel forfeiture under [Section] 26." If this disposition were mandatory, the protection that Section 26 afforded to innocent lienors would be "in direct conflict with the forfeiture provisions of [Section] 3450" and would supersede them in all situations to which both statutes could apply.[58]

The government argued that the mandatory language should not be interpreted literally. In the government's view, the phrasing of Section 26 "was not intended to do more than state generally the duty resting on all law enforcement officers to enforce the law, but which leaves them free when the same act or transaction constitutes an offense under different statutes, to proceed under either one."[59]

The Supreme Court conceded that the mandatory word "shall" could sometimes mean "may" when "used in a statute prospectively affecting governmental action." But it gave a number of reasons for concluding that Section 26 did not use "shall" in this fashion. First, the detailed steps of Section 26, which, "if followed, lead unavoidably to forfeiture under that section and no other," suggested a "definite purpose" to protect innocent owners in all forfeitures of vehicles used to transport intoxicating liquor. Second, the contention urged by the government would allow the forfeiture of the interest of innocent property owners "in practically every case where a transporting vehicle is seized," a result inconsistent with the congressional decision to protect innocent persons in prohibition forfeitures. Third, *Port Gardner* and *Commercial Credit* had already held that the language of Section 26 requiring forfeiture upon conviction of the person in charge of the vehicle was mandatory. In the Court's view, "[n]o tenable ground of distinction" existed for holding "that the preceding requirement of the section, that the proceeding against the person arrested 'shall be under the provisions of this title,' [was] any less so."[60]

Noting that its conclusion was "not without support in the legislative history of [Section] 26," the Court specifically mentioned two items. When the clause protecting innocent lienors was added in a House floor amendment, the amendment's sponsor indicated that the purpose was "to save from forfeiture the interest of innocent lienors and owners alike." In addition, the *Richbourg* Court referred to the language of the Senate Report on the Volstead Act. It declared that the act authorized the seizure of vehicles being used to transport intoxicating liquor, "the property seized to be disposed of under the direction of the court as provided in [Section] 26."[61]

The decision in *Richbourg* signaled an important practical change for those charged with enforcing prohibition. The earlier cases of *Port Gardner* and *Commercial Credit* had emphasized a prosecutorial election of remedies in obtaining the Volstead Act conviction, an election requirement that found textual support in the Willis-Campbell Act.[62] By contrast, *Richbourg* effectively denied the prosecutor any alternative by holding that all forfeitures falling within the scope of Section 26 of the Volstead Act had to be effected under its procedures. Thus, as a practical matter, *Richbourg* precluded the use of the general forfeiture provisions in the very cases where they would have proved most useful, those involving the use of automobiles to carry intoxicating liquors.

Richbourg also involved a significant rhetorical shift as well. The Court's opinion manifested a new solicitude for "innocent" property owners. In construing Section 26, the Court emphasized that continued recourse to R.S. § 3450 after passage of the Volstead Act "would have imposed an increased and heavy burden on many innocent persons." It therefore concluded that Congress must have intended the "carefully chosen language of Section 26" to preclude the imposition of that burden and to ensure that all "innocent third persons" received the protections granted by Section 26.[63]

Richbourg precluded resort to Section 3450 in most automobile cases, but it did not eliminate all disputes over the scope of forfeiture authority in prohibition cases. Revenue and customs laws contained other forfeiture provisions, and a series of decisions rendered in the October 1931 term confirmed that the federal government could still make prohibition-related forfeitures under several of those statutes.

The first in this group of decisions involved the seizure and forfeiture of "a bar, back bar, and other saloon furnishings" at a "so-called soft-drink parlor, [which was] in fact used for the sale of intoxicating liquor as beverages." The evidence at the forfeiture trial also established that "at the time and place of the seizure," the person in charge of the premises possessed and was selling liquor on which the required tax had not been paid.[64]

The authority alleged for forfeiture was R.S. § 3453,[65] another general forfeiture provision of the revenue laws. That section contained three clauses, whose provisions were summarized by the Supreme Court as follows:

> The first authorizes forfeiture of taxable "articles" found in the possession, custody or control of any person "for the purpose of being sold or removed by him in fraud of the internal revenue laws." The second authorizes forfeiture of "raw materials found in the possession of any person intending to manufacture the same into articles of a kind subject to tax," with intent to defraud the revenue. The third forfeits "all tools, implements, instruments, and personal property whatsoever, in the

place or building, or within any yard or enclosure where such articles or raw materials are found."[66]

The bulk of the Court's opinion explained the rejection of the defendant's argument that the forfeiture statute did not apply to him. The defendant offered a plausible linguistic argument based on the grammatical construction of Section 3453. Because the second and third clauses of the section were part of the same sentence, the defendant contended that "such articles" in the third clause should be limited to the articles described in the second clause, that is, those that were manufactured on the premises.

Justice Stone began the explanation of his rejection of the defendant's construction of Section 3453 by noting that a "strained reading" to avoid forfeiture was not appropriate. "Statutes to prevent fraud on the revenue are construed less narrowly, even though a forfeiture results, than penal statutes and others involving forfeitures." Justice Stone then gave two affirmative reasons for accepting the government's alternate reading of the statute: the government's construction was supported by the legislative history of the provision and "the uniform construction given to the section with respect to this question by the lower federal courts for more than sixty years."[67]

After deciding that the forfeiture statute in the revenue laws applied, the Court curtly dismissed, in a single paragraph, the suggestion that arrest and prosecution of the person in control of the furnishings under the Volstead Act barred the forfeiture. The *Richbourg* doctrine was inapplicable because Section 26 of the Volstead Act, on which the doctrine was based, only covered forfeitures of vehicles used to transport intoxicating liquor. Consequently, nothing in the Volstead Act was "necessarily or directly in conflict with the application" of the provisions of R.S. § 3453 to the case before the Court.[68]

Later in the same term, the Court turned to a set of forfeitures less easily distinguished from *Richbourg*, those in which vehicles and vessels carrying intoxicating liquors were forfeited for violating customs and navigations laws. Nonetheless, a series of opinions by Justice Cardozo did manage to distinguish them. In each case the Court held that the *Richbourg* requirement that liquor forfeitures proceed under Section 26 did not apply when the conduct leading to the forfeiture violated customs or navigation laws.

General Motors Acceptance Corp. v. United States[69] was the lead opinion. In it the Court ruled that Section 26 did not repeal the forfeiture provisions of the customs laws in liquor importation and transportation cases. In each of the four cases consolidated in *General Motors*, customs officers had observed an automobile crossing the border from Mexico and had discovered liquor in the automobile "at an official stopping point" of the customs service. The officers arrested the drivers for violating the Tariff Act of 1930[70] by "unlawfully importing liquor into the United States and facilitating the transportation of such liquor." At the same time, they seized the vehicles carrying the liquor. The defendant subsequently pleaded guilty to the importation charge,[71] and the United States Attorney initiated forfeiture proceedings under sections of the customs law that did not protect the interest of innocent owners.[72]

Justice Cardozo's opinion began from the apparently unchallenged premise that the defendants could properly be convicted for violating the criminal provisions of the Tariff Act even though their conduct also violated the Volstead Act. That starting point lead the Court directly to the conclusion that the government could also choose the forfeiture provision on which it preferred to rely. Justice Cardozo expressly declined the invitation to "hold that prosecution of the offender may be based at the election of the Government on the one act or the other, but that forfeiture of the implements used in his offending may be based on only one of them" because such a holding would "withdraw from the tariff acts remedies and sanctions existing for the better part of the century."[73]

The *General Motors* opinion emphasized that the Volstead Act itself recognized a distinction between importation and transportation. Section 26 was, however, directed only against transportation, "though the conduct that it does cover may be an incident of smuggling." Furthermore, separate provisions in the customs laws authorized forfeitures in cases of unlawful importation. As a result of these separate authorizations, the government had a choice when the same conduct constituted illegal transportation and unlawful importation: It could elect to seize and to forfeit the property under the customs laws or under the Volstead Act. The choice, the Court emphasized, was one "for the government." Neither the owner of the property nor the offender had "the privilege of choice between forfeiture upon the footing of the illegal transportation and forfeiture upon the footing of a smuggled importation."[74]

Justice Cardozo gave two reasons for refusing to extend *Richbourg* to the importation cases. First, the arrest and arraignment of the opera-

tor of the *Richbourg* vehicle on a charge of illegal transportation represented "a clear election to go forward under the provisions of the
prohibition act and not under any other." Second, the revenue violation alleged in *Richbourg* was moving intoxicating liquor from one
place to another within the United States with intent to evade the tax
on spirituous liquors. That offense was "more nearly identical" with
the crime of illegal transportation within the United States than was
"a wrongful importation and violation of the customs," the violation
alleged in *General Motors*. Removal with intent to evade was distinguishable from unlawful transportation "by the quality of the intent"
alone. Importation was differentiated "by the nature of the act" as
well.[75]

A contemporaneous decision extended the *General Motors* rule to
include violations of navigation as well as customs laws. It upheld the
forfeiture of a seagoing vessel for carrying intoxicating liquor in violation of a condition of the license under which the vessel operated.
According to the Court, the basis of the forfeiture of the vessel was
"not a breach of the [Volstead] Act or any movement or transportation, lawful or unlawful." Instead, the government acted to forfeit the
vehicle for a distinct act, that of "engaging in a business other than the
fishing trade in violation of the license."[76]

General Motors and its companions furnished the Supreme Court
its final opportunity to mold forfeiture doctrine in the prohibition
context. Within a year after *General Motors* was decided, the Twenty-
first Amendment had repealed national prohibition. As a result, the
number of Supreme Court forfeiture decisions dropped off sharply,
although property forfeitures have remained a significant part of
American law to the present.[77]

An Analysis of the Decisional Pattern

When the forfeiture decisions are viewed as a group, the trend they
manifest follows the general pattern of the Supreme Court decisions
from the prohibition era. The movement from the 1921 decision to
Port Gardner in 1926 to *Richbourg* in 1930 follows the pattern observed in other areas. It evidences a growing willingness to articulate
doctrines that limit the government's enforcement alternatives.

The first forfeiture opinion of the prohibition era came in 1921. In
that case, the Court showed a sensitivity to the practical difficulties of

law enforcement that was typical of early prohibition cases. Although the seizure involved in that case occurred before the enactment of the Eighteenth Amendment and the Volstead Act, wartime prohibition had already banned the production of the whiskey that was being transported. Thus, the effect of the decision was to permit the government to use a general forfeiture provision of the revenue laws to enforce a statutory prohibition applicable to intoxicating liquor. That permission understandably encouraged federal prosecutors to resort to the same forfeiture provisions to strengthen enforcement of the new statutory prohibitions found in the Volstead Act.

A number of forfeiture questions surfaced in the Supreme Court during the second half of the 1920s. The Court's opinions proved as equivocal as the public's attitudes. By 1926 the public attitude toward prohibition was less euphoric, more ambivalent. A political opposition to prohibition had begun to develop, but the prohibition forces remained in firm control of the political process. The Supreme Court's opinions from the middle and late twenties manifest a similar ambiguity regarding prohibition. They reflect incipient doubts about certain techniques of prohibition enforcement and dissents became more common. Nonetheless, the Court remained willing to grant prohibition officials broad enforcement authority.

The forfeiture decisions aptly illustrate this ambiguous thrust of the Court's opinions in the last half of the 1920s. In four decisions in 1926, the Court approved forfeiture as a device for prohibition enforcement. At the same time, it began to develop the doctrine that would ultimately preclude widespread resort to the most commonly invoked forfeiture provision of the revenue laws. Two years later, the Court initiated a cautious expansion of the new doctrine it had advanced in 1926.

Numerically, the government did quite well in the 1926 decisions, for three of the four opinions endorsed the government's position with respect to property forfeitures. The Court emphatically reaffirmed the government's constitutional power to forfeit the interests that innocent persons held in property used to transport intoxicating liquor, and it also permitted a forfeiture under the Volstead Act despite the government's failure to follow the procedural requirements of Section 26 with precision. In addition, *One Ford Coupe* indicated that federal officials could use the general forfeiture provision of the revenue laws in some cases that involved prohibition violations.

Despite the government's numerical success, the most significant of the 1926 decisions proved to be *Port Gardner*, the one decision favoring a property claimant. *Port Gardner* is important because it established the doctrinal base on which *One Ford Coupe* was finally overruled in fact if not in theory.[78]

In 1926 the relationship between Section 26 of the Volstead Act and R.S. § 3450 was much more ambiguous. *Port Gardner's* limitation on governmental discretion was a very narrow one. It required the government to use the forfeiture provisions of Section 26 only when the government chose to prosecute the person in charge of the vehicle for illegally transporting intoxicating liquor in violation of the Volstead Act. Several lines of doctrinal development other than the one eventually adopted by the Court remained open. For example, the Supreme Court could have followed the lead of some lower federal courts by allowing recourse to the general forfeiture provision but construing it narrowly so that it would not cover all transportation cases.[79] Alternatively, the Court could have relied on the Willis-Campbell Act to require forfeiture under Section 26 only when the government elected to prosecute the person in charge of the property under the Volstead Act, the course Justice Cardozo later chose with respect to the customs and navigation laws. Or the Court could have adopted an election doctrine turning on whether the person in charge of the vehicle was arrested for violating the revenue laws or for violating the Volstead Act.[80]

The Court was only slightly less equivocal when it reconsidered the forfeiture issue in *Commercial Credit* two years later. *Commercial Credit* expanded *Port Gardner's* election doctrine, but it did so in the narrowest possible fashion. Conviction for violating the Volstead Act remained the event triggering the requirement that the forfeiture proceed under Section 26. *Commercial Credit* simply applied the requirement to a conviction for illegal possession of intoxicating liquor when the possession was in fact associated with illegal transportation of the liquor. Like the 1926 decisions, the *Commercial Credit* approach is consistent with the larger pattern. The Court was increasingly willing to limit the government's enforcement tactics, but it was unwilling to articulate doctrines that significantly restricted the government's power.

By the time the election issue returned to the Supreme Court in the 1930s, the Court had become far more willing to limit the enforcement options available to prohibition officials. *Richbourg* reflects that new boldness, and the continuity in result between *Richbourg* and *Com-*

mercial Credit should not obscure the contrast in approach and in rhetoric.

Unlike *Commercial Credit, Richbourg* did not simply extend the prosecutorial election rule of *Port Gardner* one more step to cover indictments or even arrests. Instead, the Court transformed the rule that made the election turn on the defendant's conduct: Section 26 was the exclusive means for forfeiture whenever a vehicle was being used to transport intoxicating liquor.

The Court's new approach arguably conflicted with the very materials on which the *Richbourg* opinion ostensibly relied. Both the Willis-Campbell Act and the legislative history of the Volstead Act seem more consistent with an approach that would allow the prosecutor to elect the forfeiture statute that was to be used.

When conduct violated the criminal provisions of the revenue laws as well as those of the Volstead Act, the Willis-Campbell Act implicitly allowed the government to prosecute the offender under either statute.[81] However, the *Richbourg* rationale apparently meant that a decision to prosecute a transportation case under the revenue laws would preclude forfeiting the vehicle under either statute. *Richbourg* forbade a forfeiture under the revenue statutes. But Section 26 required a Volstead Act conviction before its forfeiture provisions could be invoked, and the Willis-Campbell Act made the revenue conviction a bar to prosecution under the Volstead Act.

As the Court noted, language in the Senate Report on the Volstead Act indicated that "property seized [was] to be disposed of under the direction of the court as provided in [Section] 26." When read in context, however, that language did not support the Court's position that forfeiture under Section 26 was mandatory whenever a vehicle was used to transport intoxicating liquor. The portion of the report from which the quoted language was extracted described seizure as "authorized" rather than required. Moreover, the sentence that preceded the quote used the verb "may" rather than "shall" to describe the government's authority to seize a vehicle under Section 26.[82]

The *Richbourg* Court avoided these textual and historical arguments by ignoring them. Instead, it justified its new approach by inventing a new purpose for Section 26 of the Volstead Act. According to the Court, Section 26 did not involve—as the legislative record suggests[83]—an innovative expansion of the forfeiture concept beyond its traditional use in revenue and customs laws. To the contrary, the Court viewed the enactment of Section 26 as a noble effort to limit the possibility that innocent property interests might be forfeited under earlier statutes.[84] Having postulated this purpose for the section, the Court proceeded naturally to its ultimate conclusion that the government had to use Section 26 in those transportation cases to which it applied.

The changing rhetoric of the forfeiture opinions parallels the shifting decisional pattern in the Supreme Court's opinions as a whole. The first opinions of the prohibition era accepted forfeiture as a reasonable restriction on property rights that balanced the legitimate needs of government against the interests of property owners. And even though the cases from the second half of the 1920s began to fashion a statutory limit on the federal government's right to forfeit vehicles used to transport intoxicating liquor, the Court's rhetoric as well as its decisions demonstrate this period was a transitional one. The opinions reflect no special concern for innocent property owners; instead, they essentially base the new limitations on linguistic analyses of the words in the Volstead Act. By contrast, the language of *Richbourg*, the leading decision of the 1930s, emphasizes the impact on innocent parties as a prime justification for reshaping and expanding the limitations that had been developed in earlier cases.

The foregoing analysis documents the general correlation between changing public attitudes and the decisional and rhetorical drift of the forfeiture decisions, but the correlation is not perfect. At least three discontinuities deserve further analysis—the Court's willingness to permit recourse to general forfeiture statutes in the post-*Richbourg* decisions, the Court's failure to limit the initial holding affirming the government's constitutional power to forfeit the property rights of innocent persons, and the Court's adoption of an anti-prohibition position in the 1921 decision holding the criminal penalties of the revenue laws inconsistent with those of the Volstead Act. To account for these exceptions to the general pattern requires a refined explanation of the impact of prohibition as well as another acknowledgment of the independent role exerted by the "taught tradition of the law."

At first glance, the discontinuity in the post-*Richbourg* cases seems quite substantial, for these cases refused to extend *Richbourg* to require that all prohibition forfeitures be effected under Section 26. Not only did the Court allow recourse to a general provision of the revenue laws to forfeit saloon furnishings, but decisions in *General Motors* and its companions declined to apply *Richbourg* to violations of the customs and navigation laws. Inasmuch as all of these decisions favor the government, they seem to contradict the hypothesis that attitudes toward prohibition influenced the direction of doctrinal development. But when examined more closely, this last set of decisions is better understood as offering a modification rather than a challenge to the general prohibition theme. In essence, the Court was once again more willing to limit forfeiture authority when the limitation could be confined to prohibition cases and when it protected ordinary citizens rather than organized lawbreakers.

One can easily ground the Court's refusal to apply *Richbourg* to the forfeiture of saloon furnishings in the language of Section 26,[85] but the Court's broad interpretation of the statutory provision on which the government relied is less easily explained on formalistic grounds. From a linguistic perspective, the defendant's argument that the forfeiture section should be narrowly construed was far from insubstantial.[86] As a result, one is left with the question of why the Supreme Court was willing to construe the statute broadly in the final days of prohibition.

Two answers seem to merit acceptance. First, the Court was construing a general tax statute, not a prohibition law. Thus, a narrow interpretation would restrict collection procedures for other taxes as well as restrain officials trying to use the revenue laws to aid in prohibition enforcement. The *Richbourg* approach produced no such difficulties; by construing Section 26 to supersede the revenue statutes for cases involving the transportation of intoxicating liquor, the Court effectively confined its protection to the prohibition context and kept the general provision available to help enforce other revenue laws. Second, the nature of the activities prompting the seizures in the two cases differed significantly. *Richbourg* involved automotive transportation, the new American pastime of the 1920s. The furnishings case involved the operation of a saloon, the very evil that had fueled the prohibition movement in the first place. After all, equating anti-saloon sentiment with prohibition had been the great political accomplishment of the Anti-Saloon League.[87] Moreover, even those trying to repeal prohibition in the 1930s avoided the identification with the saloon. They continually repeated their wholehearted opposition to its return.[88] The Court seems to have reflected a similar attitude. It was increasingly willing to protect ordinary citizens against excesses of prohibition enforcement. It was less inclined to support and to protect organized criminal involvement in the activity that had been instrumental in consolidating prohibition strength.

The formal argument for following *Richbourg* was considerably stronger in the customs and navigation cases. In all of them, intoxicating liquors were being transported in automobiles or boats at the time of the seizures, and *Richbourg* had held that Section 26 procedures were mandatory "whenever transportation is involved."[89] Nonetheless, in *General Motors* the Court refused to require the government to proceed under Section 26 in importation cases, and it expanded that holding to include the navigation laws in a series of companion cases. Two factors seem to explain the Court's relatively restrained approach in the customs and navigation cases as compared to its approach in *Richbourg*. For one thing, the general forfeiture statutes in the customs and navigation cases did not threaten to swallow up the whole of Section 26, as did the one involved in *Richbourg*. Although transportation might be an indispensable element of the smuggling involved in *General Motors* and the other cases, the customs and navigation laws would frequently be inapplicable in transportation cases. Many, probably most, transportation cases involved liquor produced within the United States rather than liquor smuggled into the country. By contrast, virtually every transportation case would involve the removal of liquor with intent to defraud the government of the tax because the government would not permit the tax to be paid. In addition, the activity prompting the seizure in *General Motors* and its companions was similar to the one involved in the saloon furnishings case in that it was an activity condemned even by opponents of prohibition. Smuggling, like operating a saloon but unlike carrying liquor in an automobile, was not an activity in which ordinary citizens engaged.[90]

The second discontinuity—failing to limit the original constitutional holding—requires more of a qualification to the thesis that changing attitudes toward prohibition guided the development of the forfeiture decisions. Insofar as changing attitudes provided the decisive influence, one would expect that later decisions would have modified or overruled the 1921 decision, but no such development took place. To the contrary, the Court explicitly reaffirmed the rule in 1926,[91] and even the decisions of the 1930s implicitly confirmed Congress's constitutional power to forfeit the property interests of innocent persons.[92]

In fact, the discontinuity seems to reflect an influence of an aspect of legal training and tradition—the reluctance to overrule existing precedents. This reluctance to overrule also manifested itself in the

Fourth Amendment decisions, and it was typical of the Supreme Court during the prohibition era.[93]

Acknowledgment of this influence of legal training and tradition should not obscure the relatively limited role it played. The reluctance to overrule guided the course of the later judicial decisions by focusing attention on statutory rather than constitutional issues, but it did not deflect the basic direction or pattern of the decisions. That is, foreclosure of the constitutional question did not force the Court to uphold the forfeitures in the later cases. As in nonstatutory areas, the Court found ways to circumvent the early decision without overruling it.

The third discontinuity—the anti-prohibition character of the 1921 decision regarding criminal penalties—offers the most substantial challenge to the general thesis developed in these pages. Since the opinion was issued in the very first year of prohibition when support for the Eighteenth Amendment and the Volstead Act was strong, one would have anticipated the Court to support prohibition enforcement authorities. It did not. Instead, it rebuffed the attempt of prohibition officials to augment the modest penalties of the Volstead Act by relying on the stricter punishments set forth in the revenue laws.

Of course, one could dismiss the decision from the present discussion on the ground that it involved criminal penalties rather than forfeitures. That dismissal is less than satisfactory, however. The criminal penalties involved in the case were located in the same sections of the revenue laws that contained the general forfeiture provisions. Thus, the practical impact of the decision was to preclude resort to the forfeiture provisions as an aid to prohibition enforcement.

The most persuasive explanation of the 1921 decision interprets it as offering a second illustration of the way legal training and tradition influenced the decisional pattern. Despite the swift legislative response to the Supreme Court's decision, the decision prompted no discernible scholarly critique in the legal literature.[94] The reason for this scholarly indifference apparently lies in the fact that the decision involved an application of the accepted canon of construction declaring that a comprehensive criminal statute should be interpreted to repeal prior statutes covering the same subject matter and providing different penalties,[95] and the Court's application appeared unexceptional to lawyers. The decision thus provides the major counterinstance to the theme of the prohibition cases, by illustrating the ability of the "taught tradition of the law" to lead to specific decisions out of harmony with public attitudes.

One must note, however, the relatively limited impact that legal ideology exerted when the result it produced conflicted sharply with public attitudes. Congress quickly overruled the specific holding in the Willis-Campbell Act, and the Supreme Court unanimously upheld the new law the following year. Thus, the net effect of the taught tradition was to produce a specific decision out of harmony with the general pattern, not to reverse the general pattern or to affect the general direction of the prohibition enforcement effort.

The Importance of the Property Forfeiture Cases

The legislative decision to authorize property forfeitures as a method for enforcing national prohibition produced a variety of novel and difficult problems with which the Supreme Court struggled throughout the prohibition era. In resolving these problems, the Court issued thirteen separate opinions, more than half of all the forfeiture decisions it has rendered in the twentieth century. Moreover, studying these decisions provides further insight as to prohibition's impact on American law during the years when the Eighteenth Amendment was part of the Constitution.

Most fundamentally, careful analysis of the forfeiture decisions provides further confirmation of the value of focusing on changing public attitudes toward national prohibition as a guide for understanding the judicial doctrine of the prohibition era. Those changing attitudes toward prohibition appear to be the driving force in directing the course of doctrinal development. In addition, the forfeiture cases clarify the importance of other ideological concerns, the significance of the existing doctrinal framework, and the techniques through which the Supreme Court limited the impact of its decisions to the prohibition context.

The basic pattern of the forfeiture cases mirrors the one observed in nonstatutory areas. The first decision of the prohibition era gave strong encouragement to prohibition authorities. However, by the time the Court rendered the next group of opinions five years later, it began to interpret Section 26 of the Volstead Act to impose increasingly stringent restrictions on enforcement authorities (although it did continue to reaffirm the permissibility of forfeiting the interests of innocent owners). Finally, in the last years of prohibition, the Court managed to turn Section 26 on its head by ascribing to it the purpose of restricting rather than expanding the reach of the prior forfeiture statutes.

As was true in other doctrinal areas, the trend or drift of the forfeiture decisions was neither arbitrary nor mandatory. Considered as a group, the decisions moved in harmony with changing public attitudes toward prohibition; this movement cannot fairly be dismissed on the grounds that the Court's decisions were dictated by some internal logic of the law. The Court had several alternative lines of development available to it. Neither the statutory language nor the legislative history dictated the approach that the Court ultimately chose.

This indication that prohibition's influence can be discerned in forfeiture cases offers further evidence of the pervasive nature of prohibition's impact on American legal thought. To some degree, the confirmation adheres in the realization that the forfeiture cases illustrate still another area in which the developments in legal thought paralleled changing public attitudes toward prohibition. But the forfeiture cases offer more than just another example, for they exhibit the pattern in a new context from at least two perspectives. Most obviously, they indicate that the direction of statutory construction followed the doctrinal developments in nonstatutory areas. In addition, the forfeiture cases are explicitly concerned with property rights, and they demonstrate that the mutability of legal doctrine extended to property concepts as well as to purely personal rights. The addition of these two perspectives thus serves to reiterate the pervasive character of prohibition's impact and to emphasize the need for anyone seeking to understand the Supreme Court's decisions in the 1920s and early 1930s to take seriously the prohibition backdrop against which these decisions were rendered.

Not only do the forfeiture decisions confirm the importance of prohibition for understanding American legal developments, they also clarify the nature of that impact in at least two respects. First, they indicate that even though property interests were not immutable, those interests intended to occupy a preferred position on the scale of judicial values. When compared with other prohibition-era decisions, the first forfeiture cases to invalidate the enforcement tactics of prohibition authorities appeared relatively early, during the middle years of the prohibition era (*Port Gardner* in 1926 and *Commercial Credit* in 1928) rather than during the last years of prohibition when the Court recognized the defense of entrapment and expanded the scope of the protection afforded by the Fourth Amendment.[96] This early appearance of judicial protection in the forfeiture cases suggests that the prohibition-era Court was more willing to protect interests that could be grounded in property rights, a suggestion that finds support in the Court's decisions in areas not so directly related to prohibition enforcement.[97] Second, the forfeiture decisions also confirm the tendency to structure statutory interpretation in a fashion that confined the protections created to prohibition cases and that avoided endorsing organized lawlessness. The Court's decisions after 1930 offer the most vivid illustration of this tendency. In a typical transportation case, *Richbourg* was willing to announce a bold new interpretation of Section 26. But the Court was much more cautious when it was construing a general revenue statute in a case involving a saloon and when it was asked to interpret Section 26 to limit the government's ability to forfeit automobiles and boats used by smugglers. In short, the Court was more likely to expand protections for the individual in situations that might involve otherwise lawabiding citizens and not just hardened criminals and in situations that could be expected to disappear when prohibition was finally repealed.

At the same time the forfeiture cases reaffirm the importance of the prohibition backdrop, they also furnish a further caution against a reductionist, unicasual theory of the judicial decisions. In particular, the forfeiture decisions illustrate that legal training and tradition also influenced the decisional process in at least two ways. First, the Court's reluctance to overrule existing precedents operated to channel the decisional course, although it did not deflect its basic direction. Specifically, the reluctance to overrule served to preserve the rule affirming the constitutionality of forfeitures of the interests of innocent persons and to guide legal efforts to avoid the constitutional rule toward statutory issues. Second, at least one decision seems to have followed legal training and tradition to a specific decision inconsistent with the general drift of the decisions as a whole. This inconsistency serves to limit the causative claim that can legitimately be pressed for general social forces like prohibition. While these social forces may direct the general pattern of judicial decisions, they do not always dictate the precise result in individual cases.

7 / Jury Trials: Primacy of
Institutional Concerns

Two provisions in the United States Constitution guarantee criminal defendants the right to trial by jury in federal criminal proceedings. Section 2 of Article III phrases the guarantee in terms of federal court jurisdiction. It requires that "[t]he trial of all crimes, except in cases of impeachment, shall be by jury" and that "trials shall be held in the state where the said crimes shall have been committed." By contrast, the Sixth Amendment lists trial by jury as one of the individual rights guaranteed by the Bill of Rights. It extends "the right to a speedy and public trial, by an impartial jury of the State and district wherein the crime shall have been committed," as a privilege of the accused "[i]n all criminal prosecutions."[1]

The apparent reason for the repetition of the jury trial guarantee in the Bill of Rights was to silence critics of the Constitution. They had argued that, strictly construed, Article III might permit secret trials, lengthy incarceration without trial, or inconvenient places of trial.[2]

One could also argue that the "all criminal prosecutions" language of the Sixth Amendment expanded the list of offenses to which the guarantee applied,[3] but a prohibition-era study by Felix Frankfurter and Thomas Corcoran rejected that interpretation. The study concluded that the purpose of the amendment was to set forth the essential features of the trial required by Article III. It found no "suggestion" in the relevant history that the area of criminal cases in which the jury was to operate [was to] be widened."[4]

As in other aspects of federal criminal law, the prohibition era was the occasion for significant modifications with respect to jury trials. Most importantly, the large number of prohibition cases prompted the establishment of plea bargaining as the primary vehicle for disposing of prohibition cases. In addition, doctrinal changes occurred; although they were not as dramatic as those described in previous chapters, several have had an enduring influence on federal law. Finally, the report of the Wickersham Commission stimulated a number of proposals for legislative reforms of jury trial procedures.

Once again the study of the specific topic confirms the value of the prohibition backdrop for understanding how law developed during the prohibition era and what variables affected that growth. The large number of prohibition cases was the dynamic driving the developments with respect to jury trials. At the same time, the institutional impact of that large number of cases muted (although it did not eliminate) the influence of changing attitudes toward prohibition enforcement.

Jury Trial Guarantees Prior to Prohibition

Most states had jury trial guarantees in their state constitutions that were similar to the federal provisions. But practice dating back to colonial times had allowed summary proceedings for certain "petty offenses" on the ground that the guarantees did not apply to such offenses.[5] State courts had generally upheld those exceptions for petty offenses,[6] and the United States Supreme Court had endorsed the distinction in dicta.[7]

Probably because of the paucity of federal prosecutions before the twentieth century, Congress had never enacted statutory provisions dispensing with jury trial for petty federal criminal offenses. Indeed, the federal statutory provisions dealing with the right to jury trial made no express mention of criminal trials at all.[8] In general terms, the Compiled Statutes required that "[t]he trial of issues of fact" in the district courts and the circuit courts had to be "by jury" except in equity, admiralty, and bankruptcy cases.[9]

In addition to creating exceptions for petty offenses, states had limited their jury trial guarantees in at least two other ways: by permitting defendants and prosecutors to waive jury trials and by allowing courts to use their equitable powers to restrain antisocial conduct. In neither case was the trend universal among the states,[10] but in both instances a sufficient number of states had dispensed with jury trials to serve as guides for the federal government during the prohibition era.[11]

Federal precedents prior to prohibition reflect a dichotomy with respect to exceptions to the jury trial guarantees of the federal Constitution. In ordinary criminal proceedings, the Supreme Court and lower federal courts enforced the jury trial guarantee rather strictly. On the other hand, the federal courts were more tolerant of non-jury trials in contempt proceedings brought to enforce equitable decrees.

The leading opinion on the scope of the jury trial guarantee for criminal cases indicated that it established the twelve-person jury of the common law as a part of the constitutional mandate that Congress was bound to follow.[12] This emphasis on the scope of the guarantee at common law led the Court to suggest, in dicta, that Congress could dispense with jury trials for "petty offenses."[13] Congress had, however, exercised this authority to establish summary criminal proceedings for petty offenses only with respect to crimes committed in the District of Columbia.[14] By contrast, it omitted such procedures from its early regulatory statutes, even when they established rather minor criminal offenses.[15] As a result, the Supreme Court's opinions had not defined the petty offense term with much precision. The few pertinent precedents indicated that the jury trial guarantee included some misdemeanors as well as felonies, that conspiracy to extort could not be classified as a petty offense, and that some violations of the oleomargarine statute could be classified as petty.[16]

Several decisions that antedate the prohibition era involved attempts to waive trial by jury or to proceed without the presence of jurors who needed to be excused after a criminal trial had commenced. In them the federal courts indicated that Congress could allow such waivers only in situations in which the Constitution permitted it to dispense with jury trials altogether.[17] Thus, waiver was permissible for charges of violating the oleomargarine statute and the Food and Drug Act but not for carrying on the business of a distilled spirits rectifier without paying the required tax.[18] Moreover, a defendant who waived the right to a jury trial effectively lost the opportunity for appellate review. Because of the lack of statutory authorization for the waiver, it operated as an agreement to arbitrate the issue before the district court and deprived the federal appellate courts of jurisdiction to consider most factual or legal issues raised by a defendant.[19]

In contrast to the criminal procedure decisions, the Supreme Court had no difficulty in dispensing with jury trials in contempt proceedings brought against individuals who violated the terms of judicial injunctions. The common law right to trial by jury did not extend to suits in equity,[20] and so the rationale of the criminal cases did not require juries in contempt proceedings.

Federal courts made vigorous use of the contempt power in labor cases. In re Debs,[21] one of three notorious Supreme Court decisions of 1895,[22] is probably the best known of the injunction cases. Debs and his associates had been sentenced to terms of three to six months for violating an injunction that would have, in effect, required them to abandon their strike against the Pullman Company.[23] Not only did the Court uphold the permissibility of imprisoning a defendant for a contempt violation without providing for a jury trial, it relied on the jury trial guarantee as a reason for allowing enforcement by injunction. Without the injunctive remedy, the federal government would be paralyzed whenever "all the inhabitants of a state, or even a great body of them should combine" to oppose federal power. In such a situation, prosecutions for criminal violations "would be doomed in advance to failure," and "the whole interests of the nation in these respects would be at the absolute mercy of a portion of the inhabitants of that single state."[24]

Turning more directly to the jury trial issue, the Court denied that punishment for contempt involved "any invasion of the constitutional right to trial by jury." From "time immemorial," the authority to inquire "as to the disobedience" of judicial orders had been "the special function of the court." Nor was this a "technical rule." To "compel obedience to its orders," a court had to "have the right to inquire whether there has been any disobedience thereof." Indeed, "[t]o submit the question of disobedience to another tribunal, be it a jury or another court, would operate to deprive the proceeding of half of its efficacy."[25]

In *Mugler v. Kansas*[26] the Court was equally tolerant in upholding a state prohibition law that relied on injunctions as an enforcement device. Terming "untenable" the "proposition that [the] proceedings in equity" authorized by the Kansas statute were "inconsistent with due process,"[27] the Supreme Court broadly affirmed the power to use injunctions as supplements to criminal prosecutions in enforcing regulatory statutes. In addition, the Court summarily dismissed the "objection that the statute makes no provision for jury trial in cases like this one." As to this objection, it was "sufficient to say that such a mode of trial is not required in suits in equity brought to abate a public nuisance."[28]

The Enforcement Provisions of the Volstead Act

When Congress turned its attention to how prohibition was to be enforced, supporters of the Eighteenth Amendment denied that enforcement would present unique problems. For example, Wayne

Wheeler, the general counsel of the Anti-Saloon League, estimated in a letter to Senator Sheppard that a relatively modest appropriation of $5,000,000 should suffice to ensure that the country complied with the new constitutional restrictions.[29] As a result, the Volstead Act contained no real innovations with respect to jury trials, although it did appropriate a variation of the nuisance abatement provisions that had been used by Kansas and other states.

The Volstead Act added a number of offenses to the list of federal crimes. Section 3 of Title II of the act prohibited the manufacture, sale, barter, transportation, importation, exportation, furnishing, or posses- sion of any "intoxicating liquor" except "as authorized by this Act."[30] In addition, Section 21 defined any property where intoxicating li- quors were manufactured, kept, sold, or bartered in violation of the act as "a common nuisance." It also declared that any person who maintained such a nuisance was guilty of a misdemeanor.[31]

The penalties established for the new crimes under the Volstead Act were generally modest, at least for first offenders. Section 21 pre- scribed the maximum punishment for the misdemeanor of maintain- ing a common nuisance as a $1,000 fine and imprisonment for one year.[32] In addition, Section 29 established specific penalties for manufacture and sale, two of the offenses created by Section 3. For each, the maximum punishment for a first offense was a $1,000 fine or imprisonment for six months; for subsequent offenses, the maximum penalty was a $2,000 fine and imprisonment for five years. All other offenses were lumped together into a residuary penalty provision of Section 29. It established maximum penalties of a $500 fine for the first offense, a $1,000 fine and imprisonment for 90 days for a second offense, and a fine of not less than $500 and imprisonment for two years for third and subsequent offenses.[33]

Despite the large number of federal misdemeanors that it created, the Volstead Act made no special provision for trials of prohibition violations. The effect of this statutory silence was to leave the new offenses subject to the normal requirements for jury trials with respect to all issues of fact.

Not only did the Volstead Act make prohibition violations criminal, it also authorized injunctions to abate violations that it classified as nuisances. Section 22 of Title II allowed federal and state authorities to seek to enjoin any nuisance defined in the act. Any court with jurisdiction over equity cases could hear such actions, and they were to "be brought and tried as . . . action[s] in equity." If the court found the allegations of the complaint to be true, Section 22 required the issuance of a mandatory injunction to abate the nuisance and authorized a "padlock" injunction ordering that the property "shall not be occupied or used for one year."[34] In addition, Section 23 authorized federal judges to issue injunctions restraining individuals who were carrying liquor for sale or soliciting orders for the sale of liquor.[35] Finally, Section 24 gave the court power to try violations of either type of injunction "summarily" and to punish the violator by a $500 fine and imprisonment for twelve months.[36]

The Volstead Act did include some special protections for property owners. Whenever the property of an innocent owner might be adversely affected by a judgment, the act required personal service if the property owner could "be found within the jurisdiction of the court."[37] It also gave the lessors of property used in violation of the act the power to terminate the lease.[38] Finally, even when a padlock injunction was issued, the statute allowed the court, "in its discretion," to permit the property to be occupied or used if the "owner, lessee, tenant, or occupant thereof" posted a $500 to $1,000 bond "conditioned that intoxicating liquor will not thereafter be manufactured, sold, bartered, kept or otherwise disposed of therein . . . and that he will pay all fines, costs, and damages that may be assessed for any violation of [the Act] upon said property."[39]

Developments during the Prohibition Era

The Flood of Cases

Whatever prohibition supporters hoped or expected, the Eighteenth Amendment and the Volstead Act produced a flood of cases that nearly inundated the federal courts.[40] A central obstacle to the efficient handling of the new cases was the Constitution's jury trial guarantee, and defendants quickly perceived its utility. As early as 1922, one prohibition supporter claimed that defendants were in a virtual conspiracy to frustrate the judicial system by demanding their rights to trials by juries:

> There are many criminal cases pending in the United States District Court in Chicago for liquor violations. *By a practically concerted action on the part of the defendants*, they have all asked for a jury trial. If these cases were all tried out before juries, with the present force of

Federal judges and Federal Attorneys, the indictments which were returned last week by the grand jury would probably come to trial in 1924 or 1925.[41]

The basic solution to the problem of increasing caseloads was to establish a system of institutionalized plea bargaining in the federal courts. The most notorious aspect of this plea bargaining was the use of so-called "bargain days" common in many large cities.[42] On bargain days, defendants in pending cases were offered no-jail sentences in exchange for guilty pleas that would reduce the court's backlog. As a device to reduce a backlog of cases, the bargain day was efficient. As a means of fairly enforcing constitutional prohibition, it was suspect, to put the case mildly.

Plea bargaining reduced the pressure for jury trial reforms, but it did not completely eliminate the demands for change. Doctrinal growth and legislative initiatives came in at least three areas: the special procedures for abatement of nuisances, waivers of jury trials, and the use of summary proceedings for petty offenses.

Relative Stability in the Early Years of Prohibition

The first five years of prohibition were a time of relative stability with respect to jury trial issues. Congress enacted no legislative modification of the Volstead Act procedures. Moreover, the federal judiciary showed little indication to change the traditional scope of jury trial guarantees. Some scholars raised occasional objections to the Volstead Act's procedures for abating nuisances,[43] but other legal commentators enthusiastically endorsed them.[44]

Perhaps the plea bargaining system kept the backlog sufficiently manageable in the early years of the prohibition era to preclude serious efforts to limit the availability of jury trials. Or perhaps the national commitment to prohibition enforcement was sufficient to force toleration of the judicial burden. At any rate, neither Congress nor the Supreme Court showed any inclination to eliminate jury trials for any of the minor prohibition offenses that now came before the federal courts with such regularity. The Court did, however, streamline prosecutions for prohibition offenses in one respect by holding that violations of the Volstead Act were not "infamous" crimes that required a grand jury indictment.[45]

The judicial rule prohibiting waivers of jury trials apparently generated little litigation. In the one appellate case addressing the issue, the Fourth Circuit adhered to the pre-prohibition decisions. The appellate court disallowed waiver in a case where it appears to have raised the issue on its own motion.[46]

The great bulk of the litigation relevant to jury trials involved the nuisance abatement procedures of the Volstead Act. The Supreme Court did not render any opinions on the new statutory procedures. However, the issues regularly appeared in opinions of the lower federal courts, and these opinions merit brief evaluation.

A contemporary student commentator termed the lower court decisions "far from harmonious" and concluded they "furnish[ed] few clear-cut rules."[47] That overview is not completely accurate. In general, the decisions display a fairly consistent pattern of supporting enforcement authorities.

The cases involving challenges to the constitutionality of the nuisance abatement procedures provide the best evidence of the overall pattern. With near unanimity, the federal judiciary upheld the statute against a variety of constitutional challenges.[48] Moreover, the one exception to the decisions upholding the constitutionality of the procedures can properly be dismissed as an eccentric aberration. The judge construed the statute to require padlocking a private home for a year on the basis of a single sale. Having construed the statute in such an extreme fashion, the judge then declared the unusual interpretation unconstitutional.[49]

Of course, one can find isolated decisions favoring defendants on some issues of statutory construction. For example, one federal district court held that a single sale was insufficient to establish a nuisance under the Volstead Act.[50] Another declined to grant injunctions against innocent property owners whose tenants had used the property in violation of the Volstead Act.[51] But these decisions represent a distinct minority of the total, and contrary statements can be found on the precise points at issue in them.[52]

The Ambiguity of the Middle Years

As in other areas, the legislative and judicial decisions of the middle years of the prohibition era reflect ambiguity and uncertainty with respect to jury trial issues. Congress remained under the control of the

Anti-Saloon League and its prohibition allies, the response of the courts was generally cautious and equivocal, and legal scholars remained divided on jury trial issues.[53] One can, however, detect an important change from the early cases: a greater judicial willingness to protect innocent bystanders caught up in prohibition enforcement.

In Congress the second half decade of prohibition passed like the first without significant change of the statutory provisions dealing with jury trials. But other reforms in the Jones Act of 1929 created new problems for the processing of prohibition cases. The Jones Act increased dramatically the penalties for certain violations of the Volstead Act: It made the illegal manufacture, sale, transportation, importation, and exportation of intoxicating liquor felonies punishable by imprisonment for five years and a $10,000 fine. To avoid sweeping all violators into the new dragnet, Congress added a proviso declaring its intention that, in pronouncing sentence under the Jones Act, courts should distinguish "between casual or slight violations and habitual sales of intoxicating liquor or attempts to commercialize violations of the law."[54]

The Jones Act created two difficulties for the efficient disposition of most prohibition violations. First, the act made it virtually impossible to argue that these crimes were "petty offenses" to which the jury trial guarantee was inapplicable. As a practical matter, this impediment was minor. Congress had never authorized summary proceedings for petty offenses, and cases could still be rapidly processed by guilty pleas on "bargain days." The second difficulty was more substantial. By making the offenses felonies, Congress effectively overruled the Supreme Court's holding that these offenses were not "infamous" crimes within the meaning of the Fifth Amendment's grand jury provisions.[55] Thus, the new statute required that prosecutions for the offenses it covered be initiated by grand jury indictments in place of the simpler approach of filing charges by bills of information.

In an effort to defuse criticism of prohibition enforcement, President Hoover appointed the Wickersham Commission after he took office in 1929. The study group submitted its preliminary report on the enforcement of prohibition at the very end of 1929. The preliminary report recommended a number of reforms including service by publication for absent owners in nuisance abatement actions, statutory definition of the term casual or slight violations, and hearings before magistrates for petty offenses.[56] However, the decade expired before Congress had a chance to act on any of the reform suggestions. As a result, the legislative response to the Wickersham Commission proposals forms part of the history of the final years of the prohibition era.

No Supreme Court decisions from the middle years of the prohibition era directly addressed jury trial issues. The Court did, however, issue several opinions that were significant for plea bargaining and nuisance abatement.

The Supreme Court's opinion in a non-prohibition case served to reinforce the system of implicit plea bargaining that had developed in the federal district courts. The actual holding in *Kercheval v. United States*[57] favored the defendant. The Court refused to allow the prosecution to use as evidence a guilty plea that the trial court had previously allowed the defendant to withdraw. Ironically, however, the rationale that produced this prodefendant result emphasized the absolute and binding character of guilty pleas. Unlike "a mere admission or extra-judicial confession," a plea of guilty "is itself a conviction." The guilty plea, "[l]ike the verdict of a jury," is "conclusive." Nothing remains for the court "to do but [to] give judgment and sentence."[58]

The effect of *Kercheval* was to insulate plea bargains from judicial scrutiny. Once the judge accepted the defendant's plea of guilty,[59] the plea had the same status as the verdict of a jury. Unless the trial court itself allowed the plea to be withdrawn, few, if any, challenges to the court's judgment and sentence could be raised on appeal.

The Court also rendered three decisions that interpreted the nuisance abatement provisions of the Volstead Act. In them the Court offered the continuing support for prohibition authorities that is characteristic of its decisions in the second half of the 1920s. *Murphy v. United States*[60] allowed a nuisance abatement action to proceed notwithstanding the defendant's acquittal on a related criminal charge; *Duignan v. United States*[61] upheld the validity of the injunctions that Section 23 authorized for individuals who had committed sale and transportation offenses; and *Grosfield v. United States*[62] upheld a "padlock" injunction against a landlord who should have known that his tenant was violating the Volstead Act. For the most part, all three opinions involve narrow questions of statutory construction. Considered as a group, however, the decisions served as impressive validation of the permissibility of using the nuisance abatement provisions as a supplement to criminal prosecutions.

The opinions of the lower federal courts also reflect continued support for prohibition authorities. Nonetheless, one can detect some equivocal efforts at reform, particularly in the courts of appeals.

Various lower court decisions interpreting the nuisance abatement provisions of the Volstead Act show the continuing acceptance of the act's procedures that was manifest in the Supreme Court opinions.[63] Most obviously, the lower court decisions confirmed the constitutionality of the special provisions for abatement of nuisances.[64] They also regularly entered personal injunctions against the individuals in charge of the premises where intoxicating liquor was sold,[65] declined to require a criminal conviction as a prerequisite to a nuisance abatement injunction,[66] and applied the nuisance provisions to breweries as well as speakeasies.[67]

The decisions supporting prohibition enforcement do not tell the whole story, however. When the issue shifted from validity or constitutionality to narrower questions of statutory construction, the lower court opinions—especially those of the courts of appeals—reflected an attitude more sympathetic to the defendants.

The most obvious beneficiaries of this more sympathetic attitude were "innocent" owners who were not directly involved in the prohibition violations. In a number of cases, courts declined to issue "padlock" injunctions closing the property against all uses for a year,[68] and at least one decision required personal service on those with interests in the property.[69] Moreover, owners, whether or not innocent, benefited from other decisions as well. The Second and Fifth Circuits held that the provision authorizing the district court to substitute a bond for the order closing the property required that the owner be given the option of furnishing such a bond.[70] Other decisions strictly construed an injunction and required the institution of a separate proceeding to forfeit personal property seized in a place that was found to be a nuisance under the act.[71]

The rare opinions of the courts of appeal with respect to jury trial issues in criminal prosecutions display a similarly cautious spirit of innovation. Here, however, the innovations favored judicial efficiency rather than individual defendants.

The Fourth Circuit affirmed a conviction in which the defendant, with his consent, was tried before eleven members of the original jury plus a replacement for a juror who became ill. The court ruled that the procedure did not violate the traditional rule forbidding waiver of a twelve-person jury because the new jury had been resworn and all the evidence in the original trial had been read to it. Thus, the defendant was tried by a legal jury to which he had "not only made no objection" but had "affirmatively accepted."[72]

The Ninth Circuit adopted an equally narrow rationale in a 1929 decision in which it affirmed a conviction obtained in a trial where the trial judge had appointed an alternate juror who sat with the regular jurors but was dismissed prior to the beginning of deliberations. The Court conceded that "no federal statute" authorized the appointment of such an alternate, but it avoided deciding the constitutionality of using an alternate to substitute for a juror who became incapacitated. Because the alternate had been dismissed before deliberations, the constitutional right to jury of twelve was "in no wise curtailed; 12 men were regularly selected and sworn as jurors, and they alone constituted the jury from the beginning to the end of the trial."[73]

Burgeoning Reform Efforts after 1930

After 1930 the pace of reform on matters related to jury trials quickened appreciably. The Supreme Court rendered important decisions involving waiver and petty offenses, and the courts of appeals continued to read the nuisance abatement provisions narrowly. In addition, the Wickersham Commission advocated further legislative reforms. In response, Congress gave serious consideration to a number of proposals and passed new legislation dealing with alternate jurors and the definition of petty offenses before the repeal of prohibition abruptly eliminated the impetus for reform.

The Supreme Court opened the decade with two 1930 opinions by Justice Sutherland. In both he vigorously reaffirmed the rhetoric of earlier jury trial cases. At the same time, he interpreted the constitutional guarantees in ways that would allow juries to be eliminated in many prohibition cases.

The first of the 1930 opinions defined the jury trial guarantee as a personal right that could be waived by the defendant.[74] Justice Sutherland began his opinion with an acknowledgment that "statements in some of our former opinions . . ., if followed," would preclude waivers. However, he insisted that the question was one "which this court thus far has not been required definitely to answer." In providing such a definite answer, he reaffirmed earlier decisions defining the term "trial by jury" to mean "trial by jury as understood at common law" and to include "all the essential elements as they were recognized in this country and England, when the Constitution was adopted." Nonetheless, the Court held that allowing waivers did not violate these principles. Because the jury trial guarantee was "primarily for the protection of the accused," the peremptory language of Article III was designed to emphasize "that the right of trial by jury should remain inviolate," not that it was "an inseparable part of the court." Thus, the guarantee was not "jurisdictional" but merely "a right [conferred] upon the accused which he may forego at his election."[75]

The other significant Supreme Court opinion came in a non-prohibition decision with important implications for prohibition cases.[76] It involved a challenge to a conviction in the police court of the District of Columbia on a charge of reckless operation of a motor vehicle "in such manner so as to endanger property and individuals."[77] The Supreme Court ruled that the Constitution required a jury trial on that particular charge because the defendant had not been "charged with the comparatively slight offense of exceeding the 22-mile limit of speed . . . or merely with driving recklessly, . . . but with the grave offense of having driven at the forbidden rate of speed and recklessly, 'so as to endanger property and individuals.'"

Despite this holding, the Supreme Court's opinion repeated dicta of earlier cases to the effect that "petty offenses might be proceeded against summarily before a magistrate sitting without a jury." Moreover, the factors on which the Court relied in defining what was a petty offense suggested that many prohibition offenses could fall within the petty offense exception if Congress so provided. According to the Court, whether a given crime fell with the exception "depend[ed] primarily upon the nature of the offense." Furthermore, the Court indicated that two considerations lead it to classify the motor vehicle violation before it as a crime to which the constitutional guarantee applied: (1) that the offense was "not merely malum prohibitum, but in its very nature [was] malum in se"; and (2) that the offense was one that was indictable at common law "when horses, instead of gasoline, constituted the motive power."[78] Because the manufacture, transportation, and sale of alcoholic beverages were legal at common law, neither of these considerations would normally apply to those prohibition offenses whose punishments were insufficient to classify them as felonies.[79]

In contrast to the waiver and petty offense issues, the Supreme Court's opinions after 1930 contributed little to the interpretation of the nuisance abatement statutes. The nuisance issues, however, surfaced regularly in the decisions of the lower federal courts. Those decisions continued the narrow construction in favor of property owners and other defendants that had begun to develop in the second half of the 1920s.

The most noticeable development in the nuisance abatement cases was the increased emphasis on the *in personam* character of padlock proceedings. The leading opinion came from the Second Circuit.[80] Overruling the contrary holding of an earlier prohibition case, Judge Augustus Hand emphatically declared that service of process on a bartender or similar agent who was on the premises was insufficient to authorize a court to enter a padlock injunction binding on the owner or operator of the establishment.[81] Perhaps the best demonstration of the practical significance of the decision is the large number of padlock decrees that were subsequently vacated in the Southern District of New York.[82]

The trend toward construing the nuisance provisions to limit the government's abatement authority is apparent in other areas as well. Lower courts rendered a host of decisions protecting owners in padlock actions. They dismissed outright the complaint filed against an innocent owner, denied district courts the authority to place non-statutory conditions on the bond posted to reopen premises, emphasized the need for the government to prove that the violations constituting the nuisance were continuing, refused to allow a district judge, in a padlock proceeding, to order the destruction of personal property seized when a nuisance was raided, and declined to issue padlock orders when the owners of the property had taken prompt action to abate the nuisance.[83] Finally, the Second Circuit limited the length of a padlock injunction against a brewery to the time necessary to obtain a permit under the 1933 federal statute allowing the manufacture of beer and wine.[84]

Two federal circuits also limited the power of district courts to issue personal injunctions against individuals who solicited orders of intoxicating liquor. Both the First and Second Circuits held that personal injunctions under Section 23 were improper for persons who were selling liquor at fixed locations.[85]

Not every lower federal court decision involving a request for an injunction favored the defendant. Indeed, at least one post-1930 decision emphasized the need for a "liberal" construction of the Volstead Act to eliminate the use of alcoholic beverages.[86] Nonetheless, the trend of the decisions favored the defendants rather than the government, and most of the decisions favoring the government involved substantial and deliberate violations.[87]

In 1931 the Wickersham Commission issued its final report on prohibition enforcement. In the report the commission reaffirmed its earlier proposals urging service by publication, better definition of petty offenses, and summary proceedings before magistrates.[88]

Although the proposals of the Wickersham Commission stimulated a flurry of legislative activity, the end results were relatively modest. Congress did pass statutes eliminating the need for grand jury indictments for most prohibition offenses and allowing judges to name alternate jurors for protracted criminal cases. But most of the remaining suggestions died in the Senate. They then disappeared from public debate after the repeal of the Eighteenth Amendment eliminated the bulk of the crimes that had prompted the proposals for reform.

Two bills passed by the Seventy-first Congress combined to eliminate the need for grand jury indictment for most prohibition offenses. The first was a December 1930 amendment to the statutory definition of felonies and misdemeanors. It added a proviso defining as a "petty offense" any offense for which the maximum punishment could not include imprisonment at hard labor or exceed imprisonment for six months and a $500 fine. In addition, it expressly allowed the prosecution of "all such petty offenses" to be initiated by information or complaint.[89] Just a month later, Congress passed the second statute that brought most prohibition offenses within the petty offense category. It amended the Jones Act to reduce the penalties for manufacture, transportation, or first-offense sale of intoxicating liquors in quantities of less than one gallon and for assisting in sale or transportation offenses as "a casual employee." Not surprisingly the new maximum penalty for each offense was the same six-month imprisonment, $500 fine established in the statute defining petty offenses.[90]

The third statute of the 1930s was an addition to the Judicial Code. It provided legislative authorization for judges to appoint alternate jurors in criminal cases where "the trial is likely to be a protracted one." If a juror died or became too ill to serve before final submission of the case, the court could substitute one of the alternates "who shall then take his place in the jury box, and be subject to the same rules and regulations as though he had been selected as one of the original jurors."[91] In effect Congress was offering its sanction for the procedure that the Ninth Circuit had refused to confront in 1929.

Of course, none of these statutes actually restricted the right to jury trials in prohibition cases. Following the recommendation of the Wickersham Commission, the House of Representatives passed a complicated system that allowed trial by jury for petty offenses under the Volstead Act only when the defendant demanded a jury trial following a hearing before a United States Commissioner.[92] Ultimately, however, the measure died because the Senate never acted on it.

The proposal to allow service by publication in nuisance abatement actions under the Volstead Act suffered a similar fate. The House passed a bill amending the act in accordance with the recommendations of the Wickersham Commission, but the Senate took no action on it.[93]

A final proposal would have codified the Supreme Court holding that allowed defendants to waive the jury trial guarantee.[94] Introduced before the Supreme Court handed down its decision allowing waiver, the bill passed the House shortly after the Supreme Court issued its opinion,[95] and it subsequently received a favorable report from the Senate Judiciary Committee.[96] The Senate failed, however, to act on the bill before adjournment, and it was apparently not reconsidered.

In striking contrast to the judicial efficiency emphasis of the Wickersham Commission proposals, a few commentators continued to protest the use of the Volstead Act's nuisance abatement provisions on the ground that they improperly circumvented the right to jury trial in criminal cases.[97] Those complaints seem to have had no appreciable impact on Congress. Even though Congress required trial by jury for contempt charges in labor cases when it passed the Norris–La Guardia Act of 1932,[98] it never imposed such a requirement for prohibition injunctions.

By 1933 the demands for legislative reform of the Volstead Act had been displaced by the proposal and ratification of the Twenty-first Amendment repealing constitutional prohibition. When repeal became effective, the specific problems dealing with the nuisance abatement procedures disappeared. Moreover, the dramatic reduction of the criminal caseload of the federal judiciary that accompanied the repeal of prohibition eliminated the impetus for general reform of the rules applicable to jury trials, especially now that Congress was considering the far-reaching proposals of the New Deal. As a result, the end of the prohibition era found the law in its usual inconsistent state.[99] Congress had sanctioned the use of alternate jurors, but their use had not yet been approved by the Supreme Court. The Court had sanctioned waivers of jury trial without express congressional sanction, but Congress had not passed any legislation codifying the practice. In addition, the Court had indicated that Congress could dispense with jury trials for petty offenses, but Congress had not chosen to do so.

An Interpretation of the Developments of the Prohibition Era

The foregoing chronology shows that the prohibition era produced significant changes in legal doctrines and concepts relating to jury trials as well as in actual practices regarding high-volume criminal dockets. It thus provides further confirmation for the basic claim of this study: The thirteen years of constitutional prohibition should be regarded as the formative era of modern criminal law and procedure at the federal level.

Both judicial decisions and legislative enactments contributed to the intellectual developments of the prohibition era, but the judicial decisions were considerably more important. For the most part, the legislation that was enacted was minor with the more far-reaching statutory proposals tending to die in the Senate.

The most notable of the Supreme Court decisions were those explaining the scope of the constitutional right to a jury trial in ordinary criminal proceedings. Especially dramatic was the Court's redefinition of the basic nature of the constitutional guarantee in the first of its decisions in 1930. The opinion in that case converted the peremptory, jurisdictional command described in the decisions before prohibition to an individual right waivable at the election of the criminal defendant. Less dramatic but also noteworthy was the Court's reaffirmation and expansion of the petty-offense exception to the jury trial guarantee. That decision expanded the dicta recognizing the concept for very minor violations of regulatory statutes with language that had the potential for allowing summary disposition of most prohibition offenses. By emphasizing two factors (whether the offense was an indictable crime at common law and whether it was *malum in se* rather than *malum prohibitum*) that did not apply to prohibition offenses,

Justice Sutherland's opinion at least suggested, if it did not encourage, the possibility of dispensing with jury trials for minor Volstead Act violations.

When compared to the Supreme Court decisions, the successful legislative reforms dealing with jury trials were almost inconsequential. Congress did endorse the innovations of lower federal courts in appointing alternate jurors for protracted cases, but that was more of a tinkering with the mechanics of the right than any significant change in its core meaning. Similarly the amendments that added a statutory definition of "petty offense" and that lowered many of the penalties of the Jones Act to fit within the new definition only eliminated the need for grand jury indictments, not jury trials. The additional (and more important) legislation that would have allowed the use of summary trial procedures for most prohibition violations was never enacted. Finally, Congress even lost interest in providing legislative sanction for waivers of jury trials once the Supreme Court approved the procedure by judicial fiat.

Judicial developments relating to nuisance abatement proceedings also illustrate the changing substance of the law of the prohibition era. Here, however, the lower court decisions that were spread over the entire period are more instructive than the Supreme Court decisions that are bunched in the cautious middle years of the prohibition experiment. Those lower court decisions, like the Supreme Court decisions, adhered to earlier decisions affirming the permissibility of using equity procedures to supplement criminal law enforcement. Nonetheless, they reflect an increasing tendency to favor defendants with narrow constructions of the statutory provisions, especially (but not exclusively) in cases involving property owners who do not appear to have been directly involved in any criminal activity.

Congress appears to have been reasonably satisfied with the trend of the nuisance abatement decisions. On the one hand, it declined to grant the right to a jury trial to those accused of violating prohibition injunctions as it did for similar violations of labor injunctions. On the other, the Senate refused to adopt the recommendations of the Wickersham Commission that would have made prohibition injunctions easier to obtain.

Beyond the formal changes introduced by statutes and legal decisions, the prohibition era was also a crucial period in the development of plea bargaining in the federal courts. Plea bargains antedated prohibition even in the federal courts. During the prohibition era, however, federal trial courts appropriated and institutionalized the plea bargain to manage their expanding caseloads.

Most students of the history of plea bargaining agree that plea bargaining emerged in urban courts of the United States during the nineteenth century. The legal establishment generally opposed plea bargaining,[100] but the practice became more common in the late nineteenth century and in the early decades of the twentieth century.[101] Rising caseloads were but one factor that encouraged the growth of plea bargaining. Other factors that scholars have identified as important include the changing character of jury trials,[102] the increasing professionalization of police and prosecutors,[103] the expansion of regulatory offenses that were less morally objectionable than traditional crimes,[104] and the increasing use of imprisonment as the standard punishment for crimes.[105]

Plea bargaining is a more recent phenomenon in the federal courts, although the increase in guilty pleas is a long-term trend that antedates prohibition and that has continued to the present.[106] Plea bargaining made its first substantial impact on federal judicial statistics in 1916, but the percentage of guilty pleas increased rapidly after the enactment of the Eighteenth Amendment and the Volstead Act. "By 1925, the percentage of convictions by guilty plea had reached almost 90, approximately the same level as that of recent years."[107] The prohibition era's rapid expansion of criminal caseloads mandated increased use of guilty pleas to keep the federal district courts from developing hopeless backlogs. Not surprisingly, therefore, the numbers and percentages of guilty pleas for prohibition violations increased significantly during the years when the Eighteenth Amendment was part of the federal Constitution. Furthermore, the "bargain" terminology itself seems to have become common with Volstead Act violations.[108]

The legal establishment continued to criticize plea bargaining during the prohibition era. In a study of the criminal justice system in Cleveland, Roscoe Pound and Felix Frankfurter "concluded that a discretionary system of justice, in which plea bargaining was a central figure, had undermined public confidence."[109] Similarly, the Wickersham Commission determined—near the end of the prohibition era—that "[t]he effect of the huge volume of liquor prosecutions, which has come to [federal] courts under prohibition, has injured their dignity, impaired their efficiency, and endangered the wholesome respect for them which once obtained."[110]

The opposition of the legal establishment appears to have affected the form as well as the fact of plea bargaining. Because plea bargaining was not officially condoned, plea bargains tended to be implicit rather than explicit. Indeed, one recent analysis of plea bargaining in the federal courts termed implicit plea bargaining "the hidden underside of elite lawyers' struggle to professionalize the courts."[111]

Close analysis of the changes summarized above both confirms and challenges the general trend of prohibition developments described in earlier chapters. Some of the changes show the general pattern common to prohibition decisions in other areas, but the jury trial developments also demonstrate the impact of an important new factor: institutional concern over increased caseloads.

The familiar pattern of early doctrinal support for the government followed first by cautious ambiguity in the middle years of the era and then by expanded protections for the individual finds expression in the Supreme Court's refusal to require a grand jury indictment for prohibition offenses and the decisions of both the Supreme Court and the lower federal courts construing the nuisance abatement provisions of the Volstead Act. Not only do these cases show the general trend to increase protections as public dissatisfaction with prohibition was growing, but the lower court decisions also increased the protections in ways that are consistent with the doctrinal approaches that the Supreme Court adopted in other areas. Thus, statutory interpretations received preference over new constitutional doctrines,[112] and courts were more willing to extend the protections to property owners.[113]

The new factor—institutional concerns over increased caseloads—quickly manifested itself in the plea bargaining system adopted by innovative lower federal courts. That system allowed the courts to process a high volume of prohibition cases without compromising the formal requirement for jury trials. Moreover, because it operated by agreement among judges, prosecutors, and defendants, no one challenged the validity of system on appeal. As a result, appellate courts were never forced to offer a coherent intellectual defense of bargaining for justice.

The Supreme Court decisions after 1930 also seem to have been influenced by institutional concerns. By embracing an interpretation of the jury trial guarantee that defined the guarantee as an individual right the defendant could forego, the Court broke sharply with existing precedents. But it also gave federal trial judges a new option for more efficient processing of prohibition cases. They now had a new bargain to offer a defendant, the opportunity to waive the right to a jury trial without admitting guilt; and *Kerchaval* ensured the permanence of any bargain that resulted in a guilty plea. The implicit assumption was surely that the court would consider the defendant's concern for judicial efficiency if the defendant were ultimately found guilty. Even more directly, the Court practically invited Congress to abolish jury trials for minor prohibition offenses by defining the petty-offense exception in terms that would exclude most Volstead Act misdemeanors from the guarantee of a jury trial. With that reform, federal courts could efficiently process prohibition violations whether or not the defendant agreed to dispense with trial by jury.

The impetus for efficiency received strong support from the Wickersham Commission, which was dominated by establishment lawyers.[114] The commission endorsed reduced penalties for minor prohibition violations, service by publication for nuisance abatement actions, and hearings of petty prohibition offenses before commissioners. Unfortunately, however, the proposal for hearings before commissioners was unduly complicated[115] because it preceded the Court's endorsement of the use of nonjury trials for petty offenses.

Congress was less enthusiastic than the commission about procedural efficiencies that would compromise the jury trial guarantee. Congress did eliminate the requirement for a grand jury indictment on petty offenses, and it allowed the use of alternate jurors for protracted cases. Furthermore, Congress probably would have established statutory waiver provisions if the Supreme Court's opinion had not preempted the issue. The Senate, however, refused to permit prohibition offenses to be heard before commissioners or to allow service by publication in nuisance abatement actions. This reluctance suggests that the institutional concern over prohibition caseloads was primarily important for the judiciary and its allies in the organized bar. The general body politic seems to have been far less impressed with these professional concerns.

Viewed in the context of the other changes of the prohibition era, the jury trial developments offer a further caution against any attempt at a unicausal explanation of legal change, even the changes in formal law. They show that institutional concerns of the participants in the legal process may generate pressures for change that run counter to those produced in the broader political process. Furthermore, they demonstrate that the institutional concerns can override and dominate broader political concerns on particular issues.

Of course, the caution against unicausal interpretation is not entirely new. Earlier chapters have confirmed that substantive concerns other than attitudes toward prohibition qualified the law's reflection of changing public attitudes. Similarly professional and institutional concerns not directly related to prohibition also influenced doctrinal developments in other areas. Professional views about the judicial process shaped the specific solutions that the courts embraced, although it did not change their basic direction; and formal legal doctrine tended to remain static when it was not challenged in litigation.

Even though the insights that come from careful study of the jury trial developments are not entirely novel, they are significant in two respects. They provide an emphatic confirmation of the need to avoid a unicausal interpretation, and they also highlight the importance of pragmatic, institutional concerns of the participants in the judicial process.

In the final analysis, the emphasis on institutional factors required by analysis of the jury trial developments does not contradict the basic thesis of the study. Formal law changed in response to a changing environment, and the nature of the new environment decisively influenced the direction of those changes. Of course, the new environment was a complex one, and understanding its complexity is essential if one is to understand the new changes. Nonetheless, appreciation of the complexity of the forces at work should not obscure the basic revelation of the study of the prohibition cases. For federal criminal law, the dominant factor in the new environment of the 1920s was the changing attitude toward prohibition that is reflected in both public and professional perceptions. Moreover, the solutions produced by those changing attitudes decisively altered the scope of federal criminal law doctrines that have provided the source for many modern concepts.

8 / The Prohibition Era and the Development of Federal Criminal Law

The "Criminal Law Revolution" of the 1950s and 1960s[1] has focused much legal scholarship on the substantive and procedural aspects of federal criminal law over the last three decades. During the same period, historians have devoted considerable attention to the American experiment with constitutional prohibition. For the most part both groups of scholars have ignored the close relationship between the two subjects.

With rare exceptions, neither legal commentators nor historians have recognized the magnitude of the changes in traditional doctrines and practices that occurred during the prohibition era. As a result, they have failed to appreciate the significance of the prohibition cases in the development of criminal law doctrines, and they have ignored the prohibition cases in writing the history of the Taft and Hughes Courts. Perhaps even more importantly, they have neglected the developments of the prohibition era as a case study for understanding how legal doctrine develops.

The Historical Importance of the Prohibition Cases

Developments in the Prohibition Era

The preceding chapters document the importance of prohibition as a period for the reshaping of criminal law doctrines at the federal level. They confirm that historians may properly look to legal doctrine for many of the most significant intellectual consequences of the attempt to legislate an end to commerce in intoxicating liquor. Indeed, it would hardly be an exaggeration to describe the decisions of the prohibition era as the first criminal law revolution in the federal courts.

In terms of volume, the judicial production of the prohibition era was substantial. The five areas described in earlier chapters accounted for more than forty Supreme Court opinions during the thirteen years that the Eighteenth Amendment was part of the Constitution, an aver-

age of over three decisions per year. In addition, a complete account-
ing of the prohibition decisions requires augmenting that total with
the other cases cited in the first chapter's listing of Supreme Court
decisions relating to prohibition as well as the thousands of cases
decided by the lower federal courts.[2]

Numbers alone fail to capture the true magnitude of the prohibition
decisions. The scope of the doctrinal changes was also major. In its
opinions, the Supreme Court ratified the new defense of entrapment
that had been developed in the lower courts, established the conceptual parameters of Fourth Amendment doctrine, applied the dual sovereignty rationale to the Fifth Amendment's ban on double jeopardy,
confirmed the constitutional rule allowing forfeiture of property interests of innocent owners and interpreted the Volstead Act to circumvent it, overruled nineteenth-century dicta describing the jury trial
guarantee as a peremptory command that could not be waived, and
invited congressional action to dispense with jury trials for most prohibition offenses. Similarly, the lower federal courts converted the
entrapment defense from an ad hoc weapon for bizarre cases to an
accepted legal defense, interpreted the Volstead Act to grant property
owners substantial protections in nuisance abatement actions, and
institutionalized a system of plea bargaining to handle the high volume of cases that prohibition had produced.

Both legal scholars and historians have ignored the doctrinal
changes of the prohibition era. At a minimum, prohibition deserves to
be acknowledged as the occasion for significant doctrinal changes
with respect to a variety of topics related to federal criminal law.

However, the evidence presented in the preceding chapters justifies
going beyond the modest description of prohibition as the occasion
for important doctrinal developments. It indicates that an understanding of the history of the prohibition era has great explanatory
power for describing the "drift" or trend of the developments with
respect to federal criminal law. Seen through the lens of changing
attitudes toward prohibition and prohibition enforcement, the cases
of the era assume a coherence that is otherwise lacking.

Two aspects of the evidence are particularly important for the claim
that changing public attitudes toward prohibition was an important
force in shaping the direction of the doctrinal modification that occurred between 1920 and 1933. First, the parallel between attitudes
toward prohibition and the pattern of legal thought persists through a
triple shift in public attitudes. Second, the pattern manifests itself in a

variety of doctrinal subcategories as well as in the Supreme Court's decisions as a whole.

Public attitudes toward prohibition exhibited three distinct phases: strong public support in the early years of the era, incipient doubts during the last half of the 1920s, and widespread opposition after 1930. A similar triple shift occurred in the Supreme Court decisions. An initial movement to strict construction of individual rights in the early prohibition cases was followed by the ambivalence of the middle years and, finally, by increased protection of the rights of individuals at the end of the prohibition era.

The triple shift supports the claim that prohibition was a significant causative factor in the development of the prohibition era. The multiple levels of correlation between changing public attitudes toward prohibition and the trend of the decisions decreases the likelihood that the correlation can be dismissed as mere coincidence. In addition, the erratic course of the decisions makes them difficult to explain by reference to other factors that do not display a similarly erratic course.

The degree to which the general trend reappears in many subcategories of the doctrinal structure furnishes additional justification for the claim about the importance of prohibition in shaping the developments. The consistency with which the pattern is repeated makes it more credible as a general explanation of the decisions. At the same time, the pervasiveness of the trend largely eliminates the possibility that the broader pattern of the cases was the product of different dynamics operating within individual subcategories.

The strongest support for using the prohibition backdrop to understand and to explain the doctrinal developments comes from the entrapment and Fourth Amendment decisions. But the correlation is not confined to cases involving those subjects. Decisions from other areas also furnish additional confirmation of the basic pattern.

In the case of entrapment, the lower federal courts fashioned a few aberrational cases into a new defense that has occupied a controversial place in American criminal law down to the present. The Supreme Court's role was less innovative, but no less important. By consistently denying certiorari in the early decisions, it gave the doctrine a chance to grow and to mature. The Court then ratified the new defense when it finally considered the question at the very end of the prohibition era.

With respect to Fourth Amendment doctrine, the Supreme Court itself rendered a number of significant decisions that are spread throughout the prohibition era. Although it was building on a more established base than the lower courts had for their entrapment decisions, the magnitude of the Supreme Court's achievement was no less impressive. By the end of the prohibition era, most of the major conceptual categories of contemporary Fourth Amendment doctrine— from open fields to wiretaps to automobile searches—had been established. Moreover, the Court's opinions show the same threefold development that mirrors changing public attitudes toward prohibition: from enthusiastic support of prohibition to doubtful ambiguity to rediscovery of the liberal rule of construction for Fourth Amendment rights.

The Supreme Court's property forfeiture decisions manifest a similar trend. At the very outset of the prohibition era, the Court unequivocally upheld the constitutionality of forfeiting the property interests of innocent owners of vehicles used to transport intoxicating liquors. During the middle years, the Court began cautiously to protect such owners under the Volstead Act. Finally, as prohibition came to a close, the Court construed the act to protect innocent owners in all transportation cases except for those involving smuggling activities.

Double jeopardy decisions also generally follow the pattern. Like other early prohibition opinions, *Lanza* strongly supported prohibition enforcement even though one can identify nineteenth-century precedents that could have been used to preclude successive prosecutions. Similarly *Hebert,* the single decision of the middle years of prohibition, avoided bold innovation; it simply reaffirmed the *Lanza* precedent. Although the dual sovereignty exception was never reconsidered, the Court did expand other double jeopardy protections in the last years of prohibition.

The jury trial cases are consistent with the general pattern in part. In the early years of prohibition, courts aided prohibition enforcement by restricting the use of juries. The lower federal courts instituted a plea bargaining system that dispensed of most cases without the necessity of a trial, and the Supreme Court almost as quickly dispensed with the necessity of grand jury indictments in prohibition cases. In addition, the developments with respect to the nuisance abatement provisions that authorized juryless equity proceedings generally followed the overall trend throughout the prohibition era. Early decisions in the lower federal courts upheld the validity of the Volstead Act provisions, and the Supreme Court agreed in a series of decisions from the second half of the 1920s. Then later decisions of the lower courts mitigated the impact of the provisions by construing the act to afford owners greater protection—cautiously during the second half of the 1920s and more boldly after 1930.

In addition to following general public attitudes toward prohibition, the Supreme Court's opinions are tied to the impact of prohibition in other ways as well. The Court most frequently expanded its protections for individuals in cases where the defendants were charged with noncommercialized violations. Also, the Court frequently confined the reach of many of its more expansive decisions by fashioning doctrines that limited their protections to those guilty of prohibition violations.

Undoubtedly individual violators of the Volstead Act aroused more sympathy than commercialized attempts to circumvent the prohibition law. Even Congress recognized the difference when it passed the Jones Act in 1929. Although the act substantially increased the penalties for prohibition violations, it directed federal judges to show leniency to those charged with casual or occasional violations.

The Supreme Court was also less willing to expand protections for criminal defendants in cases involving serious violations. The Court embraced the entrapment doctrine in a case involving a sale of a small quantity of liquor in a private home, and most of the early reversals of convictions on Fourth Amendment grounds involved minor violations. Moreover, the expansive interpretations of the prohibition against double jeopardy, the protection of the rights of property owners in forfeiture cases, and the limitations on the use of padlock injunctions generally reflect an analogous concern of avoiding harm to innocent owners who were not involved in commercialized violations. In the last years of prohibition, the Court did extend some of its Fourth Amendment protections in cases involving rather substantial violations, but these exceptions do not alter the overall tendency.

The primary means for limiting the scope of doctrines was to base them on the Volstead Act rather than on constitutional provisions or general principles of criminal law. Thus, the entrapment defense was dislodged from its initial roots in "public policy" and reexplained as an implied condition of the Volstead Act. Similarly the constitutional rule permitting forfeiture of the property interests of innocent owners remained in force, but the Court construed the Volstead Act to require protections for innocent property owners even when transportation of intoxicating liquor also violated the revenue laws. Likewise, the

Court's recognition of a petty-offense exception to the jury trial guarantee invited Congress to limit the exception to prohibition violations. The Court held the exception inapplicable to a charge of operating a motor vehicle in a manner that endangered life or property. At the same time, the Court offered a definition of "petty offense" that would allow Congress to include most Volstead Act offenses.

Obviously the impact of changing attitudes toward prohibition was not the only factor influencing the criminal law doctrines. The preceding chapters have identified a variety of other influences including judicial commitment to property rights, legal ideology, the makeup of the Supreme Court, the concept of federalism, the need for litigation as a catalyst to legal change, and the institutional concerns of the federal judiciary. In particular settings, each of these additional factors was important. Yet none of them provides as coherent a general explanation of all the cases as the prohibition framework offers. Thus, they serve to qualify and to supplement the general thesis about the importance of prohibition rather than to challenge its overall validity.

The Supreme Court during the Prohibition Era

Constitutional scholars have shown a curious ambivalence toward the Supreme Court of the prohibition era. They have roundly criticized some individual justices and warmly praised others. They have generally castigated the Court's jurisprudence, even though decisions of the 1920s prepared the ground for a number of modern constitutional doctrines.

The stereotype of the Supreme Court in the 1920s and early 1930s is distinctly negative. For example, three of the eight Supreme Court justices that constitutional scholars have identified as "failures" served during the prohibition era.[3] In addition, as noted in chapter 1, conventional wisdom has generally denigrated the Supreme Court of that era as a "super-legislature" suspicious of governmental regulations, zealous in protecting economic interests, and insensitive to civil liberties.[4]

Notwithstanding this negative image, some of the justices who served during the prohibition era have received effusive praise. Five of twelve justices that constitutional scholars identified as "great" also served during prohibition era as did two others who were designated "near great."[5] Moreover, modern scholars have frequently honored Justice Holmes (and, to a lesser extent, Justice Brandeis and Justice Stone) as the source of modern constitutional analysis that stands the Court of the 1920s and early 1930s on its head by tolerating economic and social reforms while protecting civil liberties.[6]

With respect to the Court as an institution, the prohibition decisions suggest that the Court was not as backward looking in the 1920s and 1930s as it is sometimes portrayed. Some decisions from the prohibition era have a distinctly modern cast. For example, one can identify antecedents of modern constitutional doctrine regarding subjects as diverse as federal commercial regulations, land use planning, freedom of speech, and unenumerated rights.[7]

The prohibition cases offer a useful framework for reconciling the conflicting appraisals of the Taft and the Hughes Courts before the New Deal crisis. They provide insights both with respect to individual justices and broader jurisprudential themes.

Frequently the prohibition cases confirm habits and styles that individual justices also displayed in other contexts. The rarity of prohibition opinions by Justice Van Devanter illustrates the writer's block for which he is commonly remembered.[8] Similarly, Justice Holmes's prohibition opinions reflect the brevity that is characteristic of all of his judicial writings.[9] Justice Cardozo's forfeiture opinions are likewise typical of his many contributions to legal doctrine; he reshapes the law by restating prior doctrine.[10]

The ideological positions revealed in the prohibition decisions often parallel positions observed in other contexts. Chief Justice Taft consistently favored those charged with enforcing prohibition,[11] while Justice Brandeis manifested the greatest sensitivity to the dangers of overzealous enforcement.[12] By authoring six opinions for the Court in prohibition cases, Justice Sutherland reinforced his claim to the intellectual leadership of the Court's conservative wing.[13] At the same time, Justice Butler's majority opinions in Fourth Amendment cases and his dissents regarding property forfeiture issues confirm his reputation as a defender of property rights.[14]

The prohibition decisions are less kind to Justice Holmes. For the most part, they confirm his indifference to civil liberties.[15] All of his opinions for the Court sustained government prosecutions or property forfeitures.[16] Only in his *Olmstead* dissent did he urge protection for a citizen from excessive enforcement zeal; even there he refused to make the ban on using illegal wiretaps a constitutional rule.[17] More surprisingly, none of his majority opinion were especially influential in the developments of the prohibition era. Holmes simply followed the Court's majority in its doctrinal vacillation.[18]

For the Court as a whole, the picture that emerges from the prohibition cases is a more complicated one. The Court is less rigid, more tolerant of governmental regulation, and less consistently divided along New Deal lines than conventional wisdom would suggest. Even more importantly, the dividing line between "modern" and "antiquated" views is less clear than one might expect. Although Chief Justice Taft was a consistent supporter of prohibition enforcement authorities, Justices Sutherland, Butler, and McReynolds authored many of the decisions favoring defendants. On the other hand, Justice Brandeis was a frequent opponent of enforcement excesses, but Justices Holmes and Stone generally followed the Court as a whole (except for their *Olmstead* dissents).

Perhaps, however, the prohibition opinions suggest a framework for understanding the discordant decisions of the Supreme Court during the 1920s and 1930s. As explained in the preceding chapters, the prohibition decisions reveal a Court tolerant of expanding federal power but concerned to protect the traditional roles of states in the federal system. With respect to individuals, the Court was willing to protect the rights of ordinary citizens but frequently insensitive to overzealous enforcement against commercialized criminal violations. Thus, the Court was relatively solicitous of the rights of property owners, especially innocent owners, and the Court was also willing, particularly in the final years of the prohibition era, to extend the rights of ordinary citizens caught in the increasingly unpopular net of prohibition enforcement. On the other hand, the Court remained relatively unsympathetic to those who were guilty of large-scale or commercialized violations. A similar characterization provides a plausible hypothesis for explaining the broader pattern of Supreme Court decisions during the prohibition era. The Court was tolerant of federal power to regulate interstate commerce, but unwilling to allow Congress to eviscerate the power of the states.[19] With respect to state regulations, the Court's position was more equivocal. Although the Court was occasionally willing to expand the police power to allow states to respond to problems of the twentieth century,[20] it was generally unwilling to allow states to direct wealth transfers from businesses to less productive groups like unions and consumers.[21] Similarly the Court was occasionally willing to insulate some Europeans from nativistic midwesterners,[22] but it refused to protect Asians or European radicals.[23]

Regardless of whether one accepts the preceding explanation as a definitive explanation of Supreme Court decisions during the prohibition era, the prohibition cases must be part of any satisfactory revision of the history of the Supreme Court between 1920 and 1933. Those decisions constitute a major portion of the Court's work during the period, and they demonstrate the error of dismissing the Taft and early Hughes Courts as rigidly opposed to regulatory power and insensitive to broader social forces.

Prohibition and Interpretations of American Legal History

From a broader historical perspective, the study of prohibition's impact on American law confirms the importance of noneconomic conflicts in shaping American history and, hence, in shaping American law. Without retreating to a consensual view of American history, this project cautions against an exclusively economic interpretation of the forces behind the growth of legal rules and doctrines. Prohibition was a historical epoch characterized by conflict, but the conflicting values cannot easily be explained in purely economic terms nor can they be dismissed as irrational. As historians and other scholars persuasively argued, prohibition was an incident in a broader conflict. In part, the conflict was a substantive one over the need for policies to combat increased liquor consumption. In part, the dispute concerned symbolic values intimately associated with the status of various groups in American society.[24]

The drive for national prohibition is, of course, simply one of a number of divisive issues in the history of the United States that cannot be fully explained on economic grounds, even though they have frequently had considerable economic significance. To understand the history of American law requires that American law be examined from the perspectives of the movement to abolish slavery, the segregation settlement of the late nineteenth century, the twentieth-century drive for racial equality, the controversy over abortion, and the war on drugs, to cite but a few examples. The prohibition example suggests that, at least in some areas of law, those perspectives may provide a coherence to legal developments that are otherwise discordant.

The Prohibition Decisions and Contemporary Law

Contemporary Significance of the Prohibition Developments

The developments of the prohibition era are obviously important for understanding the time in which they were rendered and the Court that rendered them. What is less immediately apparent is the enduring character of prohibition's legacy to federal criminal law. Although the historical situation that created the conflict between prohibition and the rights of criminal defendants passed, the intellectual attitudes that the conflict engendered remained in a number of areas.

Many, but certainly not all, of the doctrines described in the preceding chapters remain part of current law. In light of the developments in the prohibition era, this partial survival rate is hardly surprising. Just as the legal doctrine of the 1920s and 1930s was unable to resist the pressure of powerful new social forces, so has subsequent legal doctrine adjusted to changing social conditions. As long as doctrines served the Supreme Court's view of the needs of a changing society, they survived and, in some cases, even expanded. When the doctrines collided with perceived social needs, the Court altered them.

The Supreme Court has overruled some of the important doctrines of the prohibition era. Examples of modern doctrinal reversals include the exclusion of wiretaps from the protections afforded by the Fourth Amendment, the refusal to allow seizures of things with mere "evidential" value, and the "silver platter" doctrine that allowed federal prosecutors to use evidence from searches conducted by state officials and private individuals.[25] Nonetheless, despite these reversals, a substantial number of the prohibition solutions remain important features of contemporary law in the United States.

Federal courts still use the subjective test for entrapment announced in *Sorrells*. In the 1950s, the Supreme Court explicitly held that entrapment applied to crimes other than violations of the Volstead Act. Moreover, the Court has repeatedly adhered to that position in more recent decisions.[26]

The automobile and open fields exceptions to the warrant requirement of the Fourth Amendment furnish two additional illustrations of doctrines from the prohibition era that still constitute living parts of contemporary law. Recent cases have had to apply the doctrines in a variety of new settings.[27] Nonetheless, the basic parameters of the doctrinal concept are still those established during the prohibition era.

The dual sovereignty exception to double jeopardy is another concept from the prohibition era with current vitality. As with entrapment, the Supreme Court confirmed the exception during the 1950s. In more recent years, the Court has even extended it beyond the federal-state context in which it was originally developed.[28]

Federal courts also still follow the constitutional rules set forth in the prohibition cases with respect to property forfeitures. The *Goldsmith* rule allowing forfeiture of the interests of innocent owners whose property is used to transport contraband remains the law today,[29] and it is frequently used in drug cases.

Finally, much of the framework for defining the modern jury trial guarantees is also a legacy from the conflicts of the prohibition era. Not only did the conflicts commit the federal courts to plea bargaining as the method for processing high-volume crimes, they also laid out the boundaries within which contemporary rules concerning the scope of the Constitution's jury trial guarantee have been developed.

The prohibition influence on plea bargaining into the federal courts has largely been forgotten.[30] Yet, plea bargaining remains an essential feature of the system of criminal procedure throughout the United States, including the federal courts. As in the prohibition era, plea bargaining has allowed American courts to process large numbers of cases without formally abandoning the jury trial as the linchpin of criminal justice. Moreover, the prohibition experience at the federal level suggests that plea bargaining will continue until the day-to-day pressures on the judicial system no longer demand relief from the assumptions of the formal rules. So long as we have both an explicit constitutional guarantee of trial by jury and a large volume of serious criminal prosecutions, plea bargaining is likely to remain an accepted aspect of criminal procedure.

Equally dramatic is the extent to which the intellectual solutions of the prohibition era still dominate American concepts concerning jury trial doctrines. Contemporary jurisprudence has continued to permit modification of the mechanics of jury trials and to define the constitutional guarantee as a personal right that can be claimed or waived by the individual. Thus, the current Federal Rules of Criminal Procedure allow the use of alternate jurors for protracted cases;[31] and the rules (which were adopted by Supreme Court rule and not by legislative enactment) also permit waivers of jury trials.[32] Moreover, the petty-offense exception recognized in *Colts* has been transformed into a constitutional rule.[33] As the Supreme Court has recently reaffirmed, the judicially created rule requires jury trials only when the authorized punishment for an offense, including contempt of court, exceeds imprisonment for six months.[34] What has been forgotten is that the six-month punishment rule originated in the prohibition-era statute defining petty offenses for grand jury purposes. Finally, lower federal courts have held that the Supreme Court's magistrate rules deny the right to a jury trial for petty offenses by negative implication, although Congress has never adopted a statute dispensing with jury trials.[35]

From the standpoint of doctrinal consistency, the legacy of the prohibition cases is confusing and ambiguous. No simple characterization of the modern impact of the developments of the prohibition era is possible. Most favor the government over the individual, but some notable exceptions exist. Careful study of cases from this era reveals, however, that the inconsistency of the prohibition legacy era is neither accidental nor arbitrary.

The obvious and most important explanation for the inconsistency is the timing of the decisions. Because of the Court's reluctance to overrule decisions, decisions rendered in the 1920s generally remained viable precedents when prohibition was repealed. Many of those precedents remain part of contemporary law—for example, the automobile and open field exceptions to the Fourth Amendment's warrant requirement, the dual sovereignty exception to double jeopardy, and the rule allowing forfeiture of the property interests of innocent owners. They almost always favored the government. In contrast, precedents established after 1930—for example, Supreme Court recognition of the entrapment defense and the rediscovery of the liberal rule of construction for Fourth Amendment rights—generally favored the individual defendant. Of course, the number of the latter group of decisions with practical significance for contemporary law is considerably smaller, in large part because of the Court's use of statutory approaches in its decisions after 1930.

The jury trial developments contain the primary exception to this chronological interpretation. They require an additional explanation because their content seems primarily directed by the power of institutional factors rather than by general attitudes toward prohibition. Although the Supreme Court rendered important decisions after 1930, those decisions did not expand the individual criminal defendant's right to a jury trial. Instead, they served the needs of judicial efficiency by allowing lower courts to accept jury trial waivers and encouraging Congress to dispense with jury trials for petty offenses.

Understanding the twentieth-century origins of many of the important doctrines, concepts, and practices of federal criminal law holds obvious significance for modern legal scholars. By documenting the period of national prohibition as the formative era for a given doctrine in federal criminal law, study of the prohibition decisions reveals the specific problem that the doctrine was designed to solve. To the extent that modern problems differ from those of the prohibition era, one can persuasively argue that doctrines should be reconsidered.[36]

The Prohibition Development as a Case Study

Studying the prohibition cases also provides a helpful guide to a matter of more general jurisprudential interest: understanding how formal law—or, at least, legal doctrine—develops. Viewed in the historical context in which they were delivered, the prohibition decisions show the utility of a realistic approach that searches for doctrinal influences that transcend formal logic.

The prohibition backdrop offers a compelling explanation of why changes occurred in legal doctrine during the prohibition era. The advocates of prohibition were zealots committed to effective enforcement of the Eighteenth Amendment. When they turned their zeal to law, they advocated aggressive techniques to catch violators as well as narrow constructions of legal concepts that would thwart enforcement. Thus, they urged narrow constructions of Fourth Amendment rights, the Fifth Amendment's ban on double jeopardy, and the rights of those whose property was used to violate prohibition. At the same time, a considerable opposition to prohibition existed even during the 1920s. As the failures and abuses of prohibition began to receive more attention, opponents argued for increased legal restraints on prohibition authorities in addition to demanding the repeal of the Eighteenth Amendment. In the judicial arena, they urged acceptance of the entrapment defense, expansive protections for the Fourth and Fifth

Amendment rights as well as the rights of property owners, and commitment to jury trial guarantees.

The prohibition backdrop also provides the most persuasive explanation for the specific doctrinal changes that occurred. That is, the changing attitudes toward the prohibition experience and the changes that occurred in legal doctrines offer the best explanation of the general trend of the decisions from the prohibition era. That general pattern thereby demonstrates the primacy of these external concerns in determining the direction of legal decisions relating to federal criminal law. In a host of areas ranging from entrapment and the Fourth Amendment to property forfeitures, double jeopardy, and jury trials, the prohibition experience offers a window that brings coherence to the developments in federal criminal law during the 1920s and 1930s. Moreover, the general pattern controls statutory interpretation as well as judicial doctrines, confirming that determining the "meaning" of a statute is, like development of common law, more of a process than an event.

Of course, the correlation between public attitudes and prohibition is not a perfect one.[37] But that imperfection merely shows that a unicausal emphasis on general attitudes toward prohibition fails to capture the complexity of the legal evolution. Not only does it oversimplify the judicial response to prohibition, it also ignores other influences that affected developments in particular areas as well as the role of legal tradition in channeling the course of development.

Both the political and judicial processes showed a willingness to distinguish between casual offenders and violators who were part of institutionalized operations. Undoubtedly that distinction was a supplemental influence in shaping the doctrines of the prohibition era in areas as diverse as entrapment, the Fourth Amendment, double jeopardy, and property forfeitures. But even this more sophisticated assessment of judicial attitudes toward prohibition fails to offer a complete explanation for the prohibition decisions. Other substantive concerns as well as legal training and methodology all exerted important supplemental influences.

No responsible summary of American political history during the 1920s and early 1930s could limit itself to prohibition. As one would expect, the legal developments of the prohibition era show the impact of these other concerns. The clearest example concerns private property. The commitment to protect the rights of property owners manifests itself in a variety of contexts: interpretation of the Volstead Act's provisions relating to property forfeiture and nuisance abatement, the special statutory and judicial protections applicable to searches of private dwellings, and Supreme Court decisions in doctrinal areas other than those addressed in detail in earlier chapters of this study. Similarly the attempt to define the boundaries of federal and state power—the dominant legal issue of the 1930s[38]—was also important during the 1920s, and it affected development of the dual sovereignty exception to double jeopardy, where the Supreme Court's decisions appear to reflect an attempt to preserve separate and independent spheres of authority for the two governments. Finally, the impacts of other issues like the Red Scare following World War 1 and early attempts to suppress drug use were less pervasive, but they still occasionally influenced the Supreme Court's criminal law decisions during the prohibition era.

Beyond these substantive influences, the professional ideology of the legal profession, the "taught tradition of the law,"[39] also seems to have affected the prohibition cases. For the most part, that ideology affected form more than content, but exceptions do exist. In specific cases involving jury trials and preemption of criminal penalties, the legal ideology seems to have produced results out of harmony with the general pattern of decisions.[40] Beyond these particular decisions, the primary influence of legal methodology probably derives from the Supreme Court's extreme reluctance to overrule existing precedents during the prohibition era. As a result, the changes of the prohibition era tended to mask themselves as exceptions to previously established rules, stricter applications of those rules, or, most commonly, statutory protections that went beyond those required by the Constitution.

A final set of influences derives from an institutional factor: the volume of litigation generated by prohibition cases. Moreover, the impact of this factor was not confined to jury trials as one might expect. It also affected other doctrinal areas.

Chapter 7 details the impact of the volume of litigation on the developments of the prohibition era with respect to jury trials. The flood of Volstead Act cases threatened to overwhelm the capacity of the federal courts. Although the acceptance of plea bargaining reduced the problem to manageable levels, the number of prohibition cases continued to rise throughout the prohibition era. Thus, it is hardly surprising that the Supreme Court consistently developed doctrines that would facilitate the processing of prohibition cases. Early in the period, the Court held grand jury indictments unnecessary for

Volstead Act violations. After 1930 it allowed defendants to waive jury trials and reaffirmed the possibility that Congress could dispense with them altogether for most prohibition offenses.

The volume of litigation generated with respect to particular legal issues also influenced doctrinal development in other areas. Trickery was often necessary to obtain evidence of illegal sales of intoxicating liquor, and so prohibition cases commonly presented issues as to whether enforcement authorities had gone too far and actually instigated criminal activity. The repetition of these claims prompted lower federal courts to construct the defense of entrapment. When the Fourth Circuit broke this uniform pattern of development, the Supreme Court took the opportunity to place its imprimatur on the doctrine. Similarly surprise searches were frequently needed to obtain proof of prohibition violations, and the legality of those searches were frequently challenged on appeal. As a result, the Supreme Court had numerous opportunities to review lower court decisions, and it decided a number of cases that continually modified Fourth Amendment doctrine. By contrast, appeals of successive prosecutions by state and federal governments (and apparently successive prosecutions themselves) practically disappeared after 1926. Consequently, the Supreme Court never reconsidered its *Lanza* holding, and the dual sovereignty exception survived the prohibition era intact.

The individual judges themselves were another variable in producing the changes of the prohibition era. Somewhat surprisingly, however, the impact of individual personalities on the doctrinal changes of the period was relatively minor. The changes that occurred in judicial doctrine reflected changed attitudes of the Court as a whole, not the influence of particular judges. Individual judges did write multiple opinions in the same area, especially when the issue was similar to one addressed in a companion case or an earlier opinion. But no single justice, or group of justices, consistently protested the direction of the Court's opinions at any point in the prohibition era. In short, the original majorities were not later outvoted; they simply changed their positions.

As noted in the introductory chapter, the replacement of Chief Justice William Howard Taft with Charles Evans Hughes was a personnel change of some importance. Taft was far more committed to effective enforcement of the Eighteenth Amendment than Hughes, and the major decisions restricting prohibition authorities came after Hughes became chief justice in 1930. In addition, the opinions of the two chief

justices reflected their differing attitudes. Taft provided judicial leadership in the 1920s by authoring a number of opinions narrowly defining Fourth and Fifth Amendment rights. By contrast, Hughes wrote
the 1933 opinion in which the Supreme Court ratified the defense of
entrapment defense that had been developed in the lower federal
courts.

Notwithstanding these contributions, the identity of the chief justices was not the decisive factor in the developments of the prohibition era. In two important areas—property forfeitures and jury trials—
neither Taft nor Hughes authored any of the Court's opinions. The
lack of an opinion from a chief justice is particularly notable with
respect to property forfeitures because the Court issued more than a
dozen opinions during the prohibition era. Furthermore, both areas
underwent significant changes after 1930 in opinions written by associate justices. Justices Stone and Cardozo developed the new rules
relating to property forfeiture, while Justice Sutherland wrote both
1930 opinions that reshaped the rules regarding jury trials.

The chief justices did contribute to the law's development with
regard to searches and seizures, double jeopardy, and entrapment, but
their individual contributions were not the crucial elements even in
those areas. Taft wrote a minority of the Court's Fourth Amendment
opinions during the 1920s, and the early opinions of other justices
were similarly supportive of enforcement authorities. Moreover, the
author of the post-1930 opinions rediscovering the rule of liberal construction for Fourth Amendment rights was not Chief Justice Hughes
but the archconservative Justice McReynolds. Similarly another—
conservative Justice Sutherland—authored the more expansive double jeopardy decisions in the 1930s. Finally, Chief Justice Hughes did
not pull the Court in a liberal direction with respect to entrapment,
the one area in which he authored the Court's opinion. His majority
opinion in *Sorrells* took a much narrower view of the defense than the
one Justice Roberts urged in his separate opinion.

Recognition of the impact of factors other than the prohibition experience does not require one to ignore the dominant influence of
prohibition. While it cautions against accepting the prohibition experience as an adequate unicausal explanation for the doctrinal developments, it does not contradict the claim that the prohibition experience
was the major influence that determined the general trend of the doctrinal changes. Other factors influenced specific areas or, in the case of
professional ideology, channeled the course of the new doctrine

without changing its basic direction. But none of the influences provide nearly as persuasive an explanation of the general direction of the federal developments related to criminal law as that obtained by viewing the cases from the perspective of the prohibition experience. In sum, one who wishes to understand the federal criminal law developments from 1920 to 1933 without reference to prohibition will miss the basic driving force that determined the direction they took. Thus, it remains appropriate to describe the prohibition influence as decisive.

The ability to identify other factors that influenced the changing legal thought of the era of national prohibition does serve to highlight an important limitation of the realistic approach to judicial doctrine. The power of the approach is primarily explanatory rather than predictive. Viewing decisions with the hindsight of history, one can offer rational explanations of how various factors impacted particular decisions. But it appears impossible to quantify the influence of each of the factors to predict the outcome of future cases. As a result, the predictive value of a realistic assessment is limited to explaining overall patterns or trends. Prediction as to how those factors will impact specific decisions remains a matter of intuition rather than empirical certainty.

The predictive power with respect to patterns and trends is nonetheless significant, especially for those interested in the protections that American law affords to criminal defendants. The prohibition developments show that, at least in the area of federal criminal law, legal concepts and traditions can channel, but not restrain, fundamental social change.

At first glance, the modern significance of some of the prohibition doctrines seems somewhat inconsistent with the realistic analysis. If doctrines developed in response to changing economic, social, and political conditions, why would doctrines from the prohibition era remain part of federal law in the 1990s?

The realistic approach offers a ready explanation of the initial adherence to the prohibition doctrines. Volstead Act cases formed the great bulk of federal criminal cases during the prohibition era, and the repeal of the Eighteenth Amendment substantially reduced the volume of federal prosecutions. As the prohibition cases themselves illustrate, doctrinal development is litigation driven. Thus, doctrinal stability during a time of reduced prosecutions is predictable rather than unusual.

By contrast, the constitutionalization of state criminal procedures during the 1950s and 1960s requires closer examination. In this second criminal law revolution, the Supreme Court altered many doctrines of federal law, but it retained a number of important precedents from the prohibition era. Even here, however, the realistic assessment provides a persuasive framework for understanding which doctrines endured and which were modified.

When precedents from the prohibition era conflicted with modern needs, the Warren Court reversed or modified them. The "silver platter" doctrine, which allowed the federal governments to use evidence from state searches, was inconsistent with one of the basic thrusts of the Warren Court: the desire to impose uniform federal standards on police behavior. As a result, the Court abandoned the doctrine as early as 1960. Similarly the Court recognized the greater need for physical evidence to prosecute the expanded number of crimes now subject to federal oversight, and it abandoned the rule that refused to allow seizure of "mere" evidence. Finally, growing concern for individual privacy combined with increasingly evasive techniques of electronic surveillance to prompt the rejection of *Olmstead's* exemption of wiretaps from the constraints imposed by the Fourth Amendment.[41]

By contrast, other Supreme Court precedents from the prohibition era survived because they did not interfere with the Court's new agenda. In some cases, the precedents supported contemporary needs. For example, the dual sovereignty exception to double jeopardy allowed federal prosecutions when southern authorities acquitted those who harmed blacks or their supporters in the Civil Rights movement, and, more recently, it supported a renewed deference to state legislative authority.[42] Likewise, the open fields exception to the Fourth Amendment's warrant requirement also served new purposes. It aided enforcement of environmental regulations and apprehension of drug offenders.[43] In other areas, the continuing importance of the precedents is probably more a reflection of inertia than policy. Having been enshrined in Supreme Court opinions, they remained authoritative because important contemporary needs did not require their rejection. The entrapment defense seems to fall within this category. Having been embraced by a five-to-three majority in the prohibition era, a majority of the Court adhered to precedent because no contemporary concerns mandated reconsideration.[44]

In short, the cases from the prohibition era remain important for understanding modern law because the prohibition era stimulated the first great changes in legal doctrines of federal criminal law. As a result, the opinions of the prohibition era created new doctrines as well as expanding and altering traditional ones. Those opinions then became part of the law's taught tradition and remained controlling until new factors required their displacement.

Significantly, the prohibition cases provide little support for a teleological view of doctrinal development. The substance of federal criminal law appears to respond to changing views of prohibition, not to any consistent vision of the good society. The only constant characteristic that the criminal law doctrines display is increasing complexity. Exceptions, qualifications, and subdoctrines appear with respect to all the areas in which the courts repeatedly faced problems, and each of those areas has become even more complex in modern cases. Perhaps, then, increasing complexity is the one doctrinal response to external change that can be predicted with complete confidence.

Modern doctrinal changes in federal criminal procedure are consistent with the lessons learned from the study of prohibition experience. The constitutional aspects of federal criminal procedure have changed greatly in the years since the repeal of the Eighteenth Amendment. The realistic appraisal suggests persuasive hypotheses for understanding both the initial expansion and the more recent contraction.

Harry Kalven has argued that the Civil Rights movement decisively influenced the Supreme Court's expansion of the free speech protections of the First Amendment during the 1950s and 1960s.[45] A preliminary survey of the evidence suggests a similar hypothesis for the Supreme Court's early expansion of criminal procedural rights. Much of the initial impetus for the expansion of procedural rights appears to have been related to a concern that southern courts failed to protect blacks from mistreatment at the hands of prosecutors or other state officials. The Scottsboro rape trials of the 1930s offer the most dramatic examples. They produced important new doctrines expanding the right to counsel, forbidding racial discrimination in jury selection, and refusing to allow state procedural rules to frustrate the assertion of federal constitutional claims.[46] Likewise, several early opinions regarding self-incrimination and habeas corpus also came in cases of blacks convicted in the segregated justice system of the South.[47]

Unlike the expansive cases of the prohibition era, the Supreme Court grounded its modern protections for criminal defendants in the Constitution rather than in statutory interpretation. As a result, the influence of the Warren Court's criminal law revolution spread far beyond its civil rights origins. But public and judicial attitudes changed during the 1970s, and especially the 1980s. Predictably the scope of protections afforded to criminal defendants by the Bill of Rights contracted as the dominant concern of the federal criminal cases shifted from protection of the civil rights of minorities to suppression of drug traffic and the violence associated with that traffic.[48] The Fourth Amendment cases show the most obvious influence of the drug suppression concerns,[49] but drug cases have also prompted contractions in the scope of the right to counsel, the privilege against self-incrimination, the defense of entrapment, the prohibition against double jeopardy, and the availability of bail.[50]

An understanding of the prohibition origins of many doctrines of federal criminal law would not have enabled an observer to predict the precise course of the modern decisions. It would, however, have enabled the observer to anticipate the pattern of contraction as American society became committed to using the criminal law to suppress drug traffic. Moreover, it also warns that the contraction is likely to continue until our society finds alternate means to reduce drug abuse.

The post-prohibition history of rules relating to jury trials offers another illustration of the explanatory and predictive power of a realistic appraisal of legal rules. Throughout the twentieth century, even the formal doctrines have reiterated the lesson of the prohibition era that rules must not preclude the orderly processing of the regular business of the courts to which they apply. Thus, when the Warren Court expanded the reach of the jury trial guarantee by applying it to the states,[51] compromises proved necessary to avoid wholesale disruption of state practice. As Justice Harlan correctly noted at the time,[52] no one had ever suggested that the constitutional guarantee would have permitted the federal government to reduce the size of juries below twelve or to allow nonunanimous verdicts. But the dockets of state courts were considerably more crowded than federal dockets had ever been, and so both nonunanimous verdicts and smaller juries were approved once the Sixth Amendment was held applicable to the states.[53] Ultimately, the Supreme Court did limit the size to which the jury could be reduced; and the Court also refused to permit states to combine small juries with nonunanimous verdicts,[54] but the Court took these steps only after assuring itself that its limits would not seriously interfere with the prevailing practice in most states.[55]

Of course, decisions are never the product of any single influence. This maxim is especially true of decisions, like those of the Supreme Court, that require collegial agreement; and the prohibition decisions provide no exception to it. As noted above, other substantive concerns were undoubtedly important in shaping the prohibition decisions. Yet, none of those concerns provides nearly as complete an explanation of the federal criminal law developments as the changing attitudes toward prohibition.

Likewise, legal traditions and precedents also influenced the course of decision. But the degree of restraint imposed by these traditions and precedents was indeterminate; that is, their influence tended to expand or contract not as the result of an internal dynamic but in response to the external influences.

Once this indeterminacy of the influence of legal concepts and existing precedents is perceived, the ultimately political nature of the judicial process becomes clear. One simply cannot distinguish the judicial from the political on the ground that the constitutional language and precedents play a role, albeit indeterminate, in the judicial but not the political process. To take the Fourth Amendment as an example, the constitutional text exerted an impact on the Volstead Act[56] as well as on the Supreme Court decisions.

The actual difference between the judicial and the political is less distinct, more relative. Nonetheless, the difference is real. For institutional reasons, the judicial process tends to give greater coherence and continuity to general concepts and past precedents than do executives or legislatures.

At least four characteristics of the judicial process support this inclination to continuity. First, the judge's training and role emphasize the continuity of tradition. Judges are not free to disregard the language of a relevant text or the explanations of prior decisions as political activists may do; they must justify their decisions by reference to a received tradition. Second, individual judicial decisions are largely immune from direct challenge in electoral politics. Federal judges are appointed for life, and even in states where judges are elected, campaigns are rarely waged on the merits of a specific decision. Third, the judicial method emphasizes the element of rationality. Judges must connect the particular decision to the received tradition by a process of reasoning, and the power of the individual decision will be measured, at least in part, by the extent to which the judge is able to convince readers of the strength of the connection.

Fourth, judges (and probably most lawyers) are usually reluctant to rethink old solutions. Many modern courts are more willing to over-rule precedents than the Supreme Court was during the prohibition era, but the predominate techniques are limitation, qualification, and exception rather than rejection.[57]

As a result of these institutional characteristics, the judicial process tends to serve a conspicuously conservative political agenda. How-ever, the extent of this institutional conservatism is indeterminate. Courts can and do transform legal doctrines to reach substantive goals.

If this account of the judicial process and the nature of doctrinal change is correct, it seems to carry important implications for those who are concerned with the protection of individual rights and liber-ties in modern America. Concern for civil liberties cannot lead one to ignore the substantive proposals that require infringement of rights and liberties if they are to be successfully implemented. The substan-tive proposals themselves must be defeated if the individual rights are to be adequately protected. Neutral principles[58] or an abstract ap-proach to judicial decision making[59] may serve to help strengthen the role that the historical conception of a right plays in influencing the decisional process. But the experience with prohibition suggests that neither will suffice to impede the accomplishment of substantive goals indefinitely.

Perhaps even more importantly, this account of doctrinal develop-ment cautions against a retreat to the courts as the exclusive protec-tors of individual rights. Courts may temporarily slow the demands of electoral politics,[60] and they may also be able to prompt the political process into greater action.[61] But the story of doctrinal change during the era of national prohibition indicates that they will be unable to preserve rights and liberties in a society whose political process un-equivocally decides on a substantive course of action that demands restrictions in those values. Those concerned with preserving indi-vidual rights and liberties must enter the political arena to build a society whose substantive goals are consistent with those rights and liberties. Exclusive devotion to judicial remedies does not offer an acceptable substitute.

In sum, a realistic assessment of the political influences on doctri-nal developments offers both historians and legal scholars a powerful and useful explanatory tool. Without retreating to a reductionist or unicausal explanation of legal change, the assessment focuses on the external forces that are the primary determinants of the direction the change takes without ignoring the limited but significant role played by the legal tradition itself. If one turns from the past to the future, the approach offers a tool for predicting the pattern of decisions but not specific outcomes. Yet even that limited aid to prediction can be of great value to reformers who are concerned with the broad patterns of legal development.

Notes

1 The Prohibition Backdrop

1 The use of the term "noble experiment" to describe prohibition originated with Herbert Hoover. *See Public Papers of the Presidents of the United States: Herbert Hoover, 1929,* at 511 (1974) (address accepting the nomination of the 1928 Republican Convention): "I recently stated my position on the 18th Amendment, which I again repeat. . . . Our country has deliberately undertaken a great social and economic experiment, noble in motive and far-reaching in purpose. It must be worked out constructively."

2 The text of the amendment is reproduced below:

> *Section 1.* After one year from the ratification of this article the manufacture, sale, or transportation of intoxicating liquors within, the importation thereof into, or the exportation thereof from the United States and all territory subject to the jurisdiction thereof for beverage purposes is hereby prohibited.
>
> *Section 2.* The Congress and the several States shall have concurrent power to enforce this article by appropriate legislation.
>
> *Section 3.* This article shall be inoperative unless it shall have been ratified as an amendment to the Constitution by the legislatures of the several states, as provided in the Constitution to the states by the Congress.

3 The text of the Twenty-first Amendment reads as follows:

> *Section 1.* The eighteenth article of amendment to the Constitution of the United States is hereby repealed.
>
> *Section 2.* The transportation or importation into any State, Territory, or possession of the United States for delivery or use therein of intoxicating liquors, in violation of the laws thereof, is hereby prohibited.
>
> *Section 3.* This article shall be inoperative unless it shall have been ratified as an amendment to the Constitution by conventions in the several States, as provided in the Constitution, within seven years from the date of the submission hereof to the States by the Congress.

4 *See* South Dakota v. Dole, 483 U.S. 203 (1987) (upholding congressional power to condition federal highway funds on raising the legal age for purchasing intoxicating liquors).

5 Aaron and Musto, Temperance and Prohibition in America in *Alcohol and Public Policy: Beyond the Shadow of Prohibition* 127, 176 (Moore

and Gerstein eds., 1981). One recent commentary described the modern attitude as follows:

> In recent years another reversal is evident. Social scientists are again blaming alcohol. . . . Of course, they do not promote prohibition; that extremity is still remembered with negative affect. But they do recommend a policy of controls, that government should interfere with the availability of alcohol to the entire population. One critic has called this recommendation neo-prohibition. Perhaps a more just term is "inhibition."

Keller, Alcohol Problems and Policies in Historical Perspective, in *Law, Alcohol, and Order: Perspectives on National Prohibition* (D. Kyvig ed., 1985).

6 N.Y. *Times*, Dec. 8, 1993, § A at 23, col. 5.

7 R. Hofstadter, *The Age of Reform* 287 (1955).

8 A. Sinclair, *Prohibition: The Era of Excess* (1963).

9 J. Timberlake, *Prohibition and the Progressive Movement in the United States 1900–1920* (1963).

10 *See, e.g.,* Aaron & Musto, *supra* note 5; P. Carter, *Another Part of the Twenties* 91 (1977); C. Chambers, *Seedtime of Reform* 76 (1963); N. Clark, *Deliver Us from Evil: An Informal History of American Prohibition* 5, 10 (1976); K. Kerr, *Organized for Reform: A New History of the Anti-Saloon League* 7, 13 (1985); D. Kyvig, *Repealing National Prohibition* 5–10 (1979); Swindler, A Dubious Constitutional Experiment, in *Law, Alcohol, and Order: Perspectives on National Prohibition, supra* note 5; *cf.* J. Blocker, *American Temperance Movements: Cycles of Reform* xiii (1989) (describing prohibition as "clearly a middle class reform"). *But see* S. Cashman, *Prohibition: The Lie of the Land* 19–21 (1981).

11 J. Gusfield, *Symbolic Crusade: Status Politics and the American Temperance Movement* (1963).

12 *See, e.g.,* Clark, *supra* note 10, at 134–35.

13 J. Blocker, *supra* note 10, at 119; N. Clark, *supra* note 10 at 146–47; D. Kyvig, *supra* note 10, at 22–24.

14 *Compare* Nelli, American Syndicate Crime: A Legacy of Prohibition, in *Law, Alcohol, and Order: Perspectives on National Prohibition, supra* note 5, at 23, *with* Haller, Bootleggers as Businessmen: From City Slums to City Builders, in *id.* at 139. *See also* S. Cashman, *supra* note 10, *passim;* A. Sinclair, *supra* note 8, at 415.

15 K. Kerr, *supra* note 10; P. Odegard, *Pressure Politics: The Story of the Anti-Saloon League* (1928).

16 A. Sinclair, *supra* note 8, at 28; Aaron & Musto, *supra* note 5, at 127, 173–74.

17 N. Clark, *supra* note 10, at 199–205.

18 D. Kyvig, *supra* note 10, at 199–200; A. Sinclair, *supra* note 8, at 243.

19 D. Kyvig, *supra* note 10, at 201; A. Sinclair, *supra* note 8, at 243.

20 Drescher, Labor and Prohibition: The Unappreciated Impact of the Eighteenth Amendment, in *Law, Alcohol, and Order, supra* note 5, at 35.

21 E.g., N. Clark, *supra* note 10, at 195; D. Kyvig, *supra* note 10, at 29–30; A. Sinclair, *supra* note 8, at 211–12. *See also* National Comm'n on Law Observance and Enforcement, *Report on the Enforcement of the Prohibition Laws of the United States* 55–58 (1931)[hereinafter referred to as *Prohibition Enforcement Report*]; H. Asbury, *The Great Illusion: An Informal History of Prohibition* 168–73 (1950); H. Johnston, *What Rights Are Left?* 57 (1930); C. Merz, *The Dry Decade* 303 (1931); M. Tillit, *The Price of Prohibition* 53–54 (1932). For a summary of the impact of prohibition on the caseload of the United States Court of Appeals for the Seventh Circuit, see Solomon, Regulating the Regulators: Prohibition Enforcement in the Seventh Circuit, in *Law, Alcohol, and Order, supra* note 5, at 83–84.

22 E.g., D. Kyvig, *supra* note 10, at 34 (identifying *Olmstead v. United States*, 277 U.S. 438 (1928), as "[t]he last major Supreme Court decision concerning prohibition enforcement."). Legal scholars have also largely ignored the impact of the prohibition experience in shaping American law. E.g., Currie, The Constitution in the Supreme Court: 1921–30, 1986 Duke L.J. 65 (discussing prohibition's influence on Supreme Court's decisions of the 1920s only with respect to decisions directly construing the Eighteenth Amendment). For an attempt to study the impact of prohibition enforcement on the judicial decisions of a court of appeals, see Solomon, *supra* note 21.

23 J. Blocker, *supra* note 10, at 3–8; J. Krout, *The Origins of Prohibition* 71–82 (1925); W. Rorabaugh, *The Alcoholic Republic: An American Tradition* 25–27 (1979); Aaron & Musto, *supra* note 5, at 131–39.

24 J. Blocker, *supra* note 10, at 8–11; W. Rorabaugh, *supra* note 23, at 61–92.

25 J. Blocker, *supra* note 10, at 11–29; W. Rorabaugh, *supra* note 23, at 191–96, I. Tyrrell, *Sobering Up: From Temperance to Prohibition in Antebellum America, 1800–1860,* at 25–29, 11–114 (1979).

26 Aaron & Musto, *supra* note 5, at 139–40; J. Blocker, *supra* note 10, at 30–48; N. Clark, *supra* note 10, at 32–34; J. Krout, *supra* note 23, at 104, 182–222; I. Tyrrell, *supra* note 25, at 159–90.

27 1851 Laws of Maine, ch. 211; *see* N. Clark, *supra* note 10, at 2, 45.

28 J. Blocker, *supra* note 10, at 50–59; I. Tyrrell, *supra* note 25, at 252–89; Aaron & Musto, *supra* note 5, at 140–41.

29 *Compare* J. Blocker, *supra* note 10, at 59, *and* I. Tyrrell, *supra* note 25, at 307–09, *with* N. Clark, *supra* note 10, at 48, *and* K. Kerr, *supra* note 10, at 85–93.

30 J. Blocker, *supra* note 10, at 85–93.

31 Aaron & Musto, *supra* note 5, at 146–48; *see generally* J. Blocker, *"Give Wind Thy Fears"* (1985).

32 J. Blocker, *supra* note 10, at 97–100; N. Clark, *supra* note 10, at 93–97; K. Kerr, *supra* note 10, *passim;* P. Odegard, *supra* note 15, *passim;* Aaron & Musto, *supra* note 5, at 155–57. For the "official" history of the league, see E. Cherrington, *The Story of the Anti-Saloon League* (1910).

33 P. Odegard, *supra* note 15, at 38. *Accord,* N. Clark, *supra* note 10, at 93 (The Anti-Saloon League's choice of its name was significant for "the American middle class conscience, which was not yet willing to accept alcohol alone as the antibourgeois symbol but was increasingly distributed by the reality of the saloon.").

34 H. Asbury, *supra* note 21, at 182.

35 J. Blocker, *supra* note 10, at 104; C. Merz, *supra* note 21, at 18–23.

36 U.S. Const. art. I, § 8, cl. 3.

37 Leisy v. Hardin, 135 U.S. 100 (1890).

38 26 Stat. 313 (1890).

39 Wilkinson v. Rahrer, 140 U.S. 545 (1891).

40 *See, e.g.,* Kernmeyer v. Kansas, 236 U.S. 568 (1915).

41 37 Stat. 699 (1913).

42 Act of Mar. 3, 1917, 64th Cong., 2d Sess., ch. 162, § 5, 39 Stat. 1069. The author of the amendment, Senator Reed of Missouri, was a bitter opponent of prohibition, and his purpose was apparently to embarrass supportors of prohibition. *See* K. Kerr, *supra* note 10, at 196–97; P. Odegard, *supra* note 15, at 161–62.

43 Act of Aug. 10. 1917, 65th Cong., 1st Sess., ch. 53, 40 Stat. 276, 282; Act of Sept. 12, 1918, 65th Cong., 2d Sess., ch. 170, 40 Stat. 958; Act of Nov. 21, 1918, 65th Cong., 2d Sess., ch. 212, 40 Stat. 1046. *See generally* K. Kerr, *supra* note 10, at 199–202, 205–07.

44 S.J. Res. 17, 40 Stat. 1050 (1917); *see* J. Blocker, *supra* note 10, at 117–19; D. Kyvig, *supra* note 10, at 11–13. For a contemporary summary, see C. Merz, *supra* note 21, at 39–42.

45 For the text of the amendment, see note 2 *supra.* The original resolution omitted Section 3 of the amendment. The Senate added the provision mandating ratification within six years during its floor debate, 55 Cong. Rec. at 5661 (1917), but the time for ratification was lengthened to seven years, H. Rep. No. 211, 65th Cong., 2d Sess. 1–2 (Part I) (1918), as part of a compromise with opponents of the amendment. For contemporary descriptions of the agreement over Section 3, see C. Merz, *supra* note 21, at 30–32; P. Odegard, *supra* note 15 at 173–74.

46 Pub. L. No. 66–66, 41 Stat. 305 (1919) *et seq., codified at* 27 U.S.C.A. § 1 *et seq.* (1927).

47 27 U.S.C.A. § 12 (1927). Section 33 of Title II of the Volstead

Act, *id.* § 50, provided that possession of intoxicating liquors "by any person not legally permitted . . . to possess liquor" was "prima facie evidence that such liquor is kept for the purpose of being sold, bartered, exchanged, given away, furnished, or otherwise disposed of in violation of the [Act]."

48 *Id.* § 33.

49 More specifically, the definition of "intoxicating liquor" included "alcohol, brandy, whisky, rum, gin, beer, ale, porter, and wine, and in addition thereto any spirituous, vinous, malt or fermented liquor, liquids, and compounds, whether medicated, proprietary, patented, or not, and by whatever name called, containing one-half of one percent of alcohol by volume which are fit for use for beverage purposes. . . ." *Id.* § 4(1).

50 *Id.* § 34, 35, 40.

51 *Id.* § 46.

52 *Id.* §§ 12, 46, 50.

53 *Id.* § 39.

54 *See* §§ 26 (allowing vehicle to be returned to owner who posts a bond and requiring payment of liens held by innocent creditors) and 34 (allowing courts to substitute a bond for a padlock injunction).

55 *Id.* §§ 33, 46.

56 D. Kyvig, *supra* note 10, at 12; 1 W. Swindler, *Court and Constitution in the Twentieth Century: The Old Legality, 1899–1932* 253 (1969). *But cf.* J. Blocker, *supra* note 10, at 119 ("Prohibition probably did not command majority assent at the time of ratification of the Eighteenth Amendment, but the amendment's placement of its reform in the Constitution gave the cause much prestige and power, which were reflected in some favorable referendum results during the first years after national prohibition went into effect."). For a contemporary assessment of popular support for prohibition, see C. Merz, *supra* note 21, at 39–42.

57 For a contemporary summary of congressional action on the Volstead Act, see C. Merz, *supra* note 21, at 48–50.

58 Pub. L. No. 67–96, 42 Stat. 222 (1921).

59 N. Clark, *supra* note 10, at 166; A. Sinclair, *supra* note 8, at 275–76.

60 D. Kyvig, *supra* note 10, at 61–62, 80–97, 117. For a summary of the commission's work, see *id.* at 111–15.

61 M. Willebrandt, *The Inside of Prohibition* 20 (1929).

62 News dispatch *quoted in* C. Merz, *supra* note 21, at 297.

63 Pub. L. No. 69–75, §§ 4–6, 44 Stat. 1382–83 (1927).

64 Pub. L. No. 70–899, 45 Stat. 1446 (1929). *See* N. Clark, *supra* note 10, at 194–97.

65 M. Willebrandt, *supra* note 61, at 259.

66 J. Blocker, *supra* note 10, at 129; N. Clark, *supra* note 10, at 168; D. Kyvig, *supra* note 10, at 116, 130–31.

67 *Prohibition Enforcement Report, supra* note 21, at 83; *see generally* D. Kyvig, *supra* note 10, at 146–58.

68 A. Schlesinger, Jr., *The Crisis of the Old Order, 1919–33,* at 302 (1957).

69 *See generally* D. Kyvig, *supra* note 10, at 169–82.

70 S.J. Res. 211, 72d Cong., 2d Sess., 47 Stat. 1625 (1933).

71 Pub. L. No. 73–3, 48 Stat. 16 (1933).

72 1 W. Swindler, *supra* note 56, at 313–20.

73 *Id.* at 143–45.

74 *Id.* 1 W. Swindler, *supra* note 56, at 319–20.

75 2 W. Swindler, *supra* note 56, at 358–59, 422–24.

76 *See* 1 *id.* 28–100; Stern, The Commerce Clause and the National Economy, 1933–1946, 59 Harv. L. Rev. 883 (1946) (pt. II). The factor that ensured the ultimate triumph of an expanded vision of congressional power under the Commerce Clause was Roosevelt's appointment of seven justices between 1937 and 1941. *See* G. Gunther, *Cases and Materials on Constitutional Law* 130 n.2 (11th ed. 1985).

77 *Compare, e.g.,* United States v. Marron, 275 U.S. 192 (1927), *with* Go-Bart Importing Co. v. United States, 282 U.S. 344 (1931). For a similar pattern with respect to representatives and senators who served in Congress in both 1919 and 1933, see 1 W. Swindler, *supra* note 56, at 269.

78 Mason, Louis D. Brandeis, in 3 *The Justices of the United States Supreme Court 1789–1969,* at 2043, 2056 (L. Friedman & F. Israel eds., 1969); Burner, John H. Clarke, in *id.* at 2077, 2081; Burner, Willis Van Devanter, in *id.* at 1945, 1950.

79 President Hoover appointed Roberts despite his "alleged statement that 'Prohibition has no place in the Constitution.'" Burner, *Owen J. Roberts,* in *id.* at 2253, 2255.

80 Burner, *Pierce Butler,* in *id.* at 2183, 2184.

81 *See* F. Hicks, *William Howard Taft, Yale Professor of Law and New Haven Citizen* 145–51 (1945); H. Pringle, *The Life and Times of William Howard Taft* 861–62, 981–91 (1939).

82 Taft, Is Prohibition a Blow to Personal Liberty?, Ladies Home Journal 36 (May 1919); H. Pringle, *supra* note 81, at 981–83.

83 *See, e.g.,* W. Taft, *Presidential Addresses and State Papers* 403–08 (1910) (speech delivered in Macon, Ga., on Nov. 4, 1909).

84 *Quoted in* F. Biddle, *Mr. Justice Holmes* 168 (1986).

85 Grogan v. Hiram Walker & Sons, Ltd., 259 U.S. 80, 89 (1922).

86 A. Mason, *William Howard Taft: Chief Justice* 224 (1983).

87 277 U.S. 438, 471 (1928).

88 L. Paper, *Brandeis* 310 (1983).

89 B. Glad, *Charles Evans Hughes and the Illusions of Innocence* 82,

108 (1966); A. Sinclair, *supra* note 8, at 140–46; 1 W. Swindler, *supra* note 56, at 269.

90 *See generally* G. White, *The American Judicial Tradition* 214 (2d ed. 1985).

91 Because of Robert Cover's untimely death, the volume on the Taft Court in the Oliver Wendell Holmes Devise History of the Supreme Court has not yet been written.

92 *See, e.g.,* A. Mason, *The Supreme Court from Taft to Warren* 70 (rev. ed. 1968); F. Rodell, *Nine Men* 187–89 (1988 reprint); B. Schwartz, *A History of the Supreme Court* 217–19 (1993); 1 Swindler, *supra* note 56, at 235–36.

93 Frankfurter, The United States Supreme Court Molding the Constitution, 32 Current Hist. 235, 239 (1930); *see also* F. Frankfurter, *Mr. Justice Holmes and the Supreme Court* 97–137 (1938) (Appendix listing all cases holding state action invalid under the Fourteenth Amendment).

94 A. Mason, *supra* note 92, at 70.

95 Truax v. Corrigan, 257 U.S. 312 (1921); Bailey v. Drexel Furniture Co., 259 U.S. 20 (1922).

96 Adkins v. Children's Hospital, 261 U.S. 525 (1923); Weaver v. Palmer Bros., 270 U.S. 402 (1926); Di Santo v. Pennsylvania, 273 U.S. 34 (1924); Pennsylvania Coal Co. v. Mahon, 260 U.S. 393 (1922); St. Louis & O'Fallon R.R. v. United States; 279 U.S. 461 (1929).

97 Gitlow v. New York, 268 U.S. 652 (1925); *see also* Whitney v. California, 274 U.S. 357 (1927).

98 United States v. Schwimmer, 279 U.S. 644 (1929); Frick v. Webb, 263 U.S. 326 (1923); Webb v. O'Brien, 263 U.S. 313 (1923); Porterfield v. Webb, 263 U.S. 225 (1923); Terrace v. Thompson, 263 U.S. 197 (1923); Buck v. Bell, 274 U.S. 200 (1927); *see also* United States v. MacIntosh, 283 U.S. 605 (1931).

99 Kutler, Chief Justice Taft, National Regulation, and the Commerce Clause, 51 J. Am. Hist. 651 (1965); *see, e.g.,* Coronado Coal Co. v. United Mine Workers, 268 U.S. 295 (1925); Brooks v. United States, 267 U.S. 432 (1925); Board of Trade v. Olsen, 262 U.S. 1 (1923); Stafford v. Wallace, 258 U.S. 495 (1922); Wisconsin R.R. Comm'n v. Chicago, Burlington & Quincy R.R., 257 U.S. 563 (1922).

100 Village of Euclid v. Ambler Realty Co., 272 U.S. 365 (1926).

101 Gitlow v. New York, 268 U.S. 652 (1925).

102 Stromberg v. California, 283 U.S. 559 (1931); Fiske v. Kansas, 274 U.S. 380 (1927); Near v. Minnesota, 283 U.S. 697 (1931).

103 Pierce v. Society of Sisters, 268 U.S. 510 (1925); Meyer v. Nebraska, 262 U.S. 390 (1923).

104 *See* Commercial Credit Co. v. United States, 276 U.S. 226 (1928); Port Gardner Inv. Co. v. United States, 272 U.S. 564 (1926); United States

v. Zerbey, 271 U.S. 332 (1926); Regal Drug Corp. v. Wardell, 260 U.S. 386 (1922); Lipke v. Lederer, 259 U.S. 557 (1922); Street v. Lincoln Safe Deposit Co., 254 U.S. 88 (1920). Even with respect to property rights, however, the protection of the rights of individuals was far from absolute, especially in the early years of prohibition. E.g., United States v. One Ford Coupe Automobile, 272 U.S. 321 (1926); James Everard's Breweries v. Day, 265 U.S. 545 (1924); Corneli v. Moore, 257 U.S. 491 (1922).

105 Ruper v. Caffey, 251 U.S. 264 (1920).

106 Hawke v. Smith, 253 U.S. 221 (1920).

107 National Prohibition Cases, 253 U.S. 350, 386–87 (1920).

108 Dillon v. Gloss, 256 U.S. 368 (1921).

109 Druggan v. Anderson, 269 U.S. 36 (1925).

110 Cunard S.S. Co. v. Mellon, 262 U.S. 100 (1923).

111 United States v. Yuginovich, 256 U.S. 450 (1921); *cf.* Vigliotti v. Pennsylvania, 258 U.S. 403 (1922) (upholding the continued validity of a state liquor license law after passage of national prohibition).

112 Wyman v. United States, 263 U.S. 14 (1923); Brede v. Powers, 263 U.S. 4 (1923).

113 Hawes v. Georgia, 258 U.S. 1 (1922). Congress never established a similar presumption in the federal enforcement statute. The lack of the presumption proved fortunate for Senator Morris Sheppard, one of the sponsors of the Eighteenth Amendment. A Texas prohibition raid uncovered a still hidden away on a farm he owned. H. Asbury, *supra* note 21, at 44.

For a circuit court of appeals decision from the latter years of the prohibition era that is more favorable to property owners, see Verna v. United States, 54 F.2d 919 (7th Cir. 1931), discussed in Solomon, *supra* note 21, at 44. *Verna* reversed a conspiracy conviction where the only evidence linking the defendant to the conspiracy was his ownership of the farmland where the still was located.

114 Hester v. United States, 265 U.S. 57 (1924).

115 United States v. Lanza, 260 U.S. 377 (1922).

116 United States v. Valante, 264 U.S. 563 (1924).

117 Samuels v. McCurdy, 267 U.S. 188 (1925).

118 Lambert v. Yellowley, 272 U.S. 581 (1926).

119 Grosfield v. United States, 276 U.S. 494 (1928); *cf.* Duignan v. United States, 274 U.S. 195 (1927) (upholding the validity of the injunctions that Section 23 of the Volstead Act authorized for individuals who committed certain sale and transportation offenses); Murphy v. United States, 272 U.S. 630 (1926) (allowing nuisance abatement action to proceed notwithstanding the defendant's acquittal on a related criminal charge).

120 Olmstead v. United States, 277 U.S. 438 (1928); United States v.

Marron, 275 U.S. 192 (1927); United States v. Lee, 274 U.S. 559 (1927); Hebert v. Louisiana, 272 U.S. 312 (1926); Raffel v. United States, 271 U.S. 494 (1926); Dumbra v. United States, 268 U.S. 435 (1925); Steele v. United States, 267 U.S. 505 (1925); Steele v. United States, 267 U.S. 498 (1925); Carroll v. United States, 267 U.S. 132 (1925). *But cf.* Gambino v. United States, 275 U.S. 310 (1927); Byars v. United States, 273 U.S. 28 (1927).

121 Ford v. United States, 273 U.S. 593 (1927).

122 Ma-King Products Co. v. Blair, 271 U.S. 479 (1926).

123 United States v. One Ford Coupe Automobile, 272 U.S. 321 (1926); *cf.* Van Oster v. Kansas, 272 U.S. 465 (1926) (upholding the constitutionality of a state law that forfeited the interest of an innocent owner in property that was used to transport intoxicating liquor).

124 United States v. Sullivan, 274 U.S. 259 (1927).

125 *See* Shields v. United States, 273 U.S. 583 (1927); Tumey v. Ohio, 273 U.S. 510 (1927); United States v. Katz, 271 U.S. 354 (1926).

126 Olmstead v. United States, 277 U.S. 438 (1928); Lambert v. Yellowley, 272 U.S. 581 (1926). *See also* United States v. One Ford Coupe Automobile, 272 U.S. 321, 335 (1926) (Stone, J., concurring and Butler, McReynolds, and Sutherland, J.J., dissenting); Carroll v. United States, 267 U.S. 132, 163 (1925) (McReynolds and Sutherland, J.J., dissenting).

127 United States v. Sprague, 44 F.2d 967 (D.N.J. 1930), *rev'd*, 282 U.S. 716 (1931); *see* D. Kyvig, *supra* note 10, at 137–40.

128 United States v. Sprague, 282 U.S. 716 (1931). *See also* Rossi v. United States, 289 U.S. 89 (1933); McCormick & Co. v. Brown, 286 U.S. 131 (1932); Callahan v. United States, 285 U.S. 515 (1932); Dunn v. United States, 284 U.S. 390 (1932); Various Items of Personal Property v. United States, 282 U.S. 577 (1931); United States v. Norris, 281 U.S. 619 (1930); Danovitz v. United States, 281 U.S. 389 (1930).

129 United States v. Farrar, 281 U.S. 624 (1930).

130 United States v. Benz, 282 U.S. 304 (1931).

131 Cook v. United States, 288 U.S. 102 (1933).

132 Richbourg Motor Co. v. United States, 281 U.S. 528 (1930). *But see* United States v. The Ruth Mildred, 286 U.S. 67 (1932); General Motors Acceptance Corp. v. United States, 286 U.S. 49 (1932); United States v. Ryan, 284 U.S. 167 (1931).

133 Nathanson v. United States, 290 U.S. 41 (1933); Sgro v. United States, 287 U.S. 206 (1932); Grau v. United States, 287 U.S. 124 (1932); Taylor v. United States, 286 U.S. 1 (1932); United States v. Lefkowitz, 285 U.S. 452 (1932); Go-Bart Importing Co. v. United States, 282 U.S. 344 (1931). *But see* Husty v. United States, 282 U.S. 694 (1931).

134 United States v. La Franca, 282 U.S. 568 (1931).

135 Funk v. United States, 290 U.S. 371 (1933).

136 That attempt has not been entirely successful. In addition to the lingering influences of prohibition decisions, disagreement over the meaning of the Twenty-first Amendment itself has caused significant amount of litigation in recent years. *See, e.g.,* 324 Liquor Corp. v. Duffy, 479 U.S. 335 (1987); Brown-Forman Distillers Corp. v. New York State Liquor Authority, 476 U.S. 573 (1986); Capital Cities Cable Inc. v. Crisp, 467 U.S. 691 (1984); New York State Liquor Auth. v. Bellanca, 452 U.S. 714 (1982).

137 United States v. Chambers, 291 U.S. 217 (1934).

138 Massey v. United States, 291 U.S. 608 (1934). *But see* United States v. Mack, 295 U.S. 480 (1935) (liability on bond releasing ship seized under the Volstead Act held not to have been extinguished by repeal of the Eighteenth Amendment when the crew had pleaded guilty prior to repeal).

2 Entrapment: The Emergence of a Legal Doctrine

1 Woo Wai v. United States, 223 F. 412 (9th Cir. 1915). At the trial, one immigration official explained the aim of Fernando Sanford, the agent who conceived the scheme: "He wanted to get this man, as it were, in the door, so that the man would have to give him information." *Id.* at 413.

2 The Michigan Supreme Court claims that its decision in Sanders v. People, 38 Mich. 218 (1878), made it the first state court to embrace the entrapment defense. *See* People v. Turner, 390 Mich. 7, 210 N.W.2d 336 (1973).

3 Woo Wai v. United States, 223 F. 412, 415 (9th Cir. 1915). In addition to its entrapment ruling, the court of appeals also held that the government had failed to prove a conspiracy because the officers in the scheme never intended to commit the offense. The alternate holding attempted to expand the legal principle that a conspiracy requires an agreement between at least two persons to commit an unlawful act. This common law requirement meant that if one of two parties to a conspiracy was a police officer acting to apprehend the other party, there would be no conspiracy because the police officer never really intended to commit the offense. The distinguishing feature of Woo Wai's case is apparent: Woo Wai had other associates in the conspiracy who were not police officers. Thus, the conspiracy had the required minimum of two members. Other courts have not followed the Woo Wai extension of the conspiracy doctrine, probably because its almost inevitable effect would be to preclude a conspiracy conviction whenever any police official participated in the scheme.

4 The Ninth Circuit did not completely spin the defense from whole cloth. Apparently the entrapment doctrine grew out of the "consent" defenses available to accessories to a crime. At common law, when the principal offender had obtained permission to do what would otherwise be an illegal act, a person who assisted the principal could not be convicted as an accessory because the principal was not violating the law. For example, one was not an accessory to burglary when the principal had secured the owner's permission to enter the building burgled. See, e.g., State v. Hayes, 105 Mo. 76, 16 S.W. 514 (1891). Similarly a conspiracy conviction required an agreement by two or more persons to commit an unlawful act. If all but one of the parties to a conspiracy were police officers acting to apprehend the sole remaining conspirator, the lack of an agreement between two persons, both of whom had a bona fide intent to violate the law, precluded the formation of a conspiracy. See note 3 supra.

5 See Price v. United States, 165 U.S. 311 (1897); Andrews v. United States, 162 U.S. 420 (1896); Grimm v. United States, 156 U.S. 604 (1895).

The court did cite six state cases. See Love v. People, 160 Ill. 501, 43 N.E. 710 (1896); People v. McCord, 76 Mich. 200, 42 N.W. 1106 (1889); Sanders v. People, 38 Mich. 218 (1878); Commonwealth v. Wasson, 42 Pa. Sup. Ct. 38 (1910); Commonwealth v. Bickings, 12 Pa. Dist. R. 206 (1903); O'Brien v. State, 6 Tex. App. 665 (1879). For summaries of the holdings in each of the cases, see Mikell, The Doctrine of Entrapment in the Federal Courts, 90 Pa. L. Rev. 245 (1942).

6 See 1 J. Bishop, New Commentaries on the Criminal Law §§ 255–63, at 138–44 (8th ed. 1892); 1 W. Clark & W. Marshall, The Law of Crimes § 162, at 347–48 (1900); 1 F. Wharton, Criminal Law § 389, at 501–04 (11th ed. 1912). The Clark and Marshall text discusses the defense of entrapment, but cites only state cases in support of the doctrine. See generally De Feo, Entrapment as a Defense to Criminal Responsibility, 1 U. S. F. L. Rev. 245 (1967).

7 Criminal Law, in 12 Cyclopedia of Law & Procedure 160 (1904); Criminal Law, in 8 Ruling Case Law § 103, at 127–28 (1915). A new encyclopedia published in 1918 included some of the early federal cases. See Criminal Law, in 16 Corpus Juris § 57, at 89–91 (1918).

8 H. Black, Law Dictionary (2d ed. 1910); J. Bouvoir, Legal Dictionary (3d rev. 1915). Cf. Words & Phrases (2d ed. 1914), which omits entrapment from its list of legal terms.

9 Yick v. United States, 240 F. 60, 64–65 (9th Cir. 1917).

10 Peterson v. United States, 255 F. 433, 436 (9th Cir. 1919) (emphasis added).

11 The federal statute did not contain a requirement of scienter. This lack of a scienter requirement meant that the statute prohibited sales to Indians regardless of whether the prosecution proved that the seller knew the purchasers were Indians. A 1926 news article criticized a similar Idaho case, in which the Idaho defendant sold cigarettes to a police decoy who was seventeen years old but who appeared much older. Apparently

the state supreme court allowed the conviction to stand. Entrapment into Crime, 30 Law Notes 143 (1926).

12 Voves v. United States, 249 F. 191, 192 (7th Cir. 1918).

13 *See* Freeman v. United States, 243 F. 353 (9th Cir. 1917), *cert. denied*, 249 U.S. 600 (1919); Hanish v. United States, 227 F. 584 (7th Cir. 1915).

14 *See* Goldstein v. United States, 256 F. 813 (7th Cir. 1919); Fetter v. United States, 260 F. 142 (9th Cir. 1919).

15 Brown v. United States, 260 F. 752 (9th Cir. 1919).

16 *See* Partan v. United States, 261 F. 515 (9th Cir. 1919), *cert. denied*, 251 U.S. 561 (1920); Goldstein v. United States, 256 F. 813 (7th Cir. 1919); Jung Quez v. United States, 222 F. 766 (9th Cir. 1915); Hanish v. United States, 227 F. 584 (7th Cir. 1915).

17 *Index to Legal Periodicals and Law Library Journal* 81 (1924); Calhoun, When Entrapment Is a Bar to Conviction, 10 Va. L. Rev. 316 (1924); Criminal Law-Entrapment to Sell Liquor, 33 Yale L.J. 555 (1924).

18 Three cases did not involve offenses related to drugs or alcohol: Conway v. United States, 1 F.2d 274 (7th Cir. 1924) (mail theft); Browne v. United States, 290 F. 870 (6th Cir. 1923) (illegal sale of war materials); Martin v. United States, 278 F. 913 (2d Cir. 1921) (bribery).

19 For a description of the emergence of antinarcotics laws in the first two decades of the twentieth century and a summary of similarities and differences between the attempts to control intoxicating liquors and other drugs, see R. Bonnie and C. Whitebread, *The Marihuana Conviction: A History of Marihuana Prohibition in the United States* 6–31 (1974).

20 Murphy v. United States, 2 F.2d 599 (5th Cir. 1924) (sale of intoxicating liquor); Jordan v. United States, 2 F.2d 598 (5th Cir. 1924) (sale of intoxicating liquor); Reyff v. United States, 2 F.2d 39 (9th Cir. 1924) (possession, sale, and transportation of intoxicating liquor); Johnstone v. United States, 1 F.2d 928 (9th Cir. 1924) (sale of intoxicating liquor); Sabbatino v. United States, 298 F. 409 (2d Cir.), *cert. denied*, 266 U.S. 602, 636 (1924) (bribery of prohibition agents); De Marco v. United States, 296 F. 667 (4th Cir.), *cert. denied*, 265 U.S. 593 (1924) (bribery of prohibition agent); Rossi v. United States, 293 F. 896 (8th Cir. 1923) (contempt citation for violation of Volstead Act injunction); Ritter v. United States, 293 F. 187 (9th Cir. 1923) (sale of intoxicating liquor); Zucker v. United States, 288 F. 12 (3d Cir.), *cert. denied*, 262 U.S. 756 (1923) (conspiracy to sell intoxicating liquors); Luterman v. United States, 281 F. 374 (3d Cir. 1922) (forgery of liquor stamps); Billingsley v. United States, 274 U.S. 86 (6th Cir. 1921) (interstate transportation of intoxicating liquor); Farley v. United States, 269 F. 721 (9th Cir. 1921) (carrying on business of retail liquor establishment without paying required tax); Saucedou v. United States, 268 F. 830 (5th Cir. 1920) (sale of intoxicating liquor);

Ramsey v. United States, 268 F. 825 (6th Cir. 1920) (sale of intoxicating liquor).

21 Di Salvo v. United States, 2 F.2d 222 (8th Cir. 1924) (sale of narcotic drugs); Rosso v. United States, 1 F.2d 717 (3d Cir. 1924) (possession of cocaine); Bethea v. United States, 1 F.2d 290 (7th Cir. 1924) (sale of narcotic drugs); Simmons v. United States, 300 F. 321 (6th Cir. 1924) (sale of narcotic drugs by a physician); Newman v. United States, 299 F. 128 (4th Cir. 1924) (sale of narcotic drugs by a physician); Leon v. United States, 290 F. 384 (9th Cir.), cert. denied, 263 U.S. 710 (1923) (sale of narcotic drugs) Nutter v. United States, 289 F. 484 (4th Cir. 1923) (sale of morphine); Aultman v. United States, 289 F. 251 (5th Cir. 1923) (possession, importation, and sale of morphine and cocaine); Smith v. United States, 284 F. 673 (8th Cir.), cert. denied, 261 U.S. 617 (1923) (conspiracy to sell narcotic drugs); Lucadamo v. United States, 280 F. 653 (2d Cir. 1922) (conspiracy to sell narcotic drugs); Fisk v. United States, 279 F. 12 (6th Cir. 1922) (sale of narcotic drugs); Butts v. United States, 273 F. 35 (8th Cir. 1921) (sale of narcotic drugs); Rothman v. United States, 270 F. 31 (2d Cir. 1921) (sale of narcotic drugs by a physician and pharmacist); Fiunkin v. United States, 265 F. 1 (9th Cir. 1920) (sale of narcotic drugs).

22 Butts v. United States, 273 F. 35, 38 (8th Cir. 1921).

23 Di Salvo v. United States, 2 F.2d 222, 225 (8th Cir. 1924).

24 Id. at 26 (quoting charge of the trial judge).

25 Id.

26 Ritter v. United States, 293 F. 187, 188–89 (9th Cir. 1923).

27 Sabbatino v. United States, 298 F. 409, 411 (2d Cir.), cert. denied, 266 U.S. 602, 636 (1924); Luterman v. United States, 281 F. 374 (3d Cir. 1922); De Marco v. United States, 296 F. 667 (4th Cir. 1924); Bethea v. United States, 1 F.2d 290 (7th Cir. 1924).

28 See, e.g., Criminal Law-Trial-Entrapment as a Defense Where Criminal Intent Originates in Accused, 16 Va. L. Rev. 78 (1929); Criminal Law-Entrapment, 13 St. Louis L. Rev. 275 (1928); Foster, Criminal Law-Entrapment by Public Officer as Defense, 5 Neb. L. Bull. 422 (1927); Criminal Law-Solicitation by Officer-No Defense to Violation of Liquor Law, 12 Va. L. Rev. 426 (1926); Recent Cases, 20 Ill. L. Rev. 319 (1925).

29 E.g., 1929 Va. L. Rev. article, supra note 28; St. Louis L. Rev. article, supra note 28. But see 1926 Va. L. Rev. article, supra note 28, at 426:

Though certain courts have condemned the practice declaring that it is contrary to public policy, the decided weight of authority is to the effect that where one makes an unlawful sale of liquor he is not excused from criminality because he was induced to do the act for the sole purpose of prosecuting him.

30 *E.g.,* Note, Entrapment by Government Officials, 28 Colum. L. Rev. 1067 (1928).

31 Annotation, Entrapment to Commit Crime with View to Prosecution Therefor, 18 A.L.R. 45 (1922).

32 1 W. Clark and W. Marshall, *Law of Crimes* § 155 (3d ed. 1927). Bishop had recognized the defense in the 1923 edition of his text, *see* J. Bishop, *Criminal Law* § 926 (9th ed. 1923), but he tried to limit the doctrine's application in cases involving violations of liquor laws. *Id.* § 926(z)(c).

33 Criminal Law, in *Ruling Case Law Permanent Supplement* 2192 (1929).

34 Buckley v. United States, 33 F.2d 713 (6th Cir. 1929) (bribery of a prohibition agent); Polaski v. United States, 33 F.2d 686 (8th Cir.), *cert. denied,* 280 U.S. 591 (1929) (conspiracy to violate the Volstead Act); Robinson v. United States, 32 F.2d 505 (8th Cir. 1929) (bribery of a prohibition agent); De Mayo v. United States, 32 F.2d 472 (8th Cir. 1929) (introduction of intoxicating liquor into Indian territory); Porter v. United States, 32 F.2d 544 (8th Cir. 1929) (sale of intoxicating liquor); Ybor v. United States, 31 F.2d 42 (5th Cir. 1929) (bribery of a federal prohibition agent); Newman v. United States, 28 F.2d 681 (9th Cir. 1928), *cert. denied,* 279 U.S. 839 (1929) (bribery of a prohibition agent); Gargano v. United States, 24 F.2d 625 (5th Cir. 1928) (bribery of a prohibition agent); Driskill v. United States, 24 F.2d 525 (9th Cir. 1928) (possession and sale of intoxicating liquor); Corcoran v. United States, 19 F.2d 901 (8th Cir. 1927) (sale of intoxicating liquor); Jarl v. United States, 19 F.2d 891 (8th Cir. 1927) (transportation and sale of intoxicating liquor); Hadley v. United States, 18 F.2d 507 (8th Cir. 1927) (sale of intoxicating liquor); St. Clair v. United States, 17 F.2d 886 (8th Cir. 1927) (sale of intoxicating liquor); Silk v. United States, 16 F.2d 568 (8th Cir. 1926), *modified,* 19 F.2d 73 (1927) (transportation and sale of intoxicating liquor); Weiderman v. United States, 10 F.2d 745 (8th Cir. 1926) (sale of intoxicating liquor); Kendjerski v. United States, 9 F.2d 909 (6th Cir. 1926) (sale of intoxicating liquor); Capuano v. United States, 9 F.2d 41 (1st Cir. 1925) (bribery of prohibition agent); Lewis v. United States, 4 F.2d 520 (5th Cir. 1925) (transportation of intoxicating liquor); De Long v. United States, 4 F.2d 244 (8th Cir. 1924) (sale of intoxicating liquor); Scriber v. United States, 4 F.2d 97 (6th Cir. 1925) (bribery by prohibition agent); Orsatti v. United States, 3 F.2d 778 (9th Cir.), *cert. denied,* 268 U.S. 94 (1925) (bribery of prohibition agents).

35 Eleven of the twelve nonprohibition cases involved drugs. *See* Sargent v. United States, 35 F.2d 344 (9th Cir. 1929) (sale of morphine by a physician); Sauvin v. United States, 31 F.2d 732 (8th Cir. 1929) (possession and sale of morphine); Lawrence v. United States, 28 F.2d 608 (8th Cir. 1928) (sale of morphine); Boehm v. United States, 21 F.2d 283

(8th Cir. 1927) (sale of narcotic drugs); Cain v. United States, 19 F.2d 472 (8th Cir. 1927) (sale of morphine); Vamvas v. United States, 13 F.2d 347 (5th Cir. 1926) (sale of cocaine); C. M. Spring Drug Co. v. United States, 12 F.2d 852 (8th Cir. 1926) (sale of morphine); Perez v. United States, 10 F.2d 352 (9th Cir. 1926) (sale of morphine); Cline v. United States, 9 F.2d 621 (9th Cir. 1925) (sale of morphine); Cermak v. United States, 4 F.2d 99 (6th Cir. 1925) (sale of narcotic drugs); Napolitano v. United States, 3 F.2d 994 (1st Cir.), *cert. denied*, 269 U.S. 553 (1925) (sale of morphine). Only one decision involved neither liquor nor drugs; Ritzman v. United States, 3 F.2d 718 (D.C. Cir. 1925) (bribery of army officer).

36 Robinson v. United States, 32 F.2d 505 (8th Cir. 1929); Driskill v. United States, 24 F.2d 525 (9th Cir. 1928); Jarl v. United States, 19 F.2d 891 (8th Cir. 1927); Silk v. United States, 16 F.2d 568 (8th Cir. 1926), *modified*, 19 F.2d 73 (1927); Capuano v. United States, 9 F.2d 41 (1st Cir. 1925); Lewis v. United States, 4 F.2d 520 (5th Cir. 1925); Cermak v. United States, 4 F.2d 99 (6th Cir. 1925). The *Cermak* case, the first in the group from the second half of the 1920s, was the only one that did not involve an offense related to prohibition.

37 *See, e.g.,* Buckley v. United States, 33 F.2d 713 (6th Cir. 1929); Gargano v. United States, 24 F.2d 625 (5th Cir. 1928); Hadley v. United States, 18 F.2d 507 (8th Cir. 1927).

38 E.g., Ybor v. United States, 31 F.2d 42 (5th Cir. 1929) (evidence of defendant's knowledge of prior bribe offers admissible on entrapment issue); Shields v. United States, 26 F.2d 993 (D.C. Ct. App. 1928) (government has burden of proof on entrapment issue); Boehm v. United States, 21 F.2d 283 (8th Cir. 1927) (entrapment defense waived by failure to request entrapment instruction); Corcoran v. United States, 19 F.2d 901 (8th Cir. 1927) (entrapment defense waived by defense objection to prosecution rebuttal evidence).

39 Silk v. United States 16 F.2d 568, 570 (8th Cir. 1926), *modified*, 19 F.2d 73 (8th Cir. 1927). The *Silk* decision applied to two defendants whose trials were consolidated for trial in the district court. Both defendants were convicted of selling and transporting intoxicating liquor. At trial, one defendant—Silk—denied all involvement in the sale. The other—Meeks—admitted making certain sales, but said he made them only after prohibition agents applied great pressure. The court of appeals reversed Meeks's conviction but allowed Silk's conviction on the substantive counts to stand.

40 Jarl v. United States, 19 F.2d 891, 896 (8th Cir. 1927).

41 Robinson v. United States, 32 F.2d 505, 510 (8th Cir. 1929). The initial opinion of the court of appeals did not reverse the conviction on the entrapment issue, but on whether Robinson, a federal prohibition agent, accepted money with the intent to alter his testimony. The court held that the trial judge should have submitted the question to the jury. The court's final opinion—after a rehearing—also indicated, however, that Robinson's entrapment issue should go to the jury.

42 Capuano v. United States, 9 F.2d 41 (1st Cir. 1925). A district court jury convicted Capuano of bribing federal prohibition agents. Once again, the trial judge refused to submit an entrapment instruction in spite of sharply conflicting evidence concerning the alleged wrongdoing. Capuano testified that he began "paying off" the prohibition agents only after the agents beat him and threatened him with loss of his permit for denatured alcohol if he did not cooperate. The court of appeals reversed Capuano's conviction and remanded the case for a new trial before a properly instructed jury.

43 Lewis v. United States, 4 F.2d 520 (5th Cir. 1925). Lewis involved a scheme to transport illicit liquor from Bimini to Miami. The evidence conflicted on the question of whether the prohibition agents or the defendant initiated the negotiations. Nevertheless, the district court severely limited defense counsel's attempt to develop the point on cross-examination and refused to submit the issue to the jury. With a brief discussion that relied on Di Salvo v. United States, 2 F.2d 222 (8th Cir. 1924), the Eighth Circuit overturned the conviction and sent the case back for a new trial.

44 Cermak v. United States, 4 F.2d 99 (6th Cir. 1925). Cermak involved a narcotics conviction. The district court refused to submit the entrapment issue to the jury at Cermak's trial even though the defense offered evidence that Cermak, a drug store clerk, made the narcotics sale only after the government's addict informer pleaded with him at great length. Terming the case before it "the typical case in which the defense of entrapment should be sustained, upon the grounds of public policy stated in the Woo Wai case," the Sixth Circuit reversed the conviction and remanded the case for a new trial.

45 Driskill v. United States, 24 F.2d 525 (9th Cir. 1928). In Driskill the Ninth Circuit held that the defendant presented an entrapment issue for the jury when the informer made several pleas before the defendant consummated the sale and the officers had no reason to suspect the defendant of prior illegal sales.

46 See, e.g., Ybor v. United States, 31 F.2d 42 (5th Cir. 1929).

47 H. Black, Law Dictionary 666 (3d ed. 1933). Surprisingly, neither the 1926 edition of Bouvoir's dictionary nor its 1934 supplement define entrapment. J. Bouvoir, Legal Dictionary (4th rev. 1926 & 1934 Supp.).

48 Criminal Law, in Corpus Juris Annual Supplement (1934).

49 Corlett, Intoxicating Liquors-Entrapment as a Defense-Circumstances Justifying Apprehension through Decoys (Idaho, 1930), 33 Rocky

Mt. L. Rev. 80 (1930); Note, Entrapment as a Defense to Criminal Prosecution, 44 Harv. L. Rev. 109 (1930).

50 Boyd, Entrapment in Narcotic Law Violations, 20 Ky. L.J. 98 (1931); Harkrider, Criminal Law-Entrapment-Public Policy, 9 Tex. L. Rev. 276 (1931); Ragland, Crimes-Entrapment, 20 Ky. L.J. 96 (1931); Schimke, Criminal Law-Entrapment as a Defense in Criminal Prosecutions, 1 Idaho L.J. 93 (1931); Recent Cases, Criminal Law-Defenses-Entrapment in Liquor Cases, 45 Harv. L. Rev. 381 (1931).

51 The courts of appeals issued opinions discussing entrapment in thirteen cases between 1930 and 1933. For a listing of the opinions see note 53 infra.

52 The courts of appeals reversed convictions in two prohibition cases, Hunter v. United States, 62 F.2d 217 (5th Cir. 1932), O'Brien v. United States, 51 F.2d 674 (7th Cir. 1931), and one drug-related case, Wall v. United States, 65 F.2d 993 (5th Cir. 1933). In O'Brien the court of appeals reversed a conviction on entrapment grounds even though the district court had submitted the issue to the jury. O'Brien and his codefendants were accused of conspiring to violate the Volstead Act. A prohibition agent who operated a pool hall as a front for a bootlegging operation had originated the conspiracy. He then persuaded the defendants, most of whom were members of the Indianapolis police department, to join him in the illegal scheme. The Seventh Circuit reversed the conspiracy convictions and ordered judgments of acquittal. The court reviewed the proof presented at trial and found "no evidence in the record that any of the appellants had, prior to the opening of the pool hall, disclosed any disposition to enter into a criminal conspiracy to violate the prohibition law." Id. at 680. The lack of proof, the court held, established the entrapment defense as a matter of law; and it was improper to refer the case to the jury. For a further discussion of O'Brien, see Solomon, Regulating the Regulators; Prohibition Enforcement in the Ninth Circuit, in Law, Alcohol, and Order: Perspectives on National Prohibition 90 (D. Kyvig ed., 1985).

53 Nine of the thirteen entrapment opinions came in cases related to prohibition: Meyer v. United States, 67 F.2d 223 (9th Cir. 1933) (possession and transportation of intoxicating liquor); Bonnoyer v. United States, 63 F.2d 93 (1st Cir. 1933) (conspiracy to transport and to possess intoxicating liquor); Hunter v. United States, 62 F.2d 217 (5th Cir. 1932) (transportation and sale of intoxicating liquor); Beard v. United States, 59 F.2d 940 (8th Cir. 1932) (transportation of intoxicating liquor); Flynn v. United States, 57 F.2d 1044 (8th Cir.), cert. denied, 287 U.S. 627 (1932) (transportation and sale of intoxicating liquor); Sorrells v. United States, 57 F.2d 973 (4th Cir.), rev'd, 287 U.S. 584 (1932) (sale of intoxicating liquor); O'Brien v. United States, 51 F.2d 674 (7th Cir. 1931) (possession, transportation, and sale of intoxicating liquor); Pall v. United States, 46 F.2d 461 (4th Cir. 1931) (violation of the Volstead Act); Patton v. United States, 42 F.2d 68 (8th Cir. 1930) (conspiracy to bribe a federal prohibition agent). Three of the nonprohibition cases involved drug offenses: Wall v. United States, 65 F.2d 993 (5th Cir. 1933) (conspiracy to purchase, sell, displace, and distribute morphine and cocaine); Price v. United States, 56 F.2d 135 (7th Cir. 1932) (sale, transportation, and concealment of narcotics); Swallum v. United States, 39 F.2d 390 (8th Cir. 1930) (unlawful sale of morphine by prescription). Only one was unrelated to either alcohol or drugs. United States v. Becker, 62 F.2d 1007 (2d Cir. 1933) (shipping obscene matter in interstate commerce).

54 *See* Capuano v. United States, 9 F.2d 41 (1st Cir. 1925); Sabbatino v. United States, 298 F. 409 (2d Cir.), *cert. denied,* 266 U.S. 602, 636 (1924); Luterman v. United States, 281 F. 374 (3d Cir. 1922); Newman v. United States, 299 F. 128 (4th Cir. 1924); Lewis v. United States, 4 F.2d 520 (5th Cir. 1925); Cermak v. United States, 4 F.2d 99 (6th Cir. 1925); O'Brien v. United States, 51 F.2d 674 (7th Cir. 1931); Di Salvo v. United States, 2 F.2d 222 (8th Cir. 1924); Woo Wai v. United States, 223 F. 412 (9th Cir. 1915). *See also* footnote 1 of Judge Soper's dissenting opinion in Sorrells v. United States, 57 F.2d 973, 978 (4th Cir. 1932).

55 *Compare* O'Brien v. United States, 51 F.2d 674 (7th Cir. 1931), *with* Wall v. United States, 65 F.2d 993 (5th Cir. 1933), *and* C. M. Spring Drug Co. v. United States, 12 F.2d 852 (8th Cir. 1932). Commentators divided on whether the judge or the jury should pass on the entrapment issue. *Compare* Note, Entrapment by Government Officials, 28 Colum. L. Rev. 1067 (1928), *with* Jones, Criminal Law-Lawfulness of Conviction of Accused Entrapped by Officers of the Law-Entrapment, 20 Ill. L. Rev. 401 (1925).

56 Butts v. United States, 273 F. 35, 37–38 (9th Cir. 1921).

57 *See* Flynn v. United States, 57 F.2d 1044 (8th Cir.), *cert. denied,* 287 U.S. 627 (1932); Polski v. United States, 33 F.2d 686 (8th Cir.), *cert. denied,* 280 U.S. 591 (1929); Newman v. United States, 28 F.2d 681 (9th Cir. 1928), *cert. denied,* 279 U.S. 839 (1929); Napolitano v. United States, 3 F.2d 994 (1st Cir.), *cert. denied,* 269 U.S. 553 (1925); Orsatti v. United States 3 F.2d 778 (9th Cir.), *cert. denied,* 268 U.S. 694 (1925); Sabbatino v. United States, 298 F. 409 (2d Cir.), *cert. denied,* 266 U.S. 602, 636 (1924); De Marco v. United States, 296 F. 667 (4th Cir. 1924), *cert. denied,* 265 U.S. 593 (1925); Leon v. United States, 290 F. 384 (9th Cir.), *cert. denied,* 263 U.S. 710 (1923); Zucker v. United States, 288 F. 12 (3d Cir.), *cert. denied,* 262 U.S. 756 (1923); Smith v. United States, 284 F. 673 (8th Cir.), *cert. denied,* 261 U.S. 617 (1923); Partan v. United States, 261 F. 515 (9th Cir. 1919), *cert. denied,* 251 U.S. 561 (1920); Freeman v. United States, 243 F. 353 (9th Cir.), *cert. denied,* 249 U.S. 600 (1919). Interestingly, the government never sought certiorari in a case where a court of appeals reversed a conviction based on an entrapment defense.

58 276 U.S. 413 (1928).

59 Id. at 423–25 (dissenting opinion of Brandeis, J.).

60 Id. at 418–20 (majority opinion).

61 Sorrells v. United States, 287 U.S. 435 (1932).

62 United States v. Sorrells, Cr. No. 5972 (U.S. District Court for the Western District of North Carolina).

63 Transcript of Record, Sorrells v. United States, No. 3168 (4th Cir. 1932), at 7–9. I consulted the Fourth Circuit copy of the record because the district court records have been removed to the federal archives. Letter dated May 15, 1973, from Verne Bartlett, Deputy Clerk of Court for the Western District of North Carolina, to the author.

64 Id. at 9–16.

65 Id. at 16–20.

66 Brief for Defendant, Sorrells v. United States, No. 3168 (4th Cir. 1932), at 6–10. The defendant's brief also argued that the district court had erred by admitting evidence of a later liquor sale not charged in the indictment, id. at 5, and that the eighteen-month imprisonment imposed by the trial court violated the Eighth Amendment's proscription against cruel and unusual punishment. Id. at 10–12.

67 Brief for the United States, Sorrells v. United States, No. 3168 (4th Cir. 1932), at 7–9.

68 Sorrells v. United States, 57 F.2d 973, 974 (4th Cir. 1932).

69 299 F. 128 (4th Cir. 1924).

70 Sorrells v. United States, 57 F.2d 973, 976 (4th Cir. 1932). It is difficult to read the *Newman* case in any way except as directly contrary to the *Sorrells* opinion. A jury convicted Newman, a physician, of selling morphine, but defense and prosecution testimony presented sharply divergent versions of the circumstances surrounding the offense. The trial judge gave an entrapment instruction that submitted the issue to the jury, and the court of appeals approved the trial procedure:

> Under this conflicting testimony the court was right in refusing to tell the jury that they should acquit the defendant, because he was entrapped by the officer.
>
> As the issue of entrapment was vital, the defendant was entitled to an accurate statement of the law of entrapment. It is well settled that decoys may be used to entrap criminals, and to present opportunity to one intending or willing to commit crime. But decoys are not permissible to ensnare the innocent and law-abiding into the commission of crime. When the criminal design originates, not with the accused, but is conceived in the mind of the government officers, and the accused is by persuasion, deceitful repre-

sentation, or inducement lured into the commission of a criminal act, the government is estopped by sound public policy from prosecution.

Newman v. United States, 299 F. 128, 131 (4th Cir. 1924).

71 57 F.2d at 977 (4th Cir. 1932).

72 Id. at 978–79 (dissenting opinion of Soper, J.). In support of his position, Judge Soper cited Oliver Wendell Holmes's famous maxim: "The life of the law has not been logic; it has been experience."

73 Id. at 979–80.

74 Petition for certiorari and memorandum in support of petition, Sorrells v. United States, No. 177, Supreme Court of the United States (October 1932 Term), at 6.

75 Memorandum in response to petition for certiorari, Sorrells v. United States, No. 177, Supreme Court of the United States (October 1932 Term), at 8.

76 Sorrells v. United States, *pet. for cert. granted*, 287 U.S. 584 (1932) In addition to the entrapment issue, Sorrells's counsel also sought Supreme Court review of the lower courts' rulings that similar misdeeds of the defendant committed subsequent to the charged offense were admissible in evidence against him. When the Court granted the writ of certiorari, it limited its review to the entrapment question.

77 Brief for Petitioner, Sorrells v. United States, No. 177, Supreme Court of the United States (October 1932 Term), at 9.

78 Brief for the Government, Sorrells v. United States, No. 177, Supreme Court of the United States (October 1932 Term).

79 Sorrells v. United States, 287 U.S. 435 (1932). Justice McReynolds dissented without opinion.

80 Id. at 441.

81 Id. at 443.

82 Id. at 446.

83 Id. at 448.

84 Id. at 449–51.

85 Id. at 451.

86 Id. at 452.

87 Id. at 453.

88 Id. at 453–54.

89 Id. at 455–56.

90 Id. at 457.

91 Id.

92 Id. at 459.

93 Docket Sheet, United States v. Sorrells, Cr. No. 5972, U.S. District Court for the Western District of North Carolina; letter dated June 26,

1973, from Verne Bartlett, Deputy Clerk of Court, United States District Court for the Western District of North Carolina, to the author.

94 13 B.U. L. Rev. 293 (1933); 3 Det. L. Rev. 119 (1933); 1 Geo. Wash. L. Rev. 371 (1933); 46 Harv. L. Rev. 848 (1933); 31 Mich. L. Rev. 1159 (1933); 17 Minn. L. Rev 331 (1933); 10 N.Y.U. L. Rev. 533 (1933); 12 Or. L. Rev. 313 (1933); 1 U. Chi. L. Rev. 115 (1933); 39 W. Va. L.Q. 261 (1933); 42 Yale L.J. 802 (1933). There had been two earlier notes on the Fourth Circuit opinion in the *Sorrells* case: 17 Minn. L. Rev. 90 (1932); 41 Yale L.J. 1249 (1932).

95 *See* United States v. Ginsburg, 96 F.2d 882 (7th Cir.), *cert. denied*, 305 U.S. 620 (1938); Ratigan v. United States, 88 F.2d 919 (9th Cir.), *cert. denied*, 301 U.S. 705 (1937); Burke v. United States, 84 F.2d 40 (5th Cir. 1936); Yep v. United States, 83 F.2d 41 (10th Cir. 1936); Cantwell v. United States, 81 F.2d 31 (9th Cir. 1935); Clairborne v. United States, 77 F.2d 683 (8th Cir. 1935); Hill v. United States, 73 F.2d 223 (5th Cir. 1934); Strader v. United States, 72 F.2d 589 (10th Cir. 1934); Jindra v. United States, 69 F.2d 429 (5th Cir.), *cert. denied*, 292 U.S. 651 (1934); Hankins v. United States, 67 F.2d 317 (5th Cir. 1933), *cert. denied*, 291 U.S. 671 (1934); United States v. Becker, 62 F.2d 1007 (2d Cir. 1933). The appellate courts reversed convictions in *Yep* and *Strader* because of improper jury instructions on the entrapment issue; both of the reversals came in prosecutions for violation of drug laws.

96 Mikell, *supra* note 5.

97 Sherman v. United States, 356 U.S. 369 (1958).

98 *See, e.g.,* Mathews v. United States, 485 U.S. 58 (1988); Hampton v. United States, 425 U.S. 484 (1976); United States v. Russell, 411 U.S. 423 (1973). *See generally* Murchison, The Entrapment Defense in Federal Courts: Modern Developments, 47 Miss. L.J. 573 (1976).

99 *See, e.g.,* American Law Institute, *Model Penal Code* § 2.13 (Proposed Official Draft 1962); National Commission on Reform of Federal Criminal Law, *Proposed New Federal Criminal Code* § 702 (1971).

100 N. Clark, *Deliver Us From Evil* 159–65 (1976); D. Kyvig, *Repealing National Prohibition* 29–32 (1979). For a contemporary criticism of the congressional commitment to enforcement, see C. Merz, *The Dry Decade* 75–100 (1930).

101 H. Asbury, *The Great Illusion: An Informal History of Prohibition* 277–81 (1950); 1 W. Swindler, *Court and Constitution in the Twentieth Century* 265; C. Merz, *supra* note 100, at 197–99.

102 S. Doc. 198 69th Cong. 2d Sess. (192); C. Merz, *supra* note 100, at 194–95.

103 H. Asbury, *supra* note 101, at 211–13; D. Kyvig, *supra* note 100, at 27; C. Merz, *supra* note 100, at 194–95. *See also* I. Einstein, *Prohibition Agent No. 1* (1932).

104 For a description of the modern expansion of these technical issues, see Murchison, *supra* note 98.

105 The Supreme Court decision came only about a month before the Twenty-first Amendment was submitted to the states for ratification.

106 P. Finley, The Supreme Court Decisions, in *Mr. Dooley's Opinions* (1900) ("No matther, whether th' constitution follows th' flag or not, th' supreme court follows th' iliction returns.").

107 *See* Woodard, Reality and Social Reform: The Transition From Laissez-Faire to the Welfare State, 72 Yale L.J. 286 (1962). For leading articles on both sides of the "neutral principles" debate that has long divided constitutional scholars, *compare* Wechsler, Toward Neutral Principles in Constitutional Law, 73 Harv. L. Rev. 1 (1959), *with* Miller & Howell, The Myth of Neutrality in Constitutional Adjudication, 27 U. Chi. L. Rev. 661 (1960).

3 The Fourth Amendment, 1920–1929: A Doctrinal Explosion

1 U.S. Const. amend. IV: "The right of the people to be secure in their persons, houses, papers, and effects against unreasonable searches and seizures, shall not be violated, and no warrants shall issue, but upon oath or affirmation, and particularly describing the place to be searched, and the persons or things to be seized."

2 *See, e.g.,* J. Wigmore, *A Treatise on the Anglo-American System of Evidence in Trials at Common Law* 2184 (2d ed. 1923); Wigmore, Using Evidence Obtained By Illegal Search and Seizure, 8 A.B.A. J. 479 (1922).

3 232 U.S. 383 (1914). The Court first advanced the thesis that the admission of evidence obtained in violation of the Fourth Amendment would violate the Fifth Amendment privilege against self-incrimination in Boyd v. United States, 116 U.S. 616 (1880), but the post-*Boyd* decision in Adams v. New York, 192 U.S. 585 (1904), seemed to retreat from this position. For summaries of the Court's vacillation prior to *Weeks*, see Wigmore, A.B.A. J. article *supra* note 2, at 480; Note, Formalism, Legal Realism, and Constitutionally Protected Privacy under the Fourth and Fifth Amendments, 90 Harv. L. Rev. 945, 951–57 (1977); Comment, Search, Seizure, and the Fourth and Fifth Amendments, 31 Yale L.J. 518, 520–21 (1922).

4 232 U.S. at 393. The Court was not very precise in explaining the analytic basis for this conclusion. The first decision to suggest the exclusionary rule had argued that introduction of evidence seized in violation of the Fourth Amendment's prohibition against unreasonable searches and searches violated the owner's Fifth Amendment privilege against self-incrimination. Boyd v. United States, 116 U.S. 616, 633 (1886); *ac-*

cord, Gouled v. United States, 255 U.S. 298, 306 (1921). Wigmore, however, roundly criticized this reliance on an interrelationship between the
Fourth and Fifth Amendment rights, see Wigmore treatise, supra note 2,
at § 2264; and some commentators who praised Weeks's exclusionary rule
defended it on a different basis. They argued that it was justified as the
only reasonable means of deterring unreasonable police conduct. See,
e.g., Chaffee, Progress of the Law, 1921–1922: Evidence, 35 Harv. L. Rev.
673, 694–95 (1922). But cf. Atkinson, Admissibility of Evidence Obtained
through Unreasonable Searches and Seizures, 25 Colum. L. Rev. 11 (1925)
(accepting both justifications).

One of the most confusing aspects of the law of search and seizure was
the rule concerning the type of objection necessary to preserve a Fourth
Amendment claim. Weeks relied on the pretrial objection as a reason for
not invoking the evidentiary rule precluding consideration of collateral
issues, and the Court even distinguished Adams v. New York, 192 U.S.
585 (1904), on the ground that the defendant in Adams had offered his
objection when the seized evidence was offered at trial. 232 U.S. at 396,
criticized in Wigmore, A.B.A. J. article, supra note 2 at 481. But some later
decisions considered Fourth Amendment claims in the absence of pretrial
objections. E.g., Agnello v. United States, 269 U.S. 20 (1926) (lack of
pretrial objection ignored because the facts concerning the search were
not in dispute); Gouled v. United States, 255 U.S. 298 (1921) (lack of
pretrial objection ignored because defendant had no knowledge of the
illegal seizure until the evidence was offered at trial); Amos v. United
States, 255 U.S. 313 (1921) (application not made until after jury was
sworn ruled to be timely). See generally Atkinson, Prohibition and the
Doctrine of the Weeks Case, 23 Mich. L. Rev. 748, 753–57 (1925).

5 E.g., Boyd v. United States, 116 U.S. 616 (1886); Ex parte Jackson, 96
U.S. 727 (1877).

6 Ex parte Jackson, 96 U.S. 727 (1877); Silverthorne Lumber Co. v.
United States, 251 U.S. 385 (1919). But cf. Stroud v. United States, 251
U.S. 15, 21 (1919) (Fourth Amendment does not require exclusion of an
inmate's letters when "[t]hey came into the possession of the officials of
the penitentiary under established practice, reasonably designed to promote the discipline of the institution.").

7 232 U.S. at 390. The property origins of Fourth Amendment rights
received even greater emphasis in Boyd v. United States, 116 U.S. 616
(1886).

8 See, e.g., Silverthorne Lumber Co. v. United States, 251 U.S. 385
(1919); Ex parte Jackson, 96 U.S. 727 (1877).

9 See, e.g., Boyd v. United States, 116 U.S. 616, 623 (1880) (dictum).
This special treatment has continued in modern law. See, e.g., United
States v. Ramsey, 431 U.S. 606 (1972).

10 Silverthorne Lumber Co. v. United States, 251 U.S. 385, 392 (1919); Wilson v. United States, 221 U.S. 361, 382–83 (1911); Hale v. Heinkel, 201 U.S. 43, 74–76 (1906). *See also* Wheeler v. United States, 226 U.S. 478 (1913) (officers of dissolved corporation cannot refuse to produce corporate records that would incriminate them).

11 *See* Comment, The Meaning of the Federal Rule on Evidence Illegally Obtained, 36 Yale L.J. 537, 538–39 (1927) (counting 525 federal opinions involving both the Fourth Amendment and prohibition).

12 *See* N. Bindler, *The Conservative Court, 1910–1930* 193–95 (1986); *see generally* H. Warner, *The Life of Mr. Justice Clarke: A Testament to the Power of Liberal Dissent in America* (1959). A strong supporter of labor unions and world peace, Justice Clarke did not always vote to uphold civil liberties. *See* Abrams v. United States, 250 U.S. 616 (1919).

13 Gouled v. United States, 255 U.S. 298, 304, 306, 309 (1921).

14 Amos v. United States, 255 U.S. 313 (1921). The defendant had been convicted for violating the revenue statute that forbade moving or selling whiskey on which the prescribed federal tax had not been paid.

15 *Id.* at 316–17.

16 Burdeau v. McDowell, 256 U.S. 465, 475 (1921). Brandeis dissented in *Burdeau* in an opinion that Holmes joined.

17 265 U.S. 57 (1924).

18 *Id.* at 58. Justice Holmes did not specify what "information" prompted the agents to put Hester's house under observation, and the record provides only slightly more illumination. One of the prohibition agents testified that "we had destroyed distilleries near [Hester's] house before and we had information that he kept whiskey there," but the court struck "that statement" on the ground the agent could not "state what his information was." Hester v. United States, Transcript of Record, at 15. The agents did, in fact, search Hester's house, but Justice Holmes dismissed the search as "immaterial" because the search of the dwelling did not uncover any evidence.

19 *Id.*

20 *Id.* at 59, *citing* 4 Blackstone, *Commentaries* 223, 225, 226.

21 267 U.S. 132 (1925); *see* D. Kyvig, *Repealing National Prohibition* 33 (1979). The special treatment for automobiles has continued to the present. *See, e.g.*, California v. Acevedo, 111 U.S. 1982 (1991); California v. Carney, 471 U.S. 386 (1985); South Dakota v. Oppenheim, 428 U.S. 364 (1976); Chambers v. Maroney, 399 U.S. 42 (1970); Brinegar v. United States, 338 U.S. 160 (1949). Occasionally the Court has recognized some limits to the rule permitting searches of automobiles without a warrant. E.g., Delaware v. Prouse, 440 U.S. 648 (1979) (random checks for driver's licenses and registration certificates violate the reasonableness standard of the Fourth Amendment); Arkansas v. Sanders, 442 U.S. 753 (1979) (warrant required to search luggage taken from automobile in a valid warrantless search); United States v. Chadwick, 433 U.S. 1 (1977) (warrant required to search locked footlocker in an automobile parked at a curb).

22 267 U.S. at 134–36.

23 *Id.* at 147.

24 *Id.* at 149.

25 *Id.* at 150–53, *citing* Act of July 31, 1789, 1 Stat. 29; Act of Mar. 3, 1815, 3 Stat. 231; Rev. Stat. § 2140; Act of Mar. 3, 1899, 30 Stat. 1253. For criticism of the majority's reliance on these statutes, see F. Black, *Ill-Starred Prohibition Cases* 21–27 (1931).

26 *Id.* at 154, 156.

27 *Id.* at 160. Detroit's position as a principal point of entry for liquor smuggled from Canada was a matter of general knowledge. *See, e.g.,* Selden, Rum Row in the Middle West, in *The Twenties: Fords, Flappers & Fanatics* 105 (G. Mowry ed., 1963).

28 267 U.S. at 156–58; *see* F. Black, *supra* note 25, at 31–32 (1931). *See generally* 9 Halsbury, *Laws of England* 523, 607–17 (1909); *see also* 3 American Law Institute, *Commentaries on Torts* 40–41 (1927) [hereinafter cited as *ALI Commentaries*]; Wilgus, Arrest without a Warrant, 22 Mich. L. Rev. 541, 673–76, 703–04 (1924).

29 267 U.S. at 163–75.

30 *See* H. Asbury, *The Great Illusion: An Informal History of Prohibition* 211–13 (1950); D. Kyvig; *supra* note 21, at 27 (1979); Talley, Einstein, Rum Sleuth, in *The Twenties, supra* note 27, at 107. *See* text accompanying note 103 in chapter 2.

31 Steele v. United States, 267 U.S. 498, 504 (1925).

32 *Id.* at 499.

33 *Id.* at 502–03.

34 *Id.* at 503.

35 *Id.*

36 40 Stat. 229 (1917). This provision was one of the requirements of the Espionage Act that was incorporated by reference in the Volstead Act. 27 U.S.C.A. § 11 (1927).

37 U.S. Const. art. 2, § 2 ("inferior" officers must be appointed by the president, the courts, or department heads).

38 Steele v. United States, 267 U.S. at 505, 507 (1925) (*citing* Burnap v. United States, 252 U.S. 512 (1920)); United States v. Smith, 124 U.S. 525 (1888); United States v. Mouat, 124 U.S. 303 (1888).

To support this interpretation of the act, the Court emphasized three arguments: (1) the exclusion under the restrictive interpretation of many persons who would otherwise satisfy the language of the Espionage Act, which provided that the person to whom the warrant is issued shall be one "duly authorized to enforce or assist in enforcing any law of the United States"; (2) the use of similar phrases in various parts of the Volstead Act in circumstances that supported the broader construction; and (3) the negative implication of the provision in the Volstead Act that made it a misdemeanor for a prohibition agent to search a dwelling without a warrant.

39 Dumbra v. United States, 268 U.S. 435 (1925).

40 *Id.* at 441. The Court did criticize the agents' failure to disclose to the magistrate that the defendants had a permit to manufacture wines for nonbeverage purposes. *Id.* at 438.

41 Agnello v. United States, 269 U.S. 20, 30–31 (1925). The evidence seized in the overturned search was relevant to the guilt of only one of the four defendants. 269 U.S. at 35–36.

42 *Id.* at 32, *citing* Boyd v. United States, 116 U.S. 616, 624 *et seq.* (1880); Weeks v. United States, 232 U.S. 383, 393 (1914); Silverthorne Lumber Co. v. United States, 251 U.S. 385, 391 (1919); Gouled v. United States, 255 U.S. 298, 308 (1921); *see also id.* at 44 ("Save in certain cases as incident to arrest, there is no sanction in the decisions of the courts, Federal or state, for the search of a private dwelling house without a warrant."). For a criticism of the rule, see Comment, The Effect of the Agnello Case on "Incidental" Searches and Seizures, 35 Yale L.J. 612, 618 (1926).

43 Weeks v. United States, 232 U.S. 383, 398 (1914); National Safe Dep. Co. v. Stead, 232 U.S. 58, 71 (1914); *see also* Twining v. New Jersey, 211 U.S. 78 (1908); Ohio *ex rel.* Lloyd v. Dollison, 194 U.S. 445, 447 (1904).

44 Weeks v. United States, 232 U.S. at 386 (1914); Burdeau v. McDowell, 256 U.S. 265 (1921). Felix Frankfurter was apparently the first to coin the "silver platter" phrase. See Lustig v. United States, 338 U.S. 74 78 (1949).

45 E.g., In re Schuetze, 299 F. 827 (W.D.N.Y. 1924); United States v. Falloco, 277 F. 75 (W.D. Mo. 1922); *cf.* United States v. Bush, 269 F. 455 (W.D.N.Y. 1920) (arrest by city police does not preclude inquiry into prior search conducted by federal agents). *But see* Comment, *supra* note 3, at 538–39 (1927) (summary of cases refusing to find joint action).

46 Center v. United States, 267 U.S. 575 (1925). For a brief description of the facts in *Center*, see Gambino v. United States, 275 U.S. 310, 317 (1927).

47 Byars v. United States, 273 U.S. 28, 30–32 (1927). The Eighth Circuit affirmed Byars's conviction. 4 F.2d 507 (8th Cir. 1925), *rev'd*, 273 U.S. 28 (1927). The court acknowledged that the warrant would have been invalid if evaluated by federal standards. *Id.; accord*, 273 U.S. at 29. Nonetheless, it admitted into evidence the stamps that were seized on the ground that the Fourth Amendment did not apply to searches by non-federal investigators. According to the court of appeals, the underlying rule was clear: "[I]n order that the government may be bound by the action of the state officers, the search must have been initiated by government officers or government officers must have so far participated in that search as to make it in effect a federal undertaking." 4 F.2d at 508. Applying that rule in Byars, the court found insufficient federal involvement since state officers planned the raid without the assistance or knowledge of the federal prohibition agent, and the expedition was brought to the federal agent's notice only when it was about to start. Id.

48 Id. at 32–33 (emphasis in original).

49 Id. at 29. On use of counterfeit bonding stamps, see H. Asbury, supra note 30, at 274–75.

50 1923 N.Y. Laws c. 871; see D. Kyvig, supra note 21, at 56–57.

51 275 U.S. at 314–16; see also Comment, Prohibition Searches by New York State Police, 37 Yale L.J. 784, 785 (1928) ("[A]lthough the [New York] enforcement [statute] has been repealed, the United States attorneys have generally based their prosecutions upon evidence secured by local police.").

52 275 U.S. at 315, 317. The Court declined to determine "[w]hether the laws of the state actually imposed on the troopers the duty of aiding the Federal officials in the enforcement of the . . . Act." Id. at 317.

53 See text accompanying notes 21–27 supra.

54 Gambino v. United States, 275 U.S. 310 (1927), Transcript of Record, at 19.

55 274 U.S. 559 (1927).

56 Id. at 562.

57 Id. at 563.

58 275 U.S. 192 (1927).

59 Id. at 193–94.

60 Id. at 195–96. Adams v. New York, 192 U.S. 585 (1904), had implicitly accepted such an "incidental to warrant execution" exception, but Marron dismissed Adams as "a prosecution in a state court" that "involved no search or seizure under a law, or by an officer, of the United States." 275 U.S. at 197.

61 27 U.S.C.A. § 39 (1927); 18 U.S.C. §§ 611–31, 633 (1932 ed.).

62 275 U.S. at 196.

63 Id. at 198–99.

64 277 U.S. 438 (1928). For a harsh critique of the Olmstead decision, see Black, An Ill-Starred Prohibition Case: Olmstead v. United States, 18 Georgetown L.J. 120 (1930), reprinted in F. Black, supra note 25, at 79.

65 N. Clark, The Dry Years: Prohibition and Social Change in Washington 161 (1965). The factual summary in the text is derived from Clark's account as well as the Court's opinion and the record and briefs filed in the Supreme Court.

66 According to Olmstead, the wiretapper had originally tried to sell him a transcript of the taped conversations for ten thousand dollars. *Id.* at 168.

67 Wash. Comp. Stat. §§ 2616–18 (1922).

68 While serving his prison term, Olmstead embraced the Christian Science faith and became convinced "that liquor [was] bad for man and society." Clark, *supra* note 65, at 218.

69 19 F.2d 842 (9th Cir. 1927). The majority in the court of appeals defined the purpose of the Fourth Amendment as preventing "the invasion of homes and offices and the seizure of incriminating evidence found therein." *Id.* at 847. Without addressing the question of whether tapping telephone wires is "an unethical intrusion upon the privacy of persons who are suspected of crime," the court concluded that "it is not an act which comes within the letter of the prohibition of constitutional provisions." *Id.* Evidence obtained by wiretaps was thus indistinguishable, the court said, from secret observation or eavesdropping.

Judge Rodkin dissented. *Id.* at 848–50. He argued that the chief purpose of the Fourth and Fifth Amendments was to protect "the individual in his liberty and in the privacies of life." *Id.* at 849. The proper case for analogy was *Jackson*, for "[a] person using the telegraph or telephone [was] not broadcasting to the world," but was sealing his conversation "from the public as completely as . . . the instrumentalities employed will permit." *Id.* at 850. Thus, to further the purpose of the Fourth Amendment, he interpreted it to deny a "federal officer or federal agent . . . a right to take [a person's] message from the wires, in order that it may be used against him." *Id.*

70 *See* Green v. United States, 19 F.2d 850 (9th Cir. 1927), *rev'd*, 277 U.S. 438 (1928).

71 275 U.S. 557 (1927); 276 U.S. 609 (1928). The grant of certiorari was limited "to the question whether the use of evidence of private telephone conversations between the defendants and others, intercepted by means of wire tapping, is a violation of the Fourth and Fifth Amendments, and, therefore, not permissible in the federal courts." *Id.* at 609–10.

72 277 U.S. at 466. The chief justice also rejected the suggestion that the Court should fashion a nonconstitutional rule excluding the evidence because the wiretaps had violated state law. "The common law rule," he noted, "is that the admissibility of evidence is not affected by the illegality of the means by which it was obtained." *Id.* at 467. *Weeks*'s exclusionary rule was a narrow exception to that rule "required by constitutional limitations." *Id.* Since the constitutional limitations were inapplicable in *Olmstead*, "[t]he common law rule must apply." *Id.* at 468.

73 *Id.* at 463–65.

74 The other three dissenters were Justices Holmes, *id.* at 469; Butler, *id.* at 485; and Stone, *id.* at 488. Justice Holmes advocated relying solely on nonconstitutional grounds, while Justice Butler confined himself to the constitutional issue. Justice Stone's opinion is a single-paragraph justification for the Court's authority to consider the nonconstitutional issue; he also joined the dissents of both Brandeis and Holmes.

75 *Id.* at 471–85 (Brandeis, J., dissenting); *see generally* Warren and Brandeis, The Right to Privacy, 4 Harv. L. Rev. 193 (1890).

76 J. Rae, *The American Automobile,* at 48–52, 56–91, 238 (Tables 6 and 7); *see also* D. Boorstin, *The Americans: The Democratic Experience* 422–27, 546–55 (1973); J. Flink, *America Adopts the Automobile, 1895–1910,* at 55–60 (1970); J. Rae, *The Road and the Car in American Life* 40–59 (1971).

77 *See, e.g.,* Federal Highway Act of 1921, 42 Stat. 212; Road Aid Act of 1916, 39 Stat. 355; J. Flink, *supra* note 76, at 165–91 (summary of state regulation of registration, licensing, and speed); Chamberlin, Compulsory Insurance of Automobiles, 12 A.B.A. J. 49 (1926); *See, e.g.,* Brown, The Status of the Automobile, 17 Yale L.J. 233 (1908); Chamberlin, Automobiles and Vicarious Liability, 10 A.B.A. J. 788 (1924); Falkner, The Doctrine of Joint Adventurer in Automobile Law, 1 Wash. L. Rev. 113 (1925); McCabe, The Duty of an Automobile Owner to a Gratuitous Guest, 6 Notre Dame Law. 300 (1931); Note, The Family Car Doctrine, 15 Geo. L.J. 471 (1927). An interesting interplay between statutory and judicial developments occurred with respect to state court jurisdiction. Legislatures passed new "long-arm" statutes, and the Supreme Court modified the restraints of the Due Process Clause to accommodate them. *See generally* Murchison, Jurisdiction over Persons, Things, and Status, 41 La. L. Rev. 1053, 1061–64 (1981).

78 *E.g.,* Boyd v. United States, 286 F. 930 (4th Cir. 1923); Lambert v. United States, 282 F. 413 (9th Cir. 1922); United States v. Rembert, 284 F. 996 (S.D. Tex. 1922). For a particularly tolerant lower court decision, see United States v. Bateman, 278 F. 231, 235 (S.D. Cal. 1922) ("In view of the impossibility of procuring warrants for the search of automobiles suspected of transporting intoxicating liquors, the officers have a right, without a warrant, to stop and search automobiles, and *the finding of liquor therein justifies the search.*") (emphasis added).

79 3 *ALI Commentaries, supra* note 28, at 40.

80 *See* 45 Stat. 1446 (1929) (Jones Act); 27 U.S.C.A. § 46 (1927) (Section 29 of Title II of the Volstead Act).

81 *See* F. Black, *supra* note 25, at 45–47.

82 Fraenkel, Recent Developments in the Law of Search and Seizure, 13 Minn. L. Rev. 1 (1928); *see also* Atkinson, Mich. L. Rev. *supra* note 4, at

748–49; Carroll, The Search and Seizure Provisions of the Federal and State Constitutions, 10 Va. L. Rev. 124 (1923); Roberts, Does the Search and Seizure Clause Hinder the Proper Administration of Criminal Justice, 5 Wis. L. Rev. 195 (1929).

83 Comment, *supra* note 11, at 537 n.2.

84 Johnson, Some Constitutional Aspects of Prohibition Enforcement, 97 Cent. L.J. 113, 122–23 (1924). He argued that repeal of the Fourth Amendment would still leave a minimum common law protection against unreasonable searches and seizures.

85 *But see* Milam v. United States, 296 F. 629, 631 (4th Cir. 1924) ("The obligation to enforce the Eighteenth Amendment is no less solemn than that to give effect to the Fourth and Fifth Amendments. The Courts are therefore under the duty of deciding what is an unreasonable search of motor cars, in light of the mandate of the Constitution that intoxicating liquors shall not be manufactured, sold, or transported for beverage purposes."); United States v. Bateman, 278 F. 231, 233 (S.D. Cal. 1922) ("The Eighteenth Amendment must be considered in determining the question of what is an unreasonable search and seizure as prescribed by the Fourth Amendment. If there were no Eighteenth Amendment to the Constitution to be enforced, the court might have an entirely different idea of what is an unreasonable search or seizure as disclosed in this case.").

86 *See, e.g.,* Atkinson, Mich. L. Rev. *supra* note 4, at 749: "The Eighteenth Amendment prohibits the manufacture, transportation and sale of liquor. Does this mean that in case that other provisions of the Constitution come in the way of efficient enforcement of the prohibition amendment, they must fall so far as liquor offenses are concerned? Clearly not. . . . As a matter of fact, it seems too clear for argument that the Eighteenth Amendment is merely an enlargement of the federal power to deal with liquor offenses and never intended to alter in any way the constitutional safeguards and personal guarantees."

87 Comment, *supra* note 11, at 537 (footnotes omitted).

88 F. Black, *supra* note 25 at 15.

4 The Fourth Amendment, 1930–1933: Refinement and Discovery

1 D. Kyvig, *Repealing National Prohibition* 34 (1979).

2 Go-Bart Imp. Co. v. United States, 282 U.S. 344, 359 (1931).

3 *Id.* at 351 (1931).

4 *Id.* at 356–58. The court also noted that no objection was made to the searches of the persons of those arrested. *Id.* at 356.

5 *Id.* at 358.

6 Husty v. United States, 282 U.S. 694 (1931).

7 *Id.* at 700.

8 Pub. L. No. 70–899, 45 Stat. 1446 (1929).

9 282 U.S. at 703.

10 United States v. Lefkowitz, 285 U.S. 452 (1932).

11 *Id.* at 458–60. For a detailed listing of the items, *see id.* at 459 n.1, 460 nn.2, 3.

12 *Id.* at 463–65.

13 *Id.* at 465–67.

14 Taylor v. United States, 286 U.S. 1, 5–6 (1932).

15 *Id.* at 6. The garage, which the Court described as "a small metal building" was located "on the corner of a city lot and adjacent to the dwelling in which . . . Taylor lived." *Id.* at 5.

16 *Id.* at 6. The court also held the incident-to-arrest exception inapplicable because the garage was empty when the agents entered it. *Id.*

17 287 U.S. 124 (1932).

18 *Id.* at 128. For a contemporaneous criticism of this decision, see Note, The Probable Cause Requirement for Search Warrants, 46 Harv. L. Rev. 1307, 1310–11 (1933).

19 27 U.S.C.A. 39 (1927) (Section 25 of Title II of the Volstead Act).

20 287 U.S. at 127.

21 56 F.2d 779 (6th Cir.), rev'd, 287 U.S. 124 (1932). The court of appeals relied on one of its earlier precedents which held that the act's provision allowing dwellings to be searched for sale offenses only was "satisfied by an affidavit establishing probable cause for the charge that the premises are being used for the prosecution of commercial sales, involving not only manufacture, but storage, delivery to purchasers, the filling of orders, and, generally, the maintenance of the premises to be searched as a headquarters for supervising a selling business." *Id.* at 781 (*citing* Kasprowicz v. United States, 20 F.2d 506 (6th Cir. 1927)). In adopting this rationale for its decision, the court of appeals deliberately avoided "the question whether the manufacture of intoxicating liquor in large quantities in a dwelling house may be of such commercial character as to justify a search warrant on the theory that the dwelling is used in part for a business purpose." 56 F.2d at 781.

Applying the *Kasprowicz* standard, the court concluded that the *Grau* affidavit was sufficient to establish probable cause to believe that the dwelling was "being used for the unlawful sale of intoxicating liquor." *Id.* "One does not," the court noted, "manufacture liquor for his own use in such quantities as to require wholesale deliveries of . . . [the] ingredients of mash"; nor does whiskey manufactured for personal use ordinarily involve shipment "from the premises in cans, by automobile or truck loads" or the return of cans for refilling. *Id.*

22 286 U.S. 539 (1932). Among the decisions that conflicted with Grau were Simmons v. United States, 18 F.2d 85 (8th Cir. 1927); Giles v. United States, 284 F. 208 (1st Cir. 1922). *See* 287 U.S. at 126 n.2.

23 287 U.S. at 128. The Court conveniently ignored the Volstead Act's own direction that its provisions were to be liberally construed. 27 U.S.C.A. § 12 (1927) (Section 3 of Title II of the Act).

24 *Id.* at 128–29. Justice Roberts also asserted, in dictum, that the warrant had to be supported by evidence "competent in the trial of the offense before a jury." *Id.* at 128.

25 Sgro v. United States, 287 U.S. 206, 210–11 (1932). The ten-day limit was included in Section 11 of Title XI of the Espionage Act, 40 Stat. 229 (1917), that was incorporated into the Volstead Act by reference. 27 U.S.C.A. § 11 (1927). For a summary of the other statutory requirements that had to be satisfied in a "new" proceeding, *see* 287 U.S. at 209 n.1.

26 Nathanson v. United States, 290 U.S. 41, 44–47 (1933). The statutory requirement did not apply in *Nathanson* because the search was conducted by a customs agent pursuant to a warrant issued by a state judge. *Id.* at 44–45. The customs agent had, however, received his information "from prohibition officials and from an unnamed informer." 63 F.2d 937 (3d Cir. 1933).

27 A. Cornelius, *Law of Search and Seizure* 111 (2d ed. 1930). He claimed that the revised version incorporated "fifty late decisions by the United States Supreme Court, in which search and seizure are involved," but he did not provide a list of those decisions.

28 24 *Third Decennial Edition of the American Digest* 1157 (1929); 20 *Second Decennial Edition of the American Digest* 849 (1922); 8 *(First) Decennial Edition of the American Digest* 30 (1910); 43 *Century Edition of the American Digest* 2803 (1903).

29 47 *American Jurisprudence* 501–51 (1943); 24 *Ruling Case Law* 699–728 (1919).

30 56 *Corpus Juris* 1148–1262 (1932); 35 *Cyclopedia of Law and Practice* 1263–77 (1903).

31 *See* Weeks v. United States, 232 U.S. 383, 389–90 (1914); Boyd v. United States, 116 U.S. 625–30 (1886); A. Cornelius, *supra* note 27, at 12–15; Andrews, Historical Survey of the Law of Searches and Seizures, 34 Law Notes 42, 42–46 (1930); Wood, The Scope of the Constitutional Immunity against Search and Seizure, 34 W. Va. L.Q. 1, 1–10 (1927–28).

32 U.S. Const. amend. IV: "The right of the people to be secure *in their persons, houses, papers, and effects*, against unreasonable searches and seizures, shall not be violated. . . ." (emphasis added).

33 *See* Grau v. United States 287 U.S. 124 (1932); Amos v. United States, 255 U.S. 313 (1921).

34 Agnello v. United States, 269 U.S. at 20, 30 (1925).

35 *Compare* United States v. Lefkowitz, 285 U.S. 452 (1932), *and* Go-Bart Imp. Co. v. United States, 282 U.S. 344 (1931), *with* United States v. Marron, 275 U.S. 192 (1927).

36 *E.g.,* United States v. Lefkowitz, 285 U.S. 452, 464 (1932). The most consistent exponent of the privacy rationale was Justice Brandeis. *See* Olmstead v. United States, 277 U.S. 438, 478–79 (1928) (Brandeis, J., dissenting).

37 *E.g.,* Atkinson, *Prohibition and the Doctrine of the Weeks Case,* 23 Mich. L. Rev. 748, 757–59 (1927); Wood, *supra* note 31, at 137.

38 *See, e.g.,* Katz v. United States, 389 U.S. 347 (1967).

39 *See* Amos v. United States, 255 U.S. 313 (1921); *cf.* Grau v. United States, 287 U.S. 124 (1932) (dwelling did not lose the special protection to which it was entitled under the Volstead Act merely because intoxicating liquor was manufactured in it). *But see* Agnello v. United States, 269 U.S. 20 (1925) (warrantless searches of houses that are the sites of lawful arrests are lawful) (dictum).

40 Olmstead v. United States, 277 U.S. 438, 483 n.15 (1928) (Brandeis, J., dissenting); Olmstead v. United States, Brief for the Government, at 41; *see also* N. Clark, *The Dry Years: Prohibition and Social Change in Washington* 174 (1965); *cf.* M. Willebrandt, *The Inside of Prohibition* 231 (1929) (statement of opposition to wiretapping by Assistant Attorney General in charge of prohibition cases). A 1927 report submitted to Congress had expressed general disapproval of illegal conduct by prohibition agents, S. Doc. 198, 69th Cong., 2d Sess., pt. 1, at IV, 15; pt. 2, at 2; and wiretapping was illegal in most states. *See* Olmstead v. United States, Brief for Amicus Curia, at 11.

41 N. Clark, *supra* note 40, at 176; M. Willebrandt, *supra* note 40, at 232.

42 277 U.S. at 455–57; *see also* M. Willebrandt, *supra* note 40, at 233–36.

43 *N.Y. Times,* May 27, 1930, at 1, col. 7.

44 232 U.S. at 392.

45 United States v. Lefkowitz, 285 U.S. 452 (1932); Go-Bart Importing Co. v. United States, 282 U.S. 344 (1931); United States v. Marron, 275 U.S. 192 (1927); United States v. Lee, 274 U.S. 559 (1927); Agnello v. United States, 269 U.S. 20 (1925).

46 For an index listing that covers automobile search cases from the prohibition era, see Federal Digest, *Intoxicating Liquor* 249(g) (1941). For some extreme examples of overzealous enforcement, see F. Black, *Ill-Starred Prohibition Cases* 52–57 (1931).

47 *See* 267 U.S. at 171–74 (McReynolds, J., dissenting); *see also* F. Black, *supra* note 46, at 45–47; H. McBain, *Prohibition: Legal and Illegal* 85–86 (1928).

48 *See generally* H. Asbury, *The Great Illusion: An Informal History of Prohibition* 241–55 (1950); C. Merz, *The Dry Decade.* 113–15 (1931); A. Sinclair, *Prohibition: The Era of Excess* 198–99 (1962). For a very optimistic assessment of the government's success in routing Rum Row, *see* M. Willebrandt, *supra* note 40, at 220–30; *see also* R. Haynes, *Prohibition Inside Out* 69–86 (1923).

49 275 U.S. at 193–94 ("There were six or seven rooms containing slot machines, an ice box, tables, chairs, and a cash register. The evidence shows that the place was used for retailing and drinking intoxicating liquor. About a dozen men and women were there, and some of them were being furnished intoxicating liquors."); *see also* Marron v. United States, 8 F.2d 251, 253 (9th Cir. 1925).

50 Gambino v. United States, Transcript of Record, at 19.

51 275 U.S. at 195.

52 Taylor involved the seizure of 122 cases of whiskey, 286 U.S. at 5; and the evidence obtained in both *Go-Bart,* 282 U.S. at 351, and *Lefkowitz,* 285 U.S. at 462–63, suggested ongoing businesses of soliciting and filling orders for intoxicating liquors.

53 286 U.S. at 5.

54 *See Coke on Littleton* § 138 (1832 ed.) ("[F]or reason is the life of the law, nay the common law itself is nothing but reason, which is to be understood of an artificial perfection of reason, gotten by long study, observation, and experience, and not of every man's natural reason.").

55 *See* A. Mason, *The Supreme Court from Taft to Warren* 15–16, 50 (1968 ed.); 1 W. Swindler, *Court and Constitution in the Twentieth Century* 224–25 (1969); 2 *id.* at 37–38 (1970).

56 Comment, Prohibition Searches by New York State Police, 37 Yale L.J. 784, 789 (1928).

57 Mapp v. Ohio, 367 U.S. 343 (1961).

58 *E.g.,* Fowler v. United States, 62 F.2d 656 (7th Cir. 1932), *discussed in* Solomon, Regulating the Regulators: Prohibition Enforcement in the Seventh Circuit, in *Law, Alcohol, and Order: Perspectives on National Prohibition* 81, 89–90 (D. Kyvig ed., 1985); Crank v. United States, 61 F.2d 981 (8th Cir. 1932); Hall v. United States, 41 F.2d 54 (9th Cir. 1930); United States v. De Bousi, 32 F.2d 902 (W.D. Mass. 1929).

59 *E.g.,* Aldridge v. United States, 67 F.2d 956 (10th Cir. 1933); United States v. Myers, 46 F.2d 317 (M.D. Pa. 1931); United States v. Walker, 41 F.2d 538 (E.D. Tenn. 1930).

60 Large-scale bootleggers often had much larger quantities of stamps. *See* H. Asbury, *supra* note 48, at 275 (describing the seizure of "more than eight hundred thousand liquor labels and almost one hundred thousand internal revenue stamps" as "not an especially large haul").

61 *See* A. Sinclair, *supra* note 48, at 196. As late as 1930, only four states had repealed their enforcement statutes.

62 *See* Crank v. United States, 61 F.2d 981 (8th Cir. 1932); Hall v. United States, 41 F.2d 54 (9th Cir. 1930); United States v. De Bousi, 32 F.2d 902 (W.D. Mass. 1929).

63 *E.g.*, Aldridge v. United States, 67 F.2d 956 (10th Cir. 1933); United States v. Walker, 41 F.2d 538 (E.D. Tenn. 1930); United States v. One Ox-5 American Eagle Airplane, 38 F.2d 106 (W.D. Wash. 1930). *But see* Miller v. United States, 50 F.2d 505 (3d Cir. 1930) (evidence seized by state officers in warrantless search of building held admissible).

64 Locke v. United States, 11 U.S. (7 Cranch) 339, 348 (1813).

65 *See* Note, *supra* note 18, at 1308.

66 267 U.S. at 161, *quoting* Stacey v. Emery, 97 U.S. (7 Otto) 642, 645 (1879).

67 Dumbra v. United States, 268 U.S. 435 (1925); Steele v. United States, 267 U.S. 498 (1925); Carroll v. United States, 267 U.S. 132 (1925).

68 Gambino v. United States, 275 U.S. 310 (1927).

69 Grau v. United States, 287 U.S. 124 (1932).

70 Husty v. United States, 282 U.S. 694 (1931).

71 The procedural requirements of the Espionage Act, 40 Stat. 228 (1917), were incorporated by reference. 27 U.S.C.A. § 11 (1927) (Section 2 of Title II of the Volstead Act); *see also id.* § 39 (Section 25 of Title II allowing private dwellings to be searched only when they are used in part for business purposes).

72 Taylor v. United States, 286 U.S. 1 (1932).

73 Byars v. United States, 273 U.S. 28, 29 (1927); *see* chapter 3, notes 47–49 *supra* and accompanying text.

74 Grau v. United States, 287 U.S. 124, 128 (1932); *see* notes 17–24 *supra* and accompanying text.

75 Sgro v. United States, 287 U.S. 206, 211 (1932); *see* note 25 *supra* and accompanying text.

76 Nathanson v. United States, 290 U.S. 41, 47 (1933); *see* note 26 *supra* and accompanying text.

77 Fraenkel, Recent Developments in the Law of Search and Seizure, 13 Minn. L. Rev. 1 (1928); *see also*, Atkinson, *supra* note 37, at 748–49; Carroll, The Search and Seizure Provisions of the Federal and State Constitutions, 10 Va. L. Rev. 124 (1923); Roberts, Does the Search and Seizure Clause Hinder the Proper Administration of Criminal Justice, 5 Wis. L. Rev. 195 (1929).

78 Andrews, *supra* note 31, at 46; Fraenkel, *supra* note 77, at 2–6; Comment, The Meaning of the Federal Rule on Evidence Illegally Obtained, 36 Yale L.J. 537, 537 n.2 (1927).

79 Mapp v. Ohio, 367 U.S. 343 (1961).

80 Dumbra v. United States, 268 U.S. 435 (1925); Steele v. United States, 267 U.S. 505 (1925); Steele v. United States 267 U.S. 498 (1925); Carroll v. United States, 267 U.S. 132 (1925); Hester v. United States, 265 U.S. 57 (1924).

81 Olmstead v. United States, 277 U.S. 438 (1928); Gambino v. United States, 275 U.S. 310 (1927); United States v. Marron, 275 U.S. 192 (1927); United States v. Lee, 274 U.S. 559 (1927); Byars v. United States, 273 U.S. 28 (1927); cf. Agnello v. United States, 269 U.S. 20 (1925) (upholding search conducted incident to arrest in a case involving a violation of the Harrison Anti-Narcotic Drug Act).

82 Nathanson v. United States, 290 U.S. 41 (1933); Sgro v. United States, 287 U.S. 206 (1932); Grau v. United States, 287 U.S. 124 (1932); Taylor v. United States, 286 U.S. 1 (1932); United States v. Lefkowitz, 285 U.S. 452 (1932); Go-Bart Imp. Co. v. United States, 282 U.S. 344 (1931). But see Husty v. United States, 282 U.S. 694 (1931).

83 See generally Note, Formalism, Legal Realism, and Constitutionally Protected Privacy under the Fourth and Fifth Amendments, 90 Harv. L. Rev. 945 (1977).

84 See e.g., Roberts, supra note 77.

85 Comment, Enforcing Prohibition under the Federal Rule on Unreasonable Searches, 36 Yale L.J. 988 (1927).

86 See F. Black, supra note 46, at 142–45. For other restrictive decisions associated with the World War 1 and its aftermath, see Gilbert v. Minnesota, 254 U.S. 325 (1920); Abrams v. United States, 250 U.S. 515 (1919); Schenck v. United States, 249 U.S. 47 (1919).

87 See R. Bonnie and C. Whitebread, The Marihuana Conviction: A History of Marihuana Prohibition in the United States 8–31 (1974).

88 See A. Mason, The Supreme Court from Taft to Warren 15–16, 50 (1968); 2 id. at 37–38; G. White, The American Judicial Tradition 214 (2d ed. 1985).

89 Taylor involved the seizure of 122 cases of whiskey, 286 U.S. 1, 5 (1932); the evidence obtained in both Go-Bart Importing Co. v. United States, 282 U.S. 344, 351 (1932), and United States v. Lefkowitz, 285 U.S. 452, 462–63 (1932), suggested ongoing businesses of soliciting and filling orders for intoxicating liquors; and the search in Sgro v. United States, 287 U.S. 206 (1932) uncovered a pint of gin and three and one-half barrels of beer after the information to support the search was obtained in a prior purchase by the prohibition agent. Transcript of Record, at 2–3, 17.

90 Olmstead v. United States, 277 U.S. 438 (1928); Steele v. United States 267 U.S. 498 (1925); Carroll v. United States, 267 U.S. 132 (1925).

91 McReynolds authored three; Nathanson v. United States, 290 U.S. 41 (1933); Sgro v. United States, 287 U.S. 206 (1932); Taylor v. United States, 286 U.S. 1 (1932); Butler, two: United States v. Lefkowitz, 285 U.S.

452 (1932); Go-Bart Importing Co. v. United States, 282 U.S. 344 (1931); and Roberts and Stone, one each: Grau v. United States 287 U.S. 124 (1932) (Roberts); Husty v. United States, 282 U.S. 694 (1931) (Stone).

5   Double Jeopardy: Crystallization of an Enduring Exception

1 U.S. Const. amend. V: "[N]or shall any person be subject for the same offense to be twice put in jeopardy of life or limb." Sigler, A History of Double Jeopardy, 7 Am. J.L. Hist. 283 (1963), provides an overview of the historical antecedents for the Fifth Amendment's Double Jeopardy Clause and also describes the events leading to its inclusion in the Bill of Rights. For a modern attempt to articulate a comprehensive theory for analyzing double jeopardy problems, see Westen & Drubel, Toward a General Theory of Double Jeopardy, 1978 Sup. Ct. Rev. 81.

2 See Abbate v. United States, 359 U.S. 187 (1959); Bartkus v. United States, 359 U.S. 121 (1959); cf. Heath v. Alabama, 106 S. Ct. 433 (1985) (successive prosecutions by two states); United States v. Wheeler, 435 U.S. 313 (1978) (successive prosecutions by an Indian tribe and federal court). For a critique of modern adherence to the dual sovereignty exception, see Murchison, The Dual Sovereignty Exception to Double Jeopardy, 14 N.Y.U. Rev. L. & Soc. Change 383 (1986).

3 See, e.g., United States v. Oppenheimer, 282 U.S. 85 (1916) (judgment dismissing an indictment as barred by the statute of limitations precludes second prosecution under a new indictment for the same offense); Keel v. Montana, 213 U.S. 135 (1909) (retrial after dismissal of a deadlocked jury does not constitute double jeopardy); McDonald v. Massachusetts, 180 U.S. 311 (1901) (imposing a heavier punishment for recidivist offenders does not violate double jeopardy); In re Chapman, 166 U.S. 661 (1897) (conduct may be punished both as an indictable misdemeanor and a contempt of Congress); cf. Shevlin-Carpenter Co. v. Minnesota, 218 U.S. 57 (1911) (making the cutting of timber on state lands a crime as well as imposing double damages in civil suit does not violate the prohibition against double jeopardy).

4 United States v. Furlong, 18 U.S. (5 Wheat.) 184 (1820).

5 Id. at 196–97.

6 Id. at 197–98.

7 Nielsen v. Oregon, 212 U.S. 315 (1909).

8 Id. at 320.

9 Dowling, Concurrent Power under the Eighteenth Amendment, 6 Minn. L. Rev. 447, 457 (1922).

10 Gibbons v. Ogden, 22 U.S. (9 Wheat.) 1, 209–10 (1824); see also id. at 222–39 (concurring opinion of Johnson, J.).

11 *See, e.g.,* Schollenberger v. Pennsylvania, 171 U.S. 1 (1898); Wabash, St. L. & P. Ry. v. Illinois, 118 U.S. 557 (1886).

12 Leisy v. Hardin, 135 U.S. 100 (1890) (prior to passage of Webb-Kenyon Act, Commerce Clause of the Constitution forbade states from banning shipments of liquor into the state so long as the liquor remained within its original package); *see generally* text accompanying notes 36–41 in chapter 1.

13 For summaries of the nineteenth-century decisions, *see* G. Gunther, *Cases and Materials on Constitutional Law* 264–72 (10th ed. 1980); W. Lockhart, Y. Kamisar, & J. Choper, *Constitutional Law: Cases-Comments-Questions* 277–86 (5th ed. 1980).

14 U.S. Const. art. VI, cl. 2.

15 Gibbons v. Ogden, 22 U.S. (9 Wheat.) 1 (1824).

16 Southern Ry. Co. v. Railroad Comm'n, 236 U.S. 439 (1915).

17 Act of Mar. 2, 1893, 52d Cong., 2d Sess., 27 Stat. 531.

18 Crossley v. California, 168 U.S. 640, 641 (1898).

19 Cross v. North Carolina, 132 U.S. 131 (1889).

20 46 U.S. (5 How.) 410 (1847).

21 U.S. Const. art. I, § 8, cl. 5, 6.

22 Gilbert v. Minnesota, 254 U.S. 325 (1920).

23 U.S. Const. art. I, § 8, cl. 11; *cf. id.,* cl. 12, 13 (powers to raise and to support armies and to provide and to maintain a navy).

24 46 U.S. (5 How.) at 434–35.

25 United States v. Marigold, 50 U.S. (9 How.) 560 (1850).

26 *Id.* at 568–69.

27 S.J. Res. 17, 40 Stat. 1050 (1917).

28 S. Rep. No. 52, 65th Cong., 1st Sess. 1 (1917).

29 The Commerce Clause cases suggested that this might be the case. *See* notes 10–13 *supra* and accompanying text. For an objection to the proposed change on this ground, *see* H. Rep. No. 211, 65th Cong., 1st Sess. 4–5 (Part I) (1918).

30 S. Rep. No. 52, 65th Cong., 1st Sess. 4–5 (1917) ("National law, enacted under an amended Constitution, could prohibit importation and sale, and *in concurrence with like legislation by the States . . .,* could soon put an end to the traffic [in intoxicating liquor].") (emphasis added).

31 55 Cong. Rec. 5640, 5552 (1917) (statements of Senator Sheppard).

32 *Id.* at 5666.

33 *Id.* at 5723.

34 H. Rep. No. 211, 65th Cong., 2d Sess. 1–2 (1917) (Part I). *See* A. Sinclair, *Prohibition: The Era of Excess* 161 (1962).

35 *But see* H. Rep. No. 211, 65th Cong., 2d Sess. 4–5 (Part 3) (minority views of Representatives Gard and Steele arguing that the committee

proposal would abrogate state police powers with respect to intoxicating liquor).

36 56 Cong. Rec. 423 (1917).

37 *Id.* at 423, 425.

38 *Id.* at 424.

39 *Id.* Earlier in the same discussion he gave the following explanation of the nature of concurrent jurisdiction:

> If the State should get jurisdiction first, the State jurisdiction would apply and if the [Federal] Government should get jurisdiction first, the [Federal] jurisdiction would apply. Both would be supreme, and it would only be a question as to who got the offender first.

Id.

40 *Id.* at 461–70.

41 *Id.* at 478.

42 H. Rep. No. 91, 66th Cong., 1st Sess. (1919); S. Rep. No. 151, 66th Cong., 1st Sess. (1919).

43 58 Cong. Rec. 2429 (1919) (statement of Representative Steele); *see also* H. Rep. No. 91, 66th Cong., 1st Sess. (1919) (Part III) (minority report), *reprinted at* 58 Cong. Rec. 2294–96 (1919).

44 253 U.S. 350, 385 (1920).

45 *Id.* at 385–88.

46 *Id.* at 387.

47 State v. Smith, 101 Or. 127, 199 P. 194 (1921).

48 United States v. Peterson, 268 F. 864 (W.D. Wash. 1921), *rev'd sub nom.* United States v. Lanza, 260 U.S. 377 (1922).

49 United States v. McCann, 281 F. 880 (D. Conn. 1922); United States v. Ratzgczak, 275 F. 558 (D. Ohio 1921); United States v. Regan, 273 F. 727 (D.N.H. 1921); United States v. Boston, 273 F. 535 (D. Ala. 1921); United States v. Holt, 270 F. 639 (D.N.H. 1920).

50 Cooley v. State, 152 Ga. 469, 110 S.E. 449 (1922), *writ dismissed,* 260 U.S. 760 (1922); State v. Mosley, 122 S.C. 62, 114 S.E. 866 (1922); *cf.* Yoreman v. Commonwealth, 193 Ky. 536, 237 S.W. 6 (1922) (dictum); Ex parte Jancaary, 295 Mo. 653, 246 S.W. 241 (1922).

51 Brief for Amicus Curiae, National Prohibition Cases, 253 U.S. 350 (1920), at 54–55.

52 United States v. Peterson, 268 F. 864, 866 (W.D. Wash. 1921), *rev'd sub nom.* United States v. Lanza, 260 U.S. 377 (1922). Some of the *Peterson* defendants had been convicted of violating municipal prohibition ordinances, but the *Peterson* court ruled that these prosecutions did not bar a subsequent prosecution under the Volstead Act. For a criticism for this distinction between state laws and municipal ordinances, *see* 1 Wis. L. Rev. 371 (1922).

53 260 U.S. 377 (1922).

54 *Id.* at 379–82.

55 *Id.* at 382–84.

56 260 U.S. at 385.

57 *See* Lanier, Prohibition and Double Jeopardy, 8 Va. L. Rev.(N.S.) 740 (1923); 8 Buff. L. Rev. 188 (1923).

58 *See* Carpenter, Double Jeopardy in Cases Coming under Both the Eighteenth Amendment and State Prohibition Laws, 2 Or. L. Rev. 124 (1923); Editorial, Double Jeopardy, 27 Law Notes 4 (1923); Editorial, Twice in Jeopardy, 9 Va. L. Rev. (N.S.) 53 (1923); Note, 6 Bi-Monthly L. Rev. 98 (1923); 23 Colum. L. Rev. 395 (1923).

59 Bronaugh, Double Punishment in Prohibition Cases, 26 Law Notes 187 (1923) (hereinafter cited as Bronaugh, Double Punishment). In a later article, Bronaugh modified his analysis by asserting that *Lanza* failed to follow "the long accepted rule or doctrine of criminal jurisprudence that all criminal laws or statutes must be construed strictly against the state and favorably to the citizen." Bronaugh, Further Discussion of Double Punishment in Prohibition Cases, 27 Law Notes 9, 10 (1923). But even in this second article, he was primarily critical of the results of *Lanza* rather than its analytical framework:

> But brushing aside all legal technicalities, it matters not one iota to the poor devil accused of crime whether he is twice put in jeopardy by two federal courts or by a state court and a federal court. The result to him is the same double—punishment. And the fact that his second conviction is by judicial construction given another name or effect does not help him or save him from twice paying the penalty for the same act. For in truth and verity he is twice punished for the same offense, though by the reverse application of technical rules of construction he may not have been twice in jeopardy. Call it what you will, it is repugnant to every idea of justice and repulsive to that belief in fairness embedded in the hearts and minds of a free-born people.

60 *Id.* Bronaugh, Double Punishment, *supra* note 58, at 187.

61 *N.Y. Times*, Jan. 9, 1923, at 23, col. 2.

62 272 U.S. 312 (1926).

63 *Id.* at 313–14.

64 150 La. 209, 103 So. 742 (1924).

65 272 U.S. at 317.

66 *Id.* at 314.

67 *Id.*

68 Potts, Unmerited Criticism of the Supreme Court, 12 St. Louis U. L. Rev. 119 (1927).

69 *Id.*; Note, Constitutional Law: Double Jeopardy: Double Liability, 12 Cornell L.Q. 212 (1927); Recent Cases, Criminal Law-Former Jeopardy-

Power of the State and the Federal Government to Prosecute, 7 B.U. L.
Rev. 57 (1927); Recent Cases, Intoxicating Liquors-Eighteenth Amend-
ment-Concurrent Power of Congress and the Several States, 11 Minn. L.
Rev. 173 (1927).

70 Note, supra note 69; B.U. L. Rev., supra note 69; see also H. McBain,
Prohibition Legal and Illegal 143–54 (1928).

71 B.U. L. Rev. supra note 69, at 58.

72 Note, supra note 69, at 213.

73 B.U. L. Rev., supra note 69, at 58.

74 See Literary Digest, Nov. 20, 1926, at 18 (quoting Columbus Dispatch, Chicago Daily News, Springfield Union, Newark News, Winston-
Salem Journal, Pittsburgh Gazette Times, and Indianapolis News).

75 Id. (quoting Baltimore Sun, St. Louis Post-Dispatch, Brooklyn
Eagle, and Providence News).

76 N.Y. Times, Nov. 3, 1926, at 22, cols. 3, 4.

77 The West Key Number for the dual sovereignty doctrine contains
only two federal cases for the period between the Hebert decision and the
end of the prohibition era. See 24 Fed. Dig., Criminal Law § 201, at 231–33
(1940). Both were district court decisions, and neither actually involved
successive prosecutions. One cited Lanza as authority to reject a defendant's claim that the indictment charging him with a non-prohibition
offense, embezzlement of the funds of a national bank, was insufficient to
protect him against the possibility of a subsequent state prosecution.
United States v. Frank, 4 F. Supp. 372, 374 (W.D. Pa. 1933). The other
cited Lanza as authority for rejecting the argument that issuance of a
permit under the Volstead Act to manufacture articles with an alcoholic
content precluded application of state prohibition law against the holder
of the federal permit, but the Third Circuit reversed the district court
judgment on appeal. Gerber v. Schofield, 43 F.2d 222, 224 (E.D. Pa.),
rev'd, 43 F.2d 225 (3d Cir. 1930). Moreover, even though the Supreme
Court cited Lanza and Hebert in several post-Hebert opinions rendered
during the prohibition era, see, e.g., Asbury Truck Co. v. Railroad
Comm'n, 287 U.S. 570 (1932), aff'g 52 F.2d 263 (S.D. Cal. 1931); McCormick & Co. v. Brown, 286 U.S. 131, 141 (1932); Westfall v. United States,
274 U.S. 256, 258 (1927); Van Oster v. Kansas, 272 U.S. 465, 469 (1926),
none of those cases involved multiple prosecutions, and the remaining
citations involved per curiam orders that refused to invalidate Louisiana
convictions that were contemporaneous to Hebert. See State v. Norris, 161
La. 988, 109 So. 787 (1926), writ dismissed, 274 U.S. 719 (1927); State v.
Long, 161 La. 250, 108 So. 471 (1926), dismissed for want of a substantial
federal question, 273 U.S. 653 (1927); State v. Breaux, 161 La. 368, 108 So.
773, aff'd, 273 U.S. 645 (1926).

78 The Decennial Digest lists a number of cases that verbally acknowl-

edged the dual sovereignty doctrine during the last years of the prohibition era. *See* 9 *Fourth Decennial Digest, 1926–36*, at 247–49 (1937). However, only four of those decisions allowed state prosecutions to proceed after a prior federal prosecution for the same type of offense, and two of the four were Louisiana decisions rendered almost contemporaneously with *Hebert. See* Winslett v. State, 117 So. 5 (Ala. 1928); Crouch v. Commonwealth, 238 Ky. 5, 36 S.W.2d 653 (1931); State v. Quebadeux, 162 La. 1060, 111 So. 421 (1927); State v. Breaux, 161 La. 368, 108 La. 773, *aff'd*, 273 U.S. 645 (1926). For the most part, the remainder of the decisions refused to permit subsequent state prosecutions, e.g., People v. Spitzer, 148 Misc. 97, 266 N.Y.S. 522 (1933); People v. Wade, 127 Misc. 593, 217 N.Y.S. 486 (App. Div.), *rev'g* 126 Misc. 762, 214 N.Y.S. 781 (City Mag. Ct. 1926); contained no suggestion of multiple prosecutions by federal and state governments, e.g., People v. Skinman, 122 Ohio St. 522, 172 N.E. 367 (1930); *cf.*, People v. Papaciio, 140 Misc. 696, 251 N.Y.S. 717 (1931) (state prosecution following Italian conviction); or refused to bar the state prosecutions on the ground that the federal and state prosecutions were sufficiently distinct to have permitted multiple prosecutions by the same government. *See* Hazelwood v. State, 273 P. 1017, 1018 (Okla. 1929); Rambu v. State, 259 P. 602, 603 (Okla. 1927); People v. Arnstein, 218 App. Div. 513, 218 N.Y.S. 633 (1926); *cf.* Henderson v. State, 244 P. 1020, 1021 (Ariz. 1926) (pre-*Hebert* decision); State v. O'Brien, 170 Atl. 98, 101 (Vt. 1934) (postrepeal decision).

79 42 Stat. 223 (1921).

80 United States v. LaFranca, 282 U.S. 569 (1931).

81 Various Items of Personal Property v. United States, 282 U.S. 576, 581 (1931).

82 Grant, The Lanza Rule of Successive Prosecutions, 32 Colum. L. Rev. 1309 (1932); *see also* Grant, The Scope and Nature of Concurrent Power, 34 Colum. L. Rev. 994 (1934); Grant, Successive Prosecutions by State and Nation: Common Law and British Empire Comparisons, 4 UCLA L. Rev. 1 (1956).

83 Grant, 32 Colum. L. Rev., *supra* note 82, at 1311.

84 *Id.* at 1316–29; *see also* Grant, UCLA L. Rev., *supra* note 81.

85 Grant, 32 Colum. L. Rev., *supra* note 82, at 1331.

86 *See* L. Miller, *Double Jeopardy and the Federal System* 1 (1968).

87 *See* notes 37–39 *supra* and accompanying text.

88 Brief for Defendants in Error, United States v. Lanza, 260 U.S. 377 (1922), at 9–10 (quoting statements of Representative Webb). *See also* Reply Brief of Plaintiff in Error, United States v. Lanza, 260 U.S. 377 (1922), at 10–11.

89 Brief of Amicus Curiae, National Prohibition Cases, 253 U.S. 350 (1920), at 54–55.

90 *See, e.g.,* Wisconsin Public Intervenor v. Mortier, 111 S. Ct. 2476, 2490 (1991) (Scalia, J., concurring); United States v. Trans-Missouri Freight Assn'n, 166 U.S. 290, 318 (1897); Powell, *the Original Understanding of Original Intent,* 99 Harv. L. Rev. 885 (1985).

91 *See generally* Note, Why Learned Hand Would Never Consult Legislative History Today, 105 Harv. L. Rev. 1005, 1008–11 (1992).

92 Church of the Holy Trinity v. United States, 143 U.S. 457, 464–65 (1892).

93 Boston Sand & Gravel Co. v. United States, 278 U.S. 41, 48 (1928).

94 Richbourg Motor Co. v. United States, 281 U.S. 528, 536 (1930; *see* text accompanying notes 56–63 in chapter 6.

95 United States v. LaFranca, 282 U.S. 569 (1931).

96 Various Items of Personal Property v. United States, 282 U.S. 576 (1931).

97 United States v. LaFranca, 282 U.S. 569 (1931). For other examples of the Court's tendency during the latter years of prohibition to base its decision on its construction of the prohibition statutes, *see* Sorrells v. United States, 287 U.S. 435 (1932); Richbourg Motor Co. v. United States, 281 U.S. 528 (1930).

98 Pound, The Economic Interpretation and the Law of Torts, 53 Harv. L. Rev. 365, 366 (1939).

99 1 W. Swindler, *Court and Constitution in the Twentieth Century* 222, 388 (1969).

100 *See, e.g.,* Stafford v. Wallace, 258 U.S. 495 (1922) (extending the "current of commerce" theory to justify congressional regulation of livestock after they had been unloaded from interstate carriers); Wisconsin R.R. Comm'n v. Chicago, Burlington & Quincy R.R. Co., 257 U.S. 563 (1922) (extending the doctrine of the *Shreveport Rate Case* to allow federal regulation of intrastate portions of the passenger business of interstate carriers). *See generally* Kutler, Chief Justice Taft, National Regulation, and the Commerce Power, 51 J. Am. Hist. 651 (1965).

101 *See, e.g.,* Hill v. Wallace, 259 U.S. 44 (1922) (concluding that the tax imposed by the Futures Trading Act of 1921 was an invalid attempt to exercise the police powers reserved to the states); Bailey v. Drexel Furniture Co., 259 U.S. 20 (1922) (Child Labor Tax was an invasion of the reserved powers of the states).

102 U.S. Const. amend. X: "The powers not delegated to the United States by the Constitution, nor prohibited by it to the States, are reserved to the States respectively, or to the people."

103 N. Clark, *Deliver Us from Evil: An Informal History of Prohibition* 40–41 (1976). At least five states lacked prohibition enforcement laws by the late 1920s according to the N. Y. Times. *See N. Y. Times,* May 30, 1929, at 1, col. 5. In New York, a Democratic legislature reacted to *Lanza* by repealing the state prohibition law its Republican predecessor had passed just two years earlier. *See* Act of June 1, 1923, 1923 Laws of New York ch. 871 (repealing 1921 Laws chs. 155, 156); D. Kyvig, *Repealing National Prohibition* 55–57 (1979). Other states that repealed their enforcement laws later in the prohibition era included Montana, Nevada, and Wisconsin. *See* Act of May 29, 1929, Wisconsin Laws ch. 129 (abolishing office of state prohibition commissioner); *N.Y. Times*, May 30, 1929 at 1, col. 4 (announcing the signing of act repealing prohibition enforcement legislation); Apr. 7, 1929, at 1, col. 6 (reporting results of Wisconsin repeal referendum). In addition, Maryland apparently never adopted an enforcement law. N. Clark, *supra*, at 167.

104 *See* Note, *supra* note 69, at 213 n.8, *citing* Ariz. Pen. Code § 728 (1913); Calif. Pen. Code § 656 (1920); Idaho Comp. Stat. § 8699 (1919); Ind. Ann. Stat. § 2045–16 (1926); Miss. Ann. Code § 1164 (Hemingway 1917); N.D. Comp. Laws Ann. § 10512 (1913); Or. Law § 1388 (Olsen 1920); S.D. Rev. Code § 4516 (1919); Tex. Ann. Crim. Stat. art. 208 (Vernon 1925); Utah Comp. Laws §§ 5522, 8652 (1917); Va. Code Ann. § 4775 (1925); Wash. Comp. Stat. § 2271 (Remington 1922). The Texas statute, however, appears to apply only when the criminal act was committed in another state, not when the act violated both a federal criminal statute and was also a state crime. In addition, Montana and New York had such laws prior to the repeal of their prohibition enforcement statutes. Note, *supra* note 69, at 213 n.8, *citing* Mont. Rev. Code § 11719 (Choate 1921); N.Y. Ann. Cons. Law ch. 88, § 33 (1916).

105 *See, e.g.,* National Comm'n on Law Observance, *Report on Prohibition Enforcement,* 55–56 (1931); H. Asbury, *The Great Illusion: An Informal History of Prohibition* 167–73 (1931); H. Johnston, *What Rights Are Left?* 57 (1930). For an illustration of the impact at the state level, *see* C. Merz, *The Dry Decade* 203–05 (1930). *See also* H. McBain, *supra* note 70, at 152.

106 United States v. Hebert, Cr. No. 3932, W.D. La. (minute entry in docket book). Although the Supreme Court relied on *Lanza* in three per curiam decisions prior to *Hebert*, none of them contain any suggestion that the defendant had actually been subjected to multiple prosecutions. *See* State v. Power, 123 Me. 223, 122 Atl. 572, *dismissed for want of jurisdiction*, 269 U.S. 531 (1925); State v. Moore, 36 Idaho 565, 212 P. 349, *aff'd*, 264 U.S. 569 (1924); Chandler v. State, 89 Tex. Cr. 599, 232 S.W. 337 (1921), *aff'd*, 260 U.S. 708 (1923).

107 *See, e.g.,* L. Friedman, *A History of American Law* 10 (2d ed. 1985); S. Presser & J. Zainaldin, *Law and American History* 17 (1980); *see generally* K. Hall, *The Magic Mirror* (1989).

6 Property Forfeitures: Interpreting the Language of the Volstead Act

1 Congress had occasionally used the forfeiture device in other criminal statutes in the late nineteenth century, e.g., Sherman Antitrust Act of 1890, § 6, 26 Stat. 210; but these statutes seem to have produced few, if any, reported opinions concerning the scope of the government's forfeiture authority. These statutes were apparently prompted by the Supreme Court's upholding the forfeiture of property held by Southerners during the Civil War. *See* Tyler v. Defrees, 78 U.S. (11 Wall.) 331 (1871); McVeigh v. United States, 78 U.S. (11 Wall.) 259 (1871); *see generally* Note, Bane of American Forfeiture Law—Banished at Last, 62 Cornell L. Rev. 768, 785–88 (1977).

2 *E.g.*, R.S. § 3257 (2d ed. 1878) (attempt by distiller to defraud United States of tax due on spirits); *id.* § 3265 (setting up distillery apparatus without a permit); *id.* § 3279 (knowingly carrying distilled spirits to or from a distillery, warehouse, or store that fails to display the required sign); *id.* § 3340 (attempt by brewery to evade tax on fermented liquor); *id.* § 3343 (removing fermented liquor from brewery or warehouse without a permit); *see also id.* § 2775 (making failure to submit special report required for imported spirits and wines result in forfeiture of those spirits and wines that are not reported).

3 In addition to the provisions quoted in the text, see R.S. § 3453 (2d ed. 1878) (providing for forfeiture of goods held for sale in fraud of the internal revenue laws) and *id.* § 4377 (providing for forfeiture of licensed vessel that is employed in a trade other than one for which the vessel is licensed).

4 R.S. § 3450 (2d ed. 1878). Section 3450 read as follows:

Whenever any goods or commodities for or in respect whereof any tax is or shall be imposed, or any materials, utensils, or vessels proper or intended to be made use of for or in the making of such goods or commodities are removed, or are deposited or concealed in any place, with intent to defraud the United States of such tax, or any part thereof, all such goods and commodities, and all such materials, utensils, and vessels, respectively, shall be forfeited, and in every such case all the casks, vessels, cases, or other packages whatsoever, containing, or which shall have contained, such goods or commodities, respectively, and every vessel, boat, cart, carriage, or other conveyance whatsoever, and all horses or other animals and all things used in the removal or for the deposit or concealment thereof, respectively, shall be forfeited. And every person who removes, deposits, or conceals, is concerned in removing, depositing, or concealing any goods or commodities for or in respect whereof any tax is or shall be imposed, with intent to defraud the United States of such tax or any part thereof, shall be liable to a fine or penalty of not more than five hundred dollars. And all boilers, stills, or other vessels, tools and implements, used in distilling or rectifying, and forfeited under any of the provisions of this Title, and all condemned material, together with any engine or other machinery connected therewith, and all empty barrels, and all grain or other material suitable for distillation, shall, under the direction of the court in which the forfeiture is recovered, be sold at public auction, and the proceeds thereof, after deducting the expenses of sale, shall be disposed of according to law. And all spirits or spirituous liquors which may be forfeited under the provisions of this Title, unless herein otherwise provided, shall be disposed of by the Commissioner of Internal Revenue as the Secretary of the Treasury may direct.

5 *Id.* § 3062. The immediately preceding provision, Section 3061, gave customs officials authority to search "any vehicle, beast or person on which . . . they shall suspect there is merchandise which is subject to duty, or shall have been introduced into the United States in any manner contrary to law" and to "seize and secure the same" if they found merchandise they had reasonable cause to believe was subject to duty or unlawfully introduced into the United States. Section 3062 then provided:

Every such vehicle and beast, or either, together with teams or other motive-power used in conveying, drawing, or propelling such vehicle or merchandise, and all other appurtenances, including trunks, envelopes, covers, and all means of concealment, and all the equipage, trappings, and other appurtenances of such beast, team, or vehicle, shall be subject to seizure and forfeiture.

6 *E.g.,* United States v. Brig Malek Adhel, 43 U.S. (2 How.) 210 (1844); The Palmyra, 25 U.S. (12 Wheat.) 1 (1827); *see* Note, *supra* note 1, at 781–83.

7 Dobbins Distillery v. United States, 96 U.S. 395, 399 (1878).

8 *See, e.g.,* Dobbins Distillery v. United States, 96 U.S. 395 (1878); Henderson's Distilled Spirits, 81 U.S. (14 Wall.) 44 (1871); The Distilled Spirits, 78 U.S. (11 Wall.) 356 (1870); United States v. Seventeen Empty Barrels, 27 F. Cases 1028 (C.C.W.D. Mo. 1875) (No. 16,255); United States v. Thirty-three Barrels of Spirits, 28 F. Cases 73 (D. Mass. 1868) (No. 16,470); *see also* Note, Forfeiture of Property of Innocent Persons Used in Violation of the Law, 6 Va. L. Rev. 583, 584 (1919) (identifying "enforcement of United States internal revenue laws regarding intoxicating liquors" as "[t]he most prolific single source of forfeitures").

9 *E.g.*, 1919 Ala. Acts, No. 7, § 13; Kansas Laws 1919, c. 217, §§ 1–5; Maine Laws 1917, c. 294; 1917 S.C. Acts, No. 37, § 27; Va. Laws 1918, c. 388, § 57.

10 S. Rep. No. 151, 66th Cong., 1st Sess. 19 (1919) ("This section has precedent in Alabama . . . , Maine . . . , Oklahoma . . . , South Carolina . . . , etc."). Once the Volstead Act was enacted, a number of states used it as a model for enactment or revision of their state laws. *See, e.g.*, Cal. Stat. 1921, c. 80, § 1; Mont. Laws 1921 Ex. Sess., c. 9, § 26. For a summary of state court decisions strictly applying prohibition forfeiture procedures, see F. Black, *Ill-Starred Prohibition Cases* 97–95, 100–104 (1931).

11 27 U.S.C.A. § 40 (1927). Section 26 provided:

When the commissioner, his assistants, inspectors, or any officer of the law shall discover any person in the act of transporting, in violation of the law, intoxicating liquors in any wagon, buggy, automobile, water or air craft, or other vehicle, it shall be his duty to seize any and all intoxicating liquors found therein being transported contrary to law. Whenever intoxicating liquors transported or possessed illegally shall be seized by an officer he shall take possession of the vehicle and team or automobile, boat, air or water craft, or any other conveyance, and shall arrest any person in charge thereof. Such officer shall at once proceed against the person arrested under the provisions of this title in any court having competent jurisdiction; but the said vehicle or conveyance shall be returned to the owner upon execution by him of a good and valid bond, with sufficient sureties, in a sum double the value of the property, which said bond shall be approved by said officer and shall be conditioned to return said property to the custody of said officer on the day of trial to abide the judgment of the court. The court upon conviction of the person so arrested shall order the liquor destroyed, and unless good cause to the contrary is shown by the owner, shall order a sale by public auction of the property seized, and the officer making the sale, after deducting the expenses of keeping the property, the fee for the seizure, and the cost of the sale, shall pay all liens, according to their priorities, which are established, by intervention or otherwise at said hearing or in other proceeding brought for said purpose, as being bona fide and as having been created without the lienor having any notice that the carrying vehicle was being used or was to be used for illegal transportation of liquor, and shall pay the balance of the proceeds into the Treasury of the United States as miscellaneous receipts. All liens against property sold under the provisions of this section shall be transferred from the property to the proceeds of the sale of the property. If, however, no one shall be found claiming the team, vehicle, water or air craft, or automobile, the taking of the same, with a description thereof, shall be advertised in some newspaper published in the city or county where taken or if there be no newspaper published in such city or county, in a newspaper having circulation in the county, once a week for two weeks and by handbills posted in three public places near the place of seizure, and if no claimant shall appear within ten days after the last publication of the advertisement, the property shall be sold and the proceeds after deducting the expenses and costs shall be paid into the Treasury of the United States as miscellaneous receipts.

12 *See* 9 Va. L. Rev. 462 (1923). Section 26 provided that the court was to order forfeiture "upon conviction of the person"; it did not expressly state the crime of which the person had to be convicted.

13 As originally reported by the House Committee that drafted the Volstead Act, the provision that became Section 26 qualified the "good cause" language with the phrase "such as ignorance of the purpose for which [the owner's] . . . vehicle . . . was being used," 58 Cong. Rec. 2902 (1919); but that phrase was deleted in the Senate. H. Rep. No. 360, 66th Cong., 1st Sess. 15 (1919). Two federal district courts subsequently held that a conditional vendor's lack of knowledge of the illegal use to which the automobile was being put would not always constitute "good cause" sufficient to preclude forfeiture under Section 26. United States v. Montgomery, 289 F. 125 (D. Arizona 1922); United States v. Kane, 273 F. 275 (D. Mont. 1921). At least one state court reached a similar result in construing a state prohibition statute. *See* 32 Yale L.J. 197 (1922).

14 This provision was added in a House floor amendment. Its drafter, Representative Venable of Mississippi, justified it as follows:

I believe it is sound to treat the citizen as innocent until he is proven guilty. This takes care of the vehicle and has it forthcoming at the trial. This gives the law the process in the event he is guilty and at the same time permits the innocent man to use his vehicle and not be inconvenienced pending the time he is adjudicated not guilty.

58 Cong. Rec. 2904 (1919).

15 The protection for lienholders was added in a House floor amendment that was accepted by Representative Volstead, the floor manager of the bill. 58 Cong. Rec. 2903 (1919). The decisions were split as to whether a conditional vendor should be treated as an owner or lienor. See United States v. Sylvester, 273 F. 253 (D. Conn. 1921) (conditional vendor's interest should be protected under the provision applicable to lienholders unless the purchaser's equity were very small); Note, Rights of a Conditional Vendor under the National Prohibition Act, 72 U. Pa. L. Rev. 181 (1924).

16 58 Cong. Rec. 2904, 2905 (1919). The House Report contented itself with the general assertion that the enforcement sections of Title II contained "no new or experimental features" because "[e]very provision in it ha[d] precedents in State or Federal legislation." H. Rep. No. 91, 66th Cong., 1st Sess. 7 (1919).

17 S. Rep. No. 151, 66th Cong., 1st Sess. 19 (1919).

18 One indication of the importance of forfeitures as a method for enforcing prohibition is the number of seizures that occurred by 1930: 52,000 automobiles and 1,400 boats along with other properties in the amount of $100,000,000. *See* Williams, Forfeiture Laws, 16 A.B.A. J. 572 (1930) (quoting speech by general counsel of the Prohibition Bureau); Note, Forfeiture of Offending Vehicle Under Revenue and Prohibition Law—A Conflict in Statutes, 30 Colum. L. Rev. 1039 (1930).

19 *See generally* D. Boorstin, *The Americans: The Democratic Experience* 422–27 (1973).

20 McDonald, Automobile Forfeitures and the Eighteenth Amendment, 10 Tex. L. Rev. 140, 142–43 (1931).

21 27 U.S.C.A. § 52 (1927).

22 Neither the House Report nor the Senate Report discussed the provision that became Section 35 in detail. H. Rep. No. 91, 66th Cong., 1st Sess. (1919); S. Rep. No. 151, 66th Cong., 1st Sess. (1919). Nor did the possibility of a conflict between Sections 26 and 35 surface in the individualized consideration of the two sections in either House. *See* 58 Cong. Rec. 2902–05, 2963, 4847, 4850 (1919).

23 J. W. Goldsmith, Jr.–Grant Co. v. United States, 254 U.S. 505 (1921).

24 *Id.* at 511.

25 *Id.* at 510–13.

26 For an explanation of the government's preference for Section 3450 by the Assistant Attorney General in charge of prohibition enforcement, see Willebrandt, The National Prohibition Act in Its Relation to Section 3450, 34 Case & Comment 3 (1928).

27 *See, e.g.,* United States v. Yuginovich, 256 U.S. 450 (1921). The defendant in *Yuginovich* was charged with four violations of the revenue laws: unlawfully engaging in the business of distilling in violation of R.S. § 3257 (2d ed. 1878); failing to keep a registry sign on the premises of a distillery as required by R.S. § 3279; carrying on the business of distilling without posting the bond required by R.S. § 3281; and unlawfully making a mash in a building other than a licensed distillery in violation of R.S. § 3282. The first and third of these offenses carried maximum penalties of a $500 fine and imprisonment for three years; the second, a maximum penalty of a $500 fine; and the fourth, a maximum penalty of a $5,000 fine and imprisonment for two years. By contrast, the Volstead Act's maximum penalty for a first offense of unlawfully manufacturing intoxicating liquor was a $1,000 or six months imprisonment. 27 U.S.C.A. § 46 (1927) (Section 29 of Title II of the Volstead Act).

28 *See, e.g.,* R.S. § 3450 (2d. ed. 1878).

29 United States v. Yuginovich, 256 U.S. 450, 459–60, 463–64 (1921).

30 H. Rep. No. 224, 67th Cong., 1st Sess. 3 (1921).

31 42 Stat. 223 (1921).

32 United States v. Stafoff, 260 U.S. 477 (1923).

33 *See generally* Note, Application of Internal Revenue Laws to Forfeitures of Vehicles Used in Transporting Intoxicating Liquors, 11 Va. L. Rev. 628, 632–33 (1925); *cf.* Buddey, Forfeiture of Vehicles for Unlawful Movement of Liquor: Under the National Prohibition Act-Under the Revised Statutes, 4 B.U. L. Rev. 183, 185 (1924) ("weight of authority seems to be drifting toward the theory that 3450 has not been repealed"); *see also* Note, Forfeiture of Property of Innocent Owners Used in Transporting Liquor, 74 U. Pa. L. Rev. 170 (1925).

34 *See* United States v. One Marmon Automobile, 5 F.2d 113 (N.D. Ga. 1925); United States v. One White One-Ton Truck, 4 F.2d 413 (W.D. Wash. 1925); United States v. One Ford Coupe, 3 F.2d 64 (W.D. La. 1924); United States v. One Ford Automobile, 1 F.2d 654 (E.D. Tenn. 1924); United States v. 385 Barrels of Whiskey, 300 F. 565 (S.D.N.Y. 1924); United States v. One Cadillac Automobile, 292 F. 773 (E.D. Ill. 1923); The Cherokee, 292 F. 212 (S.D. Tex. 1923); Reo Atlanta Co. v. Stern, 279 F. 422 (N.D. Ga. 1922); The Tuscan, 276 F. 55 (S.D. Ala. 1921); United States v. One Essex Touring Automobile, 276 F. 28 (N.D. Ga. 1921); United States v. One Cole Aero Eight Automobile, 273 F. 934 (D. Mont. 1921); United States v. One Essex Touring Automobile, 266 F. 138 (N.D. Ga. 1920). For similar decisions with respect to the forfeiture provisions of the customs and navigation laws, see The Amirald, 6 F.2d 413 (D.R.I. 1925); United States v. One Durant Touring Car, 2 F.2d 478 (W.D. Tex. 1924); United States v. Two Automobiles & Five Cases of Whiskey, 2 F.2d 264 (S.D. Cal. 1924); United States v. One Ford Automobile, 292 F. 207 (S.D. Tex. 1923).

35 *See* United States v. One Buick Sedan, 1 F.2d 997 (S.D. Cal. 1924); United States v. One Buick Automobile, 300 F. 584 (S.D. Cal. 1924); *cf.* United States v. One Buick Roadster, 280 F. 517 (D. Mont. 1922) (refusing to forfeit an automobile under R.S. § 3450 when the vehicle was being used by a trespasser and neither the owner nor his bailee had authorized the use).

36 *E.g.*, The Mabenhex, 6 F.2d 415 (D.R.I. 1924); The Spray, 6 F.2d 414 (D.R.I. 1925). Other decisions reached similar results even though the government did not name Section 26. *See* United States v. Three Quarts of Whiskey, 9 F.2d 208 (S.D.N.Y. 1925); United States v. One Chevrolet Coupe, 9 F.2d 85 (E.D. Mo. 1925); United States v. Deutsch, 8 F.2d 54 (E.D. Mo. 1925); United States v. One Packard Motor Truck, 284 F. 394 (E.D. Mich. 1922); *cf.* United States v. Torres, 291 F. 139 (D. Md. 1923) (prosecution under the Volstead Act amounts to an election to use the forfeiture provisions of Section 26); United States v. One Hudson Touring

Car, 274 F. 473 (E.D. Mich. 1921), *aff'd*, 284 F. 821 (6th Cir. 1922) (post-*Yuginovich* decision holding that forfeiture provisions of R.S. § 3450 were repealed as to transportation of intoxicating liquors by subsequent passage of the inconsistent provisions of Section 26).

37 *See* United States v. One Reo Truck Automobile, 9 F.2d 529 (2d Cir. 1925); Marmon Atlanta Co. v. United States, 8 F.2d 267 (5th Cir. 1925); United States v. Milstone, 6 F.2d 481 (D.C. Cir. 1925); Commercial Credit Co. v. United States, 5 F.2d 1 (6th Cir. 1925); One Big-Six Studebaker Automobile v. United States, 289 F. 256 (9th Cir. 1923); McDowell v. United States, 286 F. 521 (9th Cir. 1923); One Ford Touring Car v. United States, 284 F. 823 (8th Cir. 1922); United States v. Federal Ins. Co., 284 F. 821 (6th Cir. 1922); Lewis v. United States, 280 F. 5 (6th Cir. 1922); United States v. One Haynes Automobile, 274 F. 926 (5th Cir. 1921); *cf.* National Bond & Inv. Co. v. United States, 8 F.2d 942 (7th Cir. 1925) (post–Willis-Campbell Act decision holding that intent to defraud the United States, an essential element for forfeiture under R.S. § 3450, could not be inferred from mere use of vehicle to transport intoxicating liquor within the United States). *But cf.* Payne v. United States, 279 F. 112 (5th Cir. 1922) (forfeiture of vehicle under R.S. § 3450 permissible when evidence justified inference that the liquor being transported had been manufactured before the Volstead Act was passed).

38 *Compare, e.g.,* United States v. One Reo Truck Automobile, 9 F.2d 529 (2d Cir. 1925) (provisions of Section 26 inconsistent with those of R.S. § 3450), *with* Commercial Credit Co. v. United States, 5 F.2d 1 (6th Cir. 1925) (passage of the Willis-Campbell Act did not revive preexisting taxes on intoxicating liquor because those taxes directly conflicted with the Volstead Act's prohibition on the issuance of liquor taxes). Several of the circuit court decisions had limited precedential value because they concerned incidents arising before the Willis-Campbell Act overruled *Yuginovich. E.g.,* One Ford Touring Car v. United States, 284 F. 823 (8th Cir. 1922); United States v. Federal Ins. Co., 284 F. 821 (6th Cir. 1922); Lewis v. United States, 280 F. 5 (6th Cir. 1922).

39 Certificate of United States Court of Appeals for the Ninth Circuit at 2–3, Port Gardner Inv. Co. v. United States, 272 U.S. 564 (1926). These were the six questions certified by the Court of Appeals:

1. Is Section 3450 of the Revised Statutes of the United States in force and effect in so far as it provides for the forfeiture of automobiles or other vehicles where the same are used or are being used for the transportation of intoxicating liquor?

2. Do the provisions of Section 3450 of the Revised Statutes of the United States authorize the forfeiture of the interest of a conditional vendor reserving title to a conveyance who is free from knowledge, blame or negligence in

the premises where the goods or commodities concerned consist of intoxicating liquors illicitly manufactured or imported, a case under the Section referred to being made out in other respects?

3. Does Section 3450 of the Revised Statutes authorize the forfeiture of
taxable goods or commodities and the carriage or other conveyance used in
the removal or for the deposit or concealment thereof where the only removal, deposit or concealment with intent to defraud the United States of
such tax that can be shown is the mere movement of such goods on a trip
other than from the original point of importation, manufacturing or bonded
warehousing?

4. In the State of Washington, where there is no place where intoxicating
liquor can be legally kept without the tax thereon being paid or otherwise,
can an automobile be said to have been guilty of being used for the removal,
deposit or concealment of intoxicating liquor with intent to defraud the
government of the tax imposed thereon where it is merely shown that the
liquor is found in the automobile and that no tax thereon has been paid?

5. Did the prosecution of the driver of the car under the National Prohibition Act constitute an election by the government to proceed under Section
26 of that Act and thereby prevent the forfeiture of the car under Section
3450 of the Revised Statutes of the United States?

6. Is there any tax on intoxicating liquor illicitly manufactured as the word
tax is meant and used in Section 3450 of the Revised Statutes of the United
States or are the so-called taxes now claimed to be collectable merely penalties?

40 United States v. Garth Motor Co., 4 F.2d 528 (5th Cir. 1925), rev'd,
272 U.S. 321 (1926).

41 Van Oster v. Kansas, 272 U.S. 465, 468–69 (1926). In the early years
of national prohibition, several state courts had construed state prohibition laws to forfeit the interests of innocent property owners. See, e.g.,
Black, Some Prohibition Cases—The Doctrine of Vicarious Liability, 78 U.
Pa. L. Rev. 518, 518–20, 522–23 (1930), reprinted in F. Black, supra note
10, at 91; 20 Colum. L. Rev. 798 (1920); 34 Harv. L. Rev. 212 (1920). But
see 8 Va. L. Rev. 59 (1921) (discussing North Carolina decision to the
contrary).

42 272 U.S. 321 (1926). Justice Stone filed a concurring opinion, and
Justice Butler dissented in an opinion that Justices McReynolds and
Sutherland joined. In his concurring opinion, Justice Stone argued "that
there conceivably may be a deposit or concealment of illicit liquor in an
automobile with intent to deprive the United States of the tax upon it,
which is not transportation within the meaning of § 26 and to that extent
the two statutes are not in conflict." He refused, however, to "subscribe to
those expressions in the opinion which seem to suggest that the two

sections are not in direct conflict, in a case where there is transportation of liquor in violation of the [Volstead] Act with intent to defraud the United States of the tax." *Id.* at 335.

Justice Butler dissented on three grounds. First, he argued that the Eighteenth Amendment repealed all taxes relating to intoxicating liquor; as a result, Section 3450 could not apply. *Id.* at 335–41. Second, he contended that a direct conflict existed between Section 26 and Section 3450 in all cases where liquor was being transported because Section 26 protected innocent property owners and Section 3450 did not. *Id.* at 341–43. Third, he concluded that the record before the Court was sufficient to demonstrate that the vehicle involved was being used to transport intoxicating liquor when it was seized. *Id.* at 344–50.

43 *Id.* at 326–30.

44 *Id.* at 330–31.

45 *Id.* at 334.

46 Dodge v. United States, 272 U.S. 530, 531–32 (1926); *accord*, United States v. One Reo Motor Truck, 6 F.2d 412 (D.R.I. 1925), *noted in* 74 U. Pa. L. Rev. 196 (1925).

47 272 U.S. 564 (1926). Justice Butler filed a concurring opinion that Justice Stone joined. He would have answered the certified question as submitted by the Ninth Circuit without limiting the holding to a case where the defendant had been convicted under the Volstead Act. He gave the following explanation of his position:

The substance of [the question left unanswered by the Court] is whether the prohibition officer discovering one in the act of transporting may disregard the plain and direct commands of [Section] 26 to proceed against the vehicle as there directed. I think he has no more right to ignore that command than he has to let the liquor and offender go. The law makes the election.

Id. at 567.

48 The certified questions are quoted in note 39 *supra*.

49 The Ninth Circuit's fifth question had asked whether *prosecution* of the driver under the Volstead Act amounted to an election to proceed under Section 26. The Supreme Court answered that disposition of the car under Section 26 was mandatory once the driver had been *convicted*.

50 *Id.* at 566. The Court specifically declined to "determine whether mere commencement of a proceeding under [Section] 26 constitutes an election." Moreover, the Court did not explain what inconsistencies rendered the two statutes incompatible. Presumably it was the protection that Section 26 afforded innocent owners but R.S. § 3450 did not. See Justice Butler's dissent in *One Ford Coupe*, which is discussed in note 42 *supra*.

51 276 U.S. 226 (1928), *noted in* 41 Harv. L. Rev. 870 (1928).

52 276 U.S. at 231–32.

53 Dissents also became more common in cases, like *One Ford Coupe,* where the Court decided in favor of the government, a development also paralleled in other areas. *See, e.g.,* Olmstead v. United States, 277 U.S. 438 (1928); Lambert v. Yellowley, 272 U.S. 581 (1926).

54 United States v. General Motors Accept. Corp., 25 F.2d 238 (5th Cir. 1928).

55 Davies Motor Co. v. United States, 35 F.2d 928 (9th Cir. 1929), *rev'd sub nom.* Richbourg Motor Co. v. United States, 281 U.S. 528 (1930); *see also* United States v. Commercial Credit Co., 20 F.2d 519 (4th Cir. 1927).

56 281 U.S. 528 (1930), *noted in* 25 Ill. L. Rev. 564 (1931); 3 U. Cin. L. Rev. 483 (1929); 79 U. Pa. L. Rev. 91 (1930).

57 J. W. Goldsmith, Jr.–Grant Co. v. United States, 254 U.S. 505 (1921); *see* text accompanying notes 23–26 *supra.*

58 281 U.S. at 533.

59 *Id.*

60 *Id.* at 534–36, *citing* Cairo & Fulton R.R. Co. v. Hecht, 95 U.S. 168 (1877); West Wisconsin R. Co. v. Foley, 94 U.S. 100 (1877).

The Court asserted, without any supporting authority, that Congress knew "that the enactment of the National Prohibition Act would enormously increase seizures of vehicles beyond those made under [Section] 3450, and that their forfeiture would place an increased and heavy burden on many persons, unless afforded some protection by the new legislators." *Id.* Undoubtedly, forfeitures did increase greatly during the prohibition era, *see* note 18 *supra;* but little, if any, evidence exists to suggest that either Congress or the prohibition lobbyists anticipated a vast number of forfeitures would be necessary to enforce the Volstead Act. *Cf.* 59 Cong. Rec. 5655 (1920) (letter from General Counsel of Anti-Saloon League to Senator Morris Sheppard estimating that "five millions a year appropriated to enforce [the Volstead Act] would be ample").

61 281 U.S. at 536, *citing* 58 Cong. Rec. 2902 (1919); S. Rep. No. 151, 66th Cong., 1st Sess. 19 (1919).

62 Act of Nov. 23, 1921, 42 Stat. 222, 223.

63 281 U.S. at 535.

64 United States v. Ryan, 284 U.S. 167, 170 (1931).

65 Section 3453 read as follows:

All goods, wares, merchandise, articles, or objects, on which taxes are imposed, which shall be found in the possession, or custody, or within the control of any person, for the purpose of being sold or removed by him in fraud of the internal revenue laws, or with design to avoid payment of said taxes, may be seized by the collector or deputy collector of the proper district, or by such other collector or deputy collector as may be specially authorized by the Commissioner of Internal Revenue for that purpose, and shall be forfeited to the United States. And all raw materials found in the possession of any person intending to manufacture the same into articles of a kind subject to tax for the purpose of fraudulently selling such manufactured articles or with design to evade the payment of said tax; and all tools, implements, instruments, and personal property whatsoever, in the place or building, or within any yard or inclosure where such articles or raw materials are found, may also be seized by any collector or deputy collector, as aforesaid, and shall be forfeited as aforesaid. The proceedings to enforce such forfeitures shall be in the nature of a proceeding in rem in the circuit court or district court of the United States for the district where such seizure is made.

66 284 U.S. at 171–72.

67 *Id.* at 174. *Ryan* avoided an overly broad construction of the section by limiting the language allowing forfeiture of "all . . . personal property" in the building where the article was sold to include only those chattels, which were "related to one or the other of the principal things, or incident to their intended use or disposition in fraud of the revenue." Applying this standard to the article seized in *Ryan* (the furnishings and equipment of a room in which tax-unpaid intoxicating liquors were dispensed), the Court concluded these chattels were subject to forfeiture because they "were incident to the sale" of the liquor and "were so related to the tax evasion at which the statute was aimed as to be clearly embraced within both its purpose and words." *Id.* at 176.

68 *Id.* at 176–77.

69 286 U.S. 49 (1932). A companion decision applied the *General Motors* distinction to a situation where the evidence of the automobiles use in smuggling was more equivocal. United States v. Commercial Credit Co., 286 U.S. 63 (1932). *Commercial Credit* upheld a forfeiture under the customs statute where the evidence "justified a finding that the cars . . . were implements or links in a continuous process of carriage from Mexico into [the United States]," although it did not clearly indicate whether the cars that were seized were loaded on the American or Mexican side of the border. *Id.* at 67.

70 Act of June 17, 1930, ch. 356, 46 Stat. 590, 639.

71 Other counts charging failures to obtain a permit, to pay duties, and to make entry at the custom house were dismissed. 286 U.S. at 54.

72 R.S. § 3061, 3062 (2d ed. 1878); *see* note 5 *supra* and accompanying text.

73 286 U.S. at 56.

74 *Id.* at 59–60.

75 *Id.* at 60–61.

76 United States v. The Ruth Mildred, 286 U.S. 67, 69 (1932). A companion case, General Import & Export Co. v. United States, 286 U.S. 70 (1932), applied the *Ruth Mildred* rationale in a libel against a ship that Coast Guard officers had seized for carrying an unmanifested cargo of intoxicating liquor. Under the provisions of the statute involved in *General Import & Export*, only the cargo—not the vessel—was subject to forfeiture.

The statutory basis for the forfeiture in *The Ruth Mildred* was R.S. § 4377 (2d ed. 1878), which provided in pertinent part as follows:

> Whenever any licensed vessel is transferred, in whole or in part, to any person who is not at the time of such transfer a citizen of and resident within the United States, or is employed in any other trade than that for which she is licensed, or is found with a forged or altered license, or one granted for any other vessel, such vessel with her tackle, apparel, and furniture, and the cargo, found on board her, shall be forfeited.

77 The Supreme Court's first significant forfeiture decision after prohibition came in 1939, and, ironically, it involved bootleg whiskey. See United States v. One 1936 Model Ford, 307 U.S. 219 (1939) (upholding a district court's mitigation of the forfeiture of an automobile under R.S. § 3450). Other modern decisions have confirmed the government's authority to forfeit property used in unlawful activities, see, e.g., Calero-Toledo v. Pearson Yacht Leasing Co., 416 U.S. 663 (1974); C. J. Hendry Co. v. Moore, 318 U.S. 133 (1943). The Court has, however, held Fourth and Fifth Amendments protections applicable in forfeiture proceedings. United States v. United States Coin & Currency, 401 U.S. 715 (1971) (Fifth Amendment privilege against self-incrimination applicable in forfeiture proceedings under 26 U.S.C § 7302); One 1958 Plymouth Sedan v. Pennsylvania, 380 U.S. 693 (1965) (evidence obtained in violation of the Fourth Amendment may not be used in forfeiture proceedings). It has also narrowly construed forfeiture provisions that affect persons not directly involved in illegal activity. United States v. Parcel of Land, Appurtenances and Improvements, 113 S. Ct. 1126 (1993) (protecting the rights of innocent owners under the Comprehensive Drug Abuse Prevention and Control Act of 1970).

For a list of the forfeiture statutes at the federal level, prior to the mid-1970s, see Recent Developments, 60 Cornell L. Rev. 467, 467 n.3 (1975). Both federal and state governments have made extensive use of the forfeiture device in drug statutes. See, e.g., 21 U.S.C. § 881 (1980); La. R.S. 40:989(A)(4) (1972). In 1970 Congress expanded the forfeiture approach as a new weapon in the battle against organized crime. See 18 U.S.C. § 1963 (1980); 21 U.S.C. § 848(a)(2) (1980); see generally Note, supra note 1, at 792–93.

78 The only possible use of the *One Ford Coupe* doctrine after *Richbourg* would be to forfeiture an automobile that was being used to conceal, but not to transport, intoxicating liquor. The likelihood of bootleggers making such use of an automobile was, at best, extremely small.

79 *See* note 35 *supra*; *see also* Va. L. Rev. Note, *supra* note 33, at 635.

80 This argument was one way that Justice Cardozo's opinion in *General Motors* distinguished the *Richbourg* holding. 286 U.S. at 60; *but see* Richbourg v. United States, 281 U.S. 528 (1930) (Section 26 procedures mandatory "whenever transportation is involved").

81 The first paragraph of Section 5 "continue[d] in force" all laws relating to the manufacture and taxation of and traffic in intoxicating liquor "except such provisions as [were] directly in conflict with" the Volstead Act, but it barred conviction under more than one law when the act charged was a violation of both the liquor laws and the Volstead Act. Under the rationale of *Richbourg*, the government could apparently elect to prosecute a defendant under the revenue laws. Choosing to prosecute under the revenue laws would, however, eliminate the possibility of forfeiting the vehicle, since the Willis-Campbell Act forbade conviction under both laws, Section 26 required a conviction before its provisions could be invoked, and *Richbourg* precluded forfeiture under the general revenue laws.

82 S. Rep. No. 151, 66th Cong., 1st Sess. 19 (1919) ("This section . . . provided that when . . . any officer discovers a person illegally transporting intoxicating liquor in an automobile or in any other vehicle, he *may* seize the same and arrest the person in charge.") (emphasis added).

83 *See* notes 16–17, *supra* and accompanying text.

84 Richbourg Motor Co. v. United States, 281 U.S. 528, 534 (1930).

85 The language of Section 26 directed officials to seize the "vehicle" a person used in transporting intoxicating liquor. In *Ryan* the property seized was not a vehicle, nor was any liquor being transported when the seizure was made unless carrying the liquor to the saloon's customers amounted to unlawful transportation.

86 *See* note 67 *supra* and accompanying text.

87 P. Odegard, *Pressure Politics: The Story of the Anti-Saloon League* 38–48 (1928). *See also* H. Asbury, *The Great Illusion: An Informal History of Prohibition* 112 (1950); N. Clark, *Deliver Us from Evil: An Informal History of Prohibition* 93 (1976); S. Cashman, *Prohibition: The Lie of the Land* 7 (1981).

88 *See, e.g.,* D. Kyvig, *Repealing National Prohibition* 58 (1979); C. Merz, *The Dry Decade* 298–99 (1931).

89 281 U.S. at 534.

90 For another example of the Court using a statutory construction approach to limit its protection to "innocent" violators, see United States

v. Sorrells, 287 U.S. 435 (1932). For another example of a less favorable decision on a statutory issue involving the relatively serious offense of manufacturing bootleg whiskey, see Danovitz v. United States, 281 U.S. 389, 395 (1930) (liberal construction of Section 25 of Title II of the Volstead Act to allow destruction of property used in the illegal manufacture of intoxicating liquor).

91 272 U.S. at 468; see note 41 *supra* and accompanying text.

92 General Motors Accept. Corp. v. United States, 286 U.S. 49, 54 (1932); Richbourg v. United States, 281 U.S. 528, 530 (1930).

93 *See* A. Mason, *The Supreme Court from Taft to Warren* 15–16, 50 (1968 ed.); 1 W. Swindler, *Court and Constitution in the Twentieth Century* 224–25 (1969); 2 *id.* at 37–38 (1970).

94 *Yuginovich* is not listed in the "Table of Cases Commented On" section of the *Index to Legal Periodicals* during the 1920–1923 period.

95 G. Endlich, *A Commentary on the Interpretation of Statutes* 317–19, 320–22 (1888); 1 J. Sutherland, *Statutes and Statutory Construction* 483–84 (2d ed. 1904).

96 In the mid-1920s, the Court occasionally decided Fourth Amendment cases adversely to the government, but these cases usually involved relatively minor violations. *See, e.g.,* Gambino v. United States, 275 U.S. 310 (1927); Byars v. United States, 273 U.S. 28 (1927).

97 *See, e.g.,* Weaver v. Palmer Bros. Co., 270 U.S. 402 (1926); Jay Burns Baking Co. v. Bryan, 264 U.S. 504 (1924); Adkins v. Children's Hospital, 261 U.S. 525 (1923); Bailey v. Drexel Furniture Co., 259 U.S. 20 (1922).

7 Jury Trials: Primacy of Institutional Concerns

1 In addition, the Seventh Amendment preserves the right of trial by jury "[i]n suits at common law, where the value in controversy shall exceed twenty dollars," and the Fifth Amendment prohibits holding anyone "to answer for a capital, or otherwise infamous crime, unless on a presentment or indictment of a Grand Jury, except in cases arising in the land or naval forces, or in the Militia, when in actual service in time of War or public danger." The grand jury provision posed a potential obstacle for the efficient processing of prohibition cases. However, two decisions of the Supreme Court in the early years of the prohibition era made the provision inapplicable to most prohibition violations, *see* Wyman v. United States, 263 U.S. 14 (1923); Brede v. Powers, 263 U.S. 4 (1923), until the Jones Act of 1929, 45 Stat. 1446, substantially increased the penalties for sales of intoxicating liquor and other violations.

2 *See* Schick v. United States, 195 U.S. 65, 78 (1904) (Harlan, J., dissenting); Frankfurter & Corcoran, Petty Federal Offenses and the Constitutional Guarantee of Trial By Jury, 39 Harv. L. Rev. 917, 970–71 (1926).

3 *See* Schick v. United States, 195 U.S. 65, 70 (1904) (discussing distinction that Blackstone draws between "crimes" and "criminal offenses"); *Ex parte* Milligan, 71 U.S. (4 Wall.) 1, 123 (1866) ("The sixth amendment . . . language [is] broad enough to embrace all persons and things.").

4 Frankfurter & Corcoran, *supra* note 2, at 971–75.

5 *Id.* at 938–65 (discussing colonial practices of Massachusetts, Connecticut, New York, New Jersey, Pennsylvania, Maryland, and Virginia).

6 E.g., Goddard v. State, 12 Comm. 448, 455 (1838); State v. Glenn, 54 Md. 572 (1880); Katz v. Eldredge, 97 N.J.L. 123, 117 Atl. 841 (1922); People ex rel. Murray v. Justices, 74 N.Y. 406 (1878); Byers v. Commonwealth, 42 Pa. St. 89 (1862); Raggdale v. Danville, 116 Va. 484, 32 S.E. 77 (1914).

7 Callan v. Wilson, 127 U.S. 540, 552 (1888): "According to many adjudicated [state] cases, arising under Constitutions which declare, generally, that the right of trial by jury shall remain inviolate, there are certain minor or petty offenses that may be proceeded against summarily, and without a jury. . . ."

8 The index to the compiled statutes only cites the constitutional provisions in relation to the accused's right to a jury in criminal proceeding. U.S. Compiled Statutes 2271 (Compact ed. 1918).

9 *Id.* §§ 1583, 1584. A judge could also empanel a jury to try issues of fact "when sitting in equity for the trial of patent causes," *id.* 1586, and, "upon the consent of the parties," in admiralty cases. *Id.* § 1585.

10 *See* Oppenheim, Waiver of Trial by Jury in Criminal Cases, 25 Mich. L. Rev. 695, 707–15 (1927) (criticizing the "minority" of state decisions that refused to allow waivers).

11 *See id.* at 699–705 (jury trials); Note, The "Padlock" Injunction, 72 U. Pa. L. Rev. 283, 284 n.2 (1923) (citing Arkansas, Iowa, Missouri, and Texas cases allowing use of injunctions to enforce prohibition).

12 Thompson v. Utah, 170 U.S. 343, 349 (1898) ("[T]he jury referred to in the original Constitution and in the [Sixth] Amendment is a jury constituted, as it was at common law, of twelve persons, neither more nor less. . . ."); *see also* Rassmussen v. United States, 197 U.S. 516, 519 (1905) ("At the bar the Government did not deny that offenses of the character of the one here prosecuted could only be tried by a *common law jury*, if the Sixth Amendment governed.") (emphasis added); *cf.* Capital Traction Co. v. Hof, 174 U.S. 1 (1899) (civil jury).

13 Callan v. Wilson, 127 U.S. 540, 552 (1880).

14 *See* D.C. Ann. Code § 44 (1924).

15 *See, e.g.,* Schick v. United States, 195 U.S. 65 (1904) (defendant

waived right to trial by jury in a case that the Court held was a petty offense for which Congress could have dispensed with jury trials).

16 Schick v. United States, 195 U.S. 65 (1904); Callan v. Wilson, 127 U.S. 540, 549 (1888) ("The jury trial guarantee [in the federal Constitution] is not to be construed as relating only to felonies, or offenses punishable in the penitentiary. It embraces as well some classes of misdemeanors, the punishment of which involves or may involve the deprivation of the liberty of the citizen"). For a listing of some lower court decisions on what constitutes a petty offense, see Frankfurter & Corcoran, supra note 2, at 980 n.287.

17 Schick v. United States, 195 U.S. 65 (1904) (allowing waiver in a case where the defendant was charged with a "petty" offense). In the waiver decisions, the federal courts did not distinguish between waiving a jury completely and waiving the right to a jury of twelve. See Patton v. United States, 281 U.S. 276, 290 (1930); Dickson v. United States, 159 F. 801, 805 (1st Cir. 1908), cert. dismissed, 213 U.S. 92 (1909).

18 Schick v. United States, 195 U.S. 65 (1904); Frank v. United States, 192 F. 864 (6th Cir. 1911); Low v. United States, 169 F. 86 (6th Cir. 1909).

19 Rogers v. United States, 141 U.S. 548 (1891); Low v. United States, 169 F. 86 (6th Cir. 1909); United States v. Louisville & Nashville R.R., 167 F. 306 (6th Cir. 1909); Dickson v. United States, 159 F. 801 (1st Cir. 1908), cert. dismissed, 213 U.S. 92 (1909).

20 E.g., Mugler v. Kansas, 123 U.S. 623, 673 (1887) (A jury trial "is not required in suits in equity to abate a public nuisance.").

21 158 U.S. 564 (1895).

22 The other two were Pollock v. Farmers Loan & Trust Co., 158 U.S. 601 (1895), which ruled the federal income tax was unconstitutional, and United States v. E.C. Knight Co., 156 U.S. 1 (1895), which narrowly construed the Sherman Antitrust Act. See generally A. Paul, Conservative Crisis and the Rule of Law 178–220 (1960).

23 See generally S. Presser & S. Zainaldin, Law and Jurisprudence in American History 680–711 (2d ed. 1989).

24 158 U.S. at 581–82.

25 Id. at 594–95.

26 123 U.S. 623 (1887).

27 Not until Duncan v. Louisiana, 391 U.S. 145 (1968), was the Sixth Amendment's jury trial requirement held applicable to the states. See Maxwell v. Dow, 170 U.S. 568 (1900).

28 Id. at 672–73. The Kansas statute declared any place where intoxicating liquors were kept to be a public nuisance. Maintaining the nuisance was an offense punishable by a $100 to $500 fine and 30 to 90 days in the county jail, and any citizen could initiate an equitable action to secure a permanent injunction to abate the nuisance. Violation of the

injunction was punishable as contempt of court by a $100 to $500 fine and by 30 to 60 days in jail. 123 U.S. at 670 (quoting Kansas statute).

29 59 Cong. Rec. 5655 (1920).

30 27 U.S.C.A. § 12 (1927). The act defined as "intoxicating liquor" any beverage containing more than one-half of 1 percent alcohol by volume. *Id.* § 4(1).

31 *Id.* § 33.

32 *Id.*

33 *Id.* § 46.

34 *Id.* § 34. The action might be brought "in the name of the United States by the Attorney General of the United States or by any United States attorney or any prosecuting attorney of any state or any subdivision thereof or by the commissioner [of the Prohibition Bureau] or his deputies or assistants." *Id.*

35 *Id.* § 35.

36 *Id.* § 38.

37 *Id.* § 62.

38 *Id.* § 37.

39 *Id.* § 34.

40 *See, e.g.,* United States v. Wadington, 29 F.2d 160, 160–61 (D. Neb. 1927); 73 Cong. Rec. 2979–80 (1931); National Commission on Law Observance and Enforcement, *Enforcement of the Prohibition Laws of the United States* 55–56 (1931) [hereinafter cited as *Final Prohibition Report*].

41 Middlekauf, The Enforcement of the Liquor Laws, 4 Ill. L.Q. 107, 115 (1922) (emphasis added).

42 *See Final Prohibition Report, supra* note 40, at 56.

43 *E.g.,* Golding, *Constitutional Question Involved in the Abatement and Injunction Sections of the National Prohibition Act,* 19 Ill. L. Rev. 71 (1924).

44 *E.g.,* Note, *supra* note 11, at 289 ("Unquestionably, the moral effect of padlock injunctions upon others who are engaging in the liquor trade will be very great.").

45 Wyman v. United States, 263 U.S. 14 (1923); Brede v. Powers, 263 U.S. 4 (1923).

46 Coates v. United States, 290 F. 134 (4th Cir. 1923).

47 Note, The Test of a Common Nuisance under the Volstead Act, 72 U. Pa. L. Rev. 289 (1923). *But see* Note, *supra* note 11 (arguing on the basis of unreported decisions that federal courts have only granted padlock injunctions in extreme cases).

48 Peter Hand Co. v. United States, 2 F.2d 449 (7th Cir. 1924); Grossman v. United States *ex rel.* Brundage, 280 F. 683 (7th Cir. 1922); United States v. American Brewing Co., 1 F.2d 1001 (E.D. Pa. 1924); United States v. Schwartz, 1 F.2d 718 (D. Mass. 1924). The overall pattern is evident with respect to issues other than those addressed in the text. For example, at least one district court granted a padlock injunction against a residence, although he allowed the defendant to continue using the premises if he posted the $1000 bond allowed by the statute, United States v. Margolis, 289 F. 161 (S.D. Cal. 1923); and two appellate courts ruled that a criminal conviction was not a prerequisite to an injunction forbidding the use of the premises. United States v. Reisenweber, 288 F. 520 (2d Cir. 1921); Lewisohn v. United States, 278 F. 421 (7th Cir. 1921), cert. denied, 258 U.S. 630 (1922). In addition, several opinions upheld jury convictions for the crime of maintaining a common nuisance. Remus v. United States, 291 F. 513 (6th Cir. 1923), cert. denied, 263 U.S. 717 (1924); Gray v. United States, 276 F. 395 (6th Cir. 1921); Young v. United States, 272 F. 967 (9th Cir. 1921); Wiggins v. United States, 272 F. 41 (2d Cir. 1921).

49 United States v. Lot 29, 296 F. 729 (D. Neb. 1924).

50 *Compare* United States v. Cohen, 260 F. 420 (E.D. Mo. 1920) (upholding statute as constitutional after construing it to require more than a simple sale).

51 United States v. Schwartz, 1 F.2d 718 (D. Mass. 1924).

52 United States v. Boynton, 297 F. 261 (E.D. Mich. 1924) (innocent owners); United States v. Eilert Brewing & Beverage Co., 278 F. 659 (D. Ohio 1921) (single sale) (dicta).

53 *Compare, e.g.,* Frankfurter & Corcoran, *supra* note 2 (documenting the historical tradition of punishing petty offenses without providing jury trials); *and* Oppenheim, *supra* note 10 (advocating that defendants be allowed to waive trial by jury); *with* H. McBain, *Prohibition: Legal and Illegal* 106–25 (1928) (arguing that the nuisance abatement provisions of the Volstead Act were unconstitutional).

54 Act of Mar. 2, 1929, ch. 473, § 1, 45 Stat. 1446.

55 Wyman v. United States, 263 U.S. 14 (1923); Brede v. Powers, 263 U.S. 4 (1923).

56 National Commission on Law Observance and Enforcement, *Preliminary Report on Observance and Enforcement of Prohibition*, H. Doc. 252, 71st Cong., 2d Sess. 5, 14, 17–25 (1930) [hereinafter cited as *Preliminary Report on Prohibition*].

57 274 U.S. 220 (1927).

58 *Id.* at 223.

59 The Court did emphasize that the Court should only accept a guilty plea if it were "made voluntarily after proper advice and with full understanding of the consequences." *Id.*

60 272 U.S. 630 (1926).

61 274 U.S. 195 (1927).

62 276 U.S. 494 (1928).

63 For other decisions that also showed judicial support for prohibition, see Engler v. United States, 25 F.2d 37 (8th Cir. 1928) (once liquor nuisance is shown to exist, owner has burden of showing that it had been abated); Schecter v. United States, 7 F.2d 881 (2d Cir. 1925) (affirming a criminal conviction for maintaining a nuisance on the basis of a single sale of intoxicating liquor).

64 Kling v. United States, 8 F.2d 730 (6th Cir. 1925), *cert. denied*, 269 U.S. 587 (1926); United States v. Duignan, 4 F.2d 983 (2d Cir. 1925), *aff'd*, 274 U.S. 195 (1927).

65 United States v. Rosoff, 27 F.2d 719 (2d Cir. 1928); Grossman v. United States *ex rel.* Brundage, 280 F. 683 (7th Cir. 1922); United States v. Chesebrough Mfg. Co., 11 F.2d 537 (S.D.N.Y. 1926). *But see* United States v. Cunningham, 37 F.2d 349 (D. Neb. 1929) (declaring Section 23 unconstitutional).

66 Denapolis v. United States, 3 F.2d 722 (5th Cir. 1925).

67 Daeuffer-Lieberman Brewing Co. v. United States, 36 F.2d 568 (3d Cir. 1929).

68 United States v. Miller, 31 F.2d 807 (S.D. Tex. 1929); United States v. All Buildings, 28 F.2d 774 (D. Kan. 1928); United States v. Gaffney, 10 F.2d 694 (2d Cir. 1926); United States v. Cheseborough Mfg. Co., 11 F.2d 537 (S.D.N.Y. 1926). *But see* Butler Hotel Co. v. United States, 35 F.2d 76 (9th Cir. 1929), *cert. denied*, 281 U.S. 733 (1930) (conditional injunction issued against innocent owner); Engler v. United States, 25 F.2d 37 (8th Cir. 1928) (formal change of tenants after prior illegal use was not sufficient to preclude issuance of an injunction).

69 United States v. McCrory, 26 F.2d 189 (2d Cir. 1928). *But see* Engler v. United States, 25 F.2d 37, 39 (8th Cir. 1928) (emphasizing *in rem* character of Section 22 proceedings).

70 United States v. Pepe, 12 F.2d 985 (2d Cir. 1926); Schlieder v. United States, 11 F.2d 345 (5th Cir. 1926); *accord*, United States v. Kelly, 24 F.2d 133 (D. Idaho 1927).

71 Dauffer-Lieberman Brewing Co. v. United States, 36 F.2d 568 (3d Cir. 1929); Webb v. United States, 14 F.2d 574 (8th Cir. 1926).

72 Grove v. United States, 3 F.2d 965 (4th Cir. 1925).

73 Gibson v. United States, 31 F.2d 19, 21–22 (9th Cir.), *cert. denied*, 279 U.S. 866 (1929).

74 Patton v. United States, 281 U.S. 276 (1930).

75 *Id.* at 287–88.

76 District of Columbia v. Colts, 282 U.S. 63 (1930).

77 *Id.* at 72.

78 *Id.* at 72–73.

79 After the 1931 amendments to the Jones Act, Act of Jan. 15, 1931, 71st Cong., 3d Sess., 46 Stat. 1036, the maximum penalties for most prohibition offenses were reduced to six months imprisonment and a $500 fine

80 United States v. Fox, 60 F.2d 685 (2d Cir. 1932); *accord*, United States v. White, 60 F.2d 958 (2d Cir. 1932). *But see* Hill v. United States, 44 F.2d 889 (D.C. Cir. 1930) (characterizing Section 22 proceedings as *in rem*).

81 60 F.2d at 688 ("[A] decree closing premises on account of liquor violations must be founded on jurisdiction over the person who at all times has the power to stop the infractions."). The overruled decision was *United States v. Johnson*, 54 F.2d 977 (2d Cir. 1932).

82 *See* United States v. Lyons, 1 F. Supp. 564 (S.D.N.Y. 1932).

83 United States v. Burtell, 51 F.2d 765 (D. Del. 1931); United States v. Carstens Packing Co., 49 F.2d 350 (W.D. Wash. 1931); Quandt Brewing Co. v. United States, 47 F.2d 199 (2d Cir. 1931); Fessler v. United States, 39 F.2d 363 (3d Cir. 1930); Crocker First Federal Trust Co. v. United States, 38 F.2d 545 (9th Cir. 1930); United States v. Mathews, 1 F. Supp. 562 (S.D.N.Y. 1932). *But cf.* United States v. Barnes, 51 F.2d 849 (D. Del. 1932) (granting injunction against an owner who had not taken steps to inform himself of the conditions of the premises or to terminate the lease after being apprised of the violations).

84 United States v. Phoenix Cereal Beverage Co., 65 F.2d 398 (2d Cir. 1933).

85 United States v. White, 60 F.2d 958 (2d Cir. 1932); United States v. Fox, 60 F.2d 685 (2d Cir. 1932); Davila v. United States, 54 F.2d 356 (1st Cir. 1931). *But see* O'Hearne v. United States, 66 F.2d 933 (D.C. Cir. 1933) (upholding contempt conviction based on Section 23 where defendant had moved his liquor business location following previous issuance of injunctions based on Sections 22 and 23).

86 Briggs v. United States, 45 F.2d 479 (6th Cir. 1930).

87 *See, e.g.*, Donato v. United States, 48 F.2d 142 (3d Cir. 1931); Hill v. United States, 44 F.2d 889 (D.C. Cir. 1930); United States v. Varele, 40 F.2d 941 (D. Idaho 1930).

88 *Final Prohibition Report, supra* note 40, at 67, 84 (Recommendations 8, 9). Only one commissioner refused to sign the report, see *id.* at 84, but all eleven of the commissioners added separate statements explaining their positions. *Id.* at 87–162.

89 Act of Dec. 16, 1930, 71st Cong., 3d Sess., 46 Stat. 1029.

90 18 U.S.C. § 541 (Compact ed. 1932 Supp.).

91 28 *id.* § 417a.

92 H.R. 9937, 71st Cong., 2d Sess. (1930). For the favorable vote of the House of Representatives, see 72 Cong. Rec. 10,071 (1930).

93 H.R. 11199, 71st Cong., 2d Sess. (1930). The vote of the House of Representatives is recorded at 74 Cong. Rec. 5660 (1931).

94 H.R. 12056, 71st Cong., 2d Sess. (1930).

95 72 Cong. Rec. 9990–91 (1930).

96 S. Rep. 1163, 71st Cong., 2d Sess. (1930).

97 *E.g.*, F. Black, *Ill-Starred Prohibition Cases* 106–23 (1931).

98 29 U.S.C. §§ 101–15 (Compact ed. 1932).

99 *See* O. Holmes, *The Common Law* 36 (1881)("[T]he law is always approaching, and never reaching, consistency. It is forever adopting new principles from life at one end, and it always retains old ones from history at the other.").

100 Alschuler, Plea Bargaining and Its History, 79 Colum. L. Rev. 1, 5 (1979).

101 *See, e.g.,* L. Friedman, *A History of American Law* 576 (2d ed. 1985); Alschuler, *supra* note 100; Haller, Plea Bargaining, the Nineteenth Century Context, 13 Law & Soc. Rev. 273 (1979); Mather, *Comments on the History of Plea Bargaining*, 13 Law & Soc. Rev. 281 (1979); *cf.* Heumann, A Note on Plea Bargaining and Case Pressure, 9 Law & Soc. Rev. 515 (1975).

102 Langbein, Understanding the Short History of Plea Bargaining, 13 Law & Soc. Rev. 261, 262 (1979).

103 Friedman, Plea Bargaining in Historical Perspective, 13 Law & Soc. Rev. 247 (1979); Haller, *supra* note 101, at 274.

104 Mather, *supra* note 101, at 282–83.

105 *Id.* at 281–82.

106 *See generally* Padgett, Plea Bargaining in the Federal Courts, 1908–34, 24 Law & Soc. Rev. 413 (1990).

107 Alschuler, *supra* note 100, at 27. In Virginia, liquor cases also increased the percentage of guilty pleas. *Id.* at 27 n.144.

108 *See* H. Johnston, *What Rights Are Left?* 27 (1930) ("'Bargain Days,' they call them now in United States District Courts"); *see also Final Prohibition Report, supra* note 40, at 56; C. Merz, *The Dry Decade* 155–57 (1931).

109 K. Hall, *The Magic Mirror: Law in American History* 254 (1989).

110 *Final Prohibition Report, supra* note 40, at 56.

111 Padgett, *supra* note 106, at 444.

112 *E.g.*, United States v. Fox, 60 F.2d 685 (2d Cir. 1932) (requiring personal service on a person with regular control of the premises in a proceeding for a nuisance abatement injunction); United States v. Pepe, 12 F.2d 985 (2nd Cir. 1926) (requiring that owner be allowed to post bond when a nuisance abatement injunction is granted).

113 *See* notes 68–71 *supra* and accompanying text; *see also* United States v. Schwartz, 1 F.2d 718 (D. Mass. 1924) (refusing to grant injunction against innocent owner); United States v. Lot 29, 296 F. 729 (D. Neb. 1924) (holding statute unconstitutional insofar as it permits padlock injunction against a home for a noncontinuing violation).

114 George Wickersham, the chairman of the commission, was a former Attorney General, and Roscoe Pound, the dean of the Harvard Law School, was a member. Other attorney members of the commission included three federal judges, one state appellate judge, and four partners in prominent law firms. The sole nonlawyer and the only woman on the commission was Ida L. Comstock, president of Radcliffe College.

115 See *Preliminary Report on Prohibition, supra* note 40, at 18–25.

8 The Prohibition Era and the Development of Federal Criminal Law

1 See generally Bureau of National Affairs, *The Criminal Law Revolution and Its Aftermath, 1960–1977* (1978).

2 For a summary of the number of prohibition cases filed in the federal district courts, see 74 Cong. Rec. 2979 (1931). A 1927 student commentary counted approximately 575 reported federal decisions discussing Fourth Amendment issues in prosecutions for violations of the liquor laws. Comment, The Meaning of the Federal Rule on Evidence Illegally Obtained, 36 Yale L.J. 536, 537 n.2 (1927).

3 H. Abraham, *Justices and Presidents: A Political History of Appointments to the Supreme Court* 413 (3d ed. 1982). Not surprisingly, the three "failures" were Van Devanter, McReynolds, and Butler.

4 The "super-legislature" appellation comes from Alpheus T. Mason. A. Mason, *The Supreme Court From Taft to Warren* 70 (rev. ed. 1968).

5 H. Abraham, *supra* note 3, at 9, 412–13. The five rated "great" were Holmes, Hughes, Brandeis, Stone, and Cardozo. The two "near greats" were Taft and Sutherland.

6 See, e.g., B. Schwartz, *A History of the Supreme Court* 219–24 (1993). Felix Frankfurter was the original architect of the effort to enshrine Holmes as the leading member of the Court prior to the New Deal. *See generally* F. Frankfurter, *Mr. Justice Holmes and the Supreme Court* (1938).

7 See, e.g., Stafford v. Wallace, 258 U.S. 495 (1922); Village of Euclid v. Ambler Realty Co., 262 U.S. 365 (1926); Gitlow v. New York, 268 U.S. 652 (1925); Pierce v. Society of Sisters, 268 U.S. 510 (1925); Meyer v. Nebraska, 262 U.S. 390 (1923).

8 See, e.g., H. Abraham, *supra* note 3, at 173; S. Novick, *Honorable Justice: The Life of Oliver Wendell Holmes* 346 (1989); B. Schwartz, *supra* note 6, at 206.

9 For an illustration of the pride Holmes took in his short opinions, see S. Novick, *supra* note 8, at 256 (quoting letter to Nina Gray).

10 For a summary of the Cardozo style, see G. White, *The American*

Judicial Tradition: Profiles of Leading American Judges 260 (rev. ed. 1985). For famous examples of the Cardozo style, see Steward Machine Co. v. Davis, 301 U.S. 548 (1937); Palsgraf v. Long Island R.R. Co., 248 N.Y. 339, 162 N.E. 99 (1928); MacPherson v. Buick Motor Co., 217 N.Y. 382, 111 N.E. 1050 (1916).

11 Dumbra v. United States, 268 U.S. 435 (1925); Steele v. United States, 267 U.S. 505 (1925); Steele v. United States, 267 U.S. 498 (1925); Carroll v. United States, 267 U.S. 132 (1925); United States v. Lanza, 260 U.S. 377 (1922).

12 *See, e.g.,* Casey v. United States, 276 U.S. 413, 423 (1928) (Brandeis, J., dissenting); Olmstead v. United States, 277 U.S. 438, 471 (Brandeis, J., dissenting); Gambino v. United States, 275 U.S. 310 (1927); Port Gardner Investment Co. v. United States, 272 U.S. 564 (1926); *but see* United States v. One Ford Coupe Automobile, 272 U.S. 321 (1926).

13 *See, e.g.,* A. Mason, *The Supreme Court From Taft to Warren* 138–40 (rev. 3d ed. 1968); 1 W. Swindler, *Court and Constitution in the Twentieth Century: The Old Legality, 1889–1932* 231 (1969); G. White, *supra* note 10, at 194–95.

14 United States v. Lefkowitz, 285 U.S. 452 (1932); Go–Bart Importing Co. v. United States, 282 U.S. 344 (1931); United States v. One Ford Coupe Automobile, 272 U.S. 321, 335 (1926) (Butler, J., dissenting); Port Gardner Investment Co. v. United States, 272 U.S. 564, 567 (1926) (Butler, J., concurring).

15 Olmstead v. United States, 277 U.S. 438, 469 (Holmes, J., dissenting).

16 Casey v. United States, 276 U.S. 413 (1928); Murphy v. United States, 272 U.S. 620 (1926); Dodge v. United States, 272 U.S. 530 (1926); Hester v. United States, 265 U.S. 57 (1924); United States v. Stafoff, 260 U.S. 477 (1923)

17 Olmstead v. United States, 277 U.S. 438, 469 (Holmes, J., dissenting).

18 The prohibition cases tend to belie Holmes's reputation as the Court's workhorse in producing opinions, *see* S. Novick, *supra* note 8, at 250–52. Justice Holmes's five majority opinions in prohibition cases exceeded the production of Justices Brandeis, Butler, and Van Devanter and equaled that of Chief Justice Taft. However, his output trailed that of Justices Stone and Sutherland, each of whom wrote six opinions for the Court.

19 *See, e.g.,* Board of Trade v. Olsen, 262 U.S. 1 (1923); Hill v. Wallace, 259 U.S. 44 (1922); Bailey v. Drexel Furniture Co., 259 U.S. 20 (1922); Stafford v. Wallace, 258 U.S. 495 (1922).

20 E.g., Village of Euclid v. Ambler Realty Co., 272 U.S. 365 (1926).

21 *See, e.g.,* Weaver v. Palmer Bros., 270 U.S. 402 (1926); Adkins v. Children's Hospital, 261 U.S. 525 (1923); Bailey v. Drexel Furniture Co., 259 U.S. 20 (1922); Truax v. Corrigan, 257 U.S. 312 (1921).

22 E.g., Fiske v. Kansas, 274 U.S. 380 (1927); Pierce v. Society of Sisters, 268 U.S. 510 (1925); Meyer v. Pierce v. Society of Sisters, 268 U.S. 510 (1925); Meyer v. Nebraska, 262 U.S. 390 (1923); *see also* Stromberg v. California, 283 U.S. 359 (1931); Near v. Minnesota, 283 U.S. 697 (1931).

23 *See, e.g.,* United States v. MacInstosh, 283 U.S. 605 (1931); United States v. Schwimmer, 279 U.S. 644 (1929); Whitney v. California, 274 U.S. 357 (1927); Gitlow v. New York, 268 U.S. 652 (1925); Frick v. Webb, 263 U.S. 326 (1923): Porterfield v. Webb, 263 U.S. 225 (123).

24 J. Gusfield, *Symbolic Crusade: Status Politics and the American Temperance Movement, passim* (1963).

25 Katz v. United States, 389 U.S. 347 (1967); Berger v. New York, 388 U.S. 41 (1967); Warden v. Hayden, 387 U.S. 294 (1967); Elkins v. United States, 364 U.S. 206 (1960).

26 *See, e.g.,* Jacobson v. United States, 112 S. Ct. 1535 (1992); Mathews v. United States, 485 U.S. 58 (1988); Hampton v. United States, 425 U.S. 484 (1976); United States v. Russell, 411 U.S. 423 (1973); Sherman v. United States, 356 U.S. 369 (1958).

27 *See, e.g.,* Florida v. Riley, 488 U.S. 445 (1989); Dow Chemical Co. v. United States, 476 U.S. 227 (1986); California v. Ciraolo, 476 U.S. 207 (1986); California v. Carney, 471 U.S. 386 (1985); Oliver v. United States, 466 U.S. 170 (1984); United States v. Ross, 456 U.S. 798 (1982); New York v. Belton, 453 U.S. 454 (1981); Coolidge v. New Hampshire, 403 U.S. 443 (1971).

28 Abbate v. United States, 359 U.S. 187 (1959); Bartkus v. United States, 359 U.S. 121 (1959). *See* Heath v. Alabama, 474 U.S. 82 (1985) (successive prosecutions by two states); United States v. Wheeler, 435 U.S. 313 (1978) (successive prosecutions by an Indian tribe and the federal government). *See generally* Murchison, The Dual Sovereignty Exception to Double Jeopardy, 14 N.Y.U. Rev. L. & Soc. Change 383, 408–35 (1986).

29 Calero-Toledo v. Pearson Yacht Leasing Co., 416 U.S. 663 (1974); *see also* C.J. Hendry Co. v. Moore, 318 U.S. 133 (1943). For a modern example of the Court's reliance on statutory construction to avoid forfeiture of the property of an "innocent owner," *see* United States v. 92 Buena Vista Ave., 113 s. ct 1126 (1993).

30 *But see* Alschuler, Plea Bargaining and Its History, 79 Colum. L. Rev. 1, 32 (1979).

31 Fed. R. Crim. Proc. 24(c) (1966). As noted in chapter 7, Congress enacted this rule in 1930. 18 U.S.C. § 417a (Compact ed. 1932). It was, however, deleted from the *United States Code* following its inclusion in the rules of procedure adopted by the Supreme Court. *See* note 32 *infra* and accompanying text.

32 Fed. R. Crim. Proc. 23(a). Federal law, 18 U.S.C. § 3771 (1988), grants the Supreme Court power to prescribe rules of criminal procedure. *Cf. id.* § 3402 (magistrate rules); 28 *id.* § 2072 (rules of civil procedure).

33 Baldwin v. New York, 399 U.S. 66 (1970).

34 Frank v. United States, 395 U.S. 147, 150 (1969); Cheff v. Schnackenberg, 384 U.S. 373 (1966) (invoking supervisory powers over the federal courts to impose the six-month rule). *See also* United States v. Nachtigal, 113 s. ct. 1072 (1993) (driving under the influence of alcohol in a national park is a petty offense to which the constitutional right to a jury trial does not apply).

35 United States v. Morrison, 425 F. Supp. 1235, 1239 (D. Md. 1977); *Rules of Procedure for the Trial of Minor Offenses before United States Magistrates*, 400 U.S. 1031 (1971); *see* Rules 2, 3(b), 5(c); 400 U.S. at 1031–35 (Black, J., dissenting from order prescribing magistrate rules). *Cf.* United States v. Bishop, 261 F. Supp. 969, 972 (N.D. Cal. 1966) (construing earlier rules to require trial by jury even for petty offenses).

36 For examples, *see* Murchison, *The Entrapment Defense in the Federal Courts: Modern Developments*, 47 Miss. L.J. 573, 612–13 (1976) (entrapment); Murchison, *Prohibition and the Fourth Amendment: A New Look at Some Old Cases*, 73 J. Crim. L. & Criminology 471, 524 (automobile exception to the Fourth Amendment's warrant requirement); Murchison, *supra* note 28, at 435 (dual sovereignty exception to double jeopardy).

37 *Cf.* Sinclair, The Use of Evolutionary Theory in Law, 64 U. Det. L. Rev. 451, 471–72 (1987) ("Biological evolution does not produce organisms perfectly adapted to or maximally efficient in their environments. Nor does evolution in law produce states of law that are optionally suited to social requirements.") (footnotes omitted).

38 *See, e.g.,* Steward Machine Co. v. Davis, 301 U.S. 548 (1937); NLRB v. Jones & Laughlin Steel Corp., 301 U.S. 1 (1937); Carter v. Carter Coal Co., 298 U.S. 238 (1936); United States v. Butler, 297 U.S. 1 (1936); Railroad Retirement Bd. v. Alton R.R., 295 U.S. 330 (1935); Schecter Poultry Corp. v. United States, 295 U.S. 495 (1935).

39 Pound, The Economic Interpretation and the Law of Torts, 53 Harv. L. Rev. 365, 366 (1940).

40 *See* United States v. Yuginovich, 256 U.S. 450 (1921); Coates v. United States, 290 F. 134 (4th Cir. 1923). *See also* United States v. Sprague, 282 U.S. 716 (1931) (Eighteenth Amendment is not void because it was ratified by state legislatures rather than conventions).

41 Katz v. United States, 389 U.S. 347 (1967); Berger v. New York, 388 U.S. 41 (1967); Warden v. Hayden, 387 U.S. 294 (1967); Elkins v. United States, 364 U.S. 206 (1960).

42 Abbate v. United States, 359 U.S. 187 (1959); Heath v. Alabama, 474 U.S. 82 (1985).

43 Florida v. Riley, 488 U.S. 445 (1989); Dow Chemical Co. v. United States, 476 U.S. 227 (1986); Air Pollution Variance Bd. v. Western Alfalfa Corp., 416 U.S. 861 (1974).

44 Masciale v. United States, 356 U.S. 386 (1958); Sherman v. United States, 356 U.S. 369 (1958). More recent entrapment cases seem consistent with the Court's reluctance to expand protections for defendants in drug cases. See Mathews v. United States, 485 U.S. 58 (1988); Hampton v. United States, 425 U.S. 484 (1976); United States v. Russell, 411 U.S. 423 (1973).

45 H. Kalven, *The Negro and the First Amendment* (1965).

46 Patterson v. Alabama, 294 U.S. 600 (1935); Norris v. Alabama, 294 U.S. 587 (1935); Powell v. Alabama, 287 U.S. 45 (1932). For a powerful description of the Scottsboro rape trials that produced these opinions, see D. Carter, *Scottsboro: A Tragedy of the American South* (2d ed. 1979).

47 E.g., Blackburn v. Alabama, 361 U.S. 199 (1960); Brown v. Allen, 344 U.S. 443 (1954); Ward v. Texas, 316 U.S. 547 (1942); Chambers v. Florida, 309 U.S. 227 (1940); Brown v. Mississippi, 297 U.S. 278 (1936).

48 *See generally* Wisotsky, Crackdown: The Emerging Drug Exception to the Bill of Rights, 38 Hastings L.J. 889 (1987).

49 E.g., Alabama v. White, 447 U.S. 667, (1990); Colorado v. Bertine, 479 U.S. 367 (1987); United States v. Leon, 468 U.S. 897 (1984); *see generally* Saltzburg, Another Victim of Illegal Narcotics: The Fourth Amendment (As Illustrated by the Open Fields Doctrine), 48 U. Pitt. L. Rev. 1 (1986).

50 *See, e.g.*, Caplin & Drysdale, Chartered v. United States, 491 U.S. 617 (1989); United States v. Salerno, 481 U.S. 739 (1987); Abernaz v. United States, 450 U.S. 333 (1981); Hampton v. United States, 425 U.S. 484 (1976); United States v. Russell, 411 U.S. 423 (1973); Harris v. New York, 401 U.S. 222 (1971).

51 Duncan v. Louisiana, 391 U.S. 145 (1968).

52 Williams v. Florida, 399 U.S. 78, 122 (1970) (Harlan, J., dissenting) ("With all respect, I consider that before today it would have been unthinkable to suggest that the Sixth Amendment's right to a trial by jury is satisfied by a jury of six, or less, as is left open by the Court's opinion . . . or by less than a unanimous verdict, a question also reserved in today's decision."); *cf.* Rochin v. California, 342 U.S. 165, 169–70 (1952)

(Frankfurter, J., for the Court) ("[T]he requirements of the Sixth and Seventh Amendments for trial by jury in the federal courts have a rigid meaning. No changes or chances can alter the content of the verbal symbol of 'jury'—a body of twelve men who must reach a unanimous conclusion if the verdict is to go against the defendant.").

53 Apodaca v. Oregon, 406 U.S. 404 (1972); Johnson v. Louisiana, 406 U.S. 356 (1972); Williams v. Florida, 399 U.S. 78 (1970).

54 Burch v. Louisiana, 441 U.S. 130 (1979) (conviction of non-petty offense by a nonunanimous jury of six persons violates the Sixth Amendment); Ballew v. Georgia, 435 U.S. 223 (1978) (five-person jury for non-petty criminal cases violates the Sixth Amendment).

55 441 U.S. at 138 ("We are buttressed in this view by the current jury practices of the several states. It appears that of those states that utilize six-member juries in trials of non-petty offenses, only two . . . also allow nonunanimous verdicts."); 435 U.S. at 244 ("[O]nly two states . . . have reduced the size of juries in certain non-petty cases to five.").

56 E.g., 27 U.S.C.A. § 39 (1927) (forbidding issuance of a warrant to search "any private dwelling occupied as such unless it is being used for the unlawful sale of intoxicating liquor, or unless it is in part used for some business purpose such as a store, shop, saloon, restaurant, hotel, or boarding house."). In addition, Section 6 of the Willis Campbell Act, Pub. L. No. 67-96, 42 Stat. 222 (1921), made it a misdemeanor for any officer of the United States to "search any private dwelling . . . without a warrant directing such search."

57 Cf. Sinclair, supra note 37, at 458 ("Tinkering with old rules is a common judicial game; replacing old rules is not.").

58 See Wechsler, Toward Neutral Principles of Constitutional Law, 73 Harv. L. Rev. 1 (1959).

59 See Dworkin, Hard Cases, 88 Harv. L. Rev. 1057 (1975). For an attempt to develop a Dworkian approach to Fourth (and Fifth) Amendment issues, see Note, Formalism, Legal Realism and Constitutionally Protected Privacy under the Fourth and Fifth Amendments, 90 Harv. L. Rev. 945 (1977).

60 Recent busing decisions, for example, may have slowed the political retreat from a national commitment to the achievement of integrated public education, see Swann v. Charlotte-Mecklenberg Bd. of Educ., 402 U.S. 1 (1971), although the Court has given ground to the changing political mood in some subsequent decisions. See, e.g., Milliken v. Bradley, 418 U.S. 717 (1974).

61 Brown v. Board of Education, 347 U.S. 483 (1954), may have exerted such an influence. Cf. Heart of Atlanta Motel, Inc. v. United States, 379 U.S. 241, 279, 291 (1964) (concurring opinions of Douglas and Goldberg, JJ., suggesting a broad congressional power under Section 5 of the Fourteenth Amendment to ban racial discrimination). The death penalty cases reflect an interesting attempt first to guide political morality and then to limit the impact of the resulting backlash. *See generally* Murchison, Toward a Perspective on the Death Penalty Cases, 27 Emory L.J. 469 (1978).

Index

Page numbers in parentheses indicate text pages where the cited endnote number is found.

About the Author

Kenneth M. Murchison is J. Denson Smith
Professor at the Paul M. Hebert Law Center
of Louisiana State University.

Library of Congress Cataloging-in-Publication Data

Murchison, Kenneth M., 1947–
Federal criminal law doctrines : the forgotten influence of
national prohibition / Kenneth M. Murchison.
p. cm
Includes index.
ISBN 0-8223-1510-6 (cloth : acid-free paper)
1. Criminal law—United States—History—20th century. 2. Liquor laws—
United States—History—20th century. 3. Prohibition—United States—
History. 4. United States—Constitutional law—Amendments—18th—
History. I. Title.
KF9219.M85   1994
345.73—dc20
[347.305]   94–18235   CIP